W9-AMA-412

Creating a
DIGITAL
Portfolio

Cynthia Baron

Hayden
Books

Creating a Digital Portfolio

©1996 Cynthia Baron

All rights reserved. Printed in the United States of America. No part of this book may be used or reproduced in any form or by any means, or stored in a database or retrieval system, without prior written permission of the publisher except in the case of brief quotations embodied in critical articles and reviews. Making copies of any part of this book for any purpose other than your own personal use is a violation of United States copyright laws. For information, address Hayden Books, 201 W. 103rd Street, Indianapolis, Indiana 46290.

Library of Congress Catalog Number: 96-77855
ISBN: 1-56830-326-2

Copyright © 1996 Hayden Books

Printed in the United States of America 1 2 3 4 5 6 7 8 9 0

ii

Warning and Disclaimer

This book is sold as is, without warranty of any kind, either express or implied. While every precaution has been taken in the preparation of this book, the author and Hayden Books assume no responsibility for errors or omissions. Neither is any liability assumed for damages resulting from the use of the information or instructions contained herein. It is further stated that the publisher and author are not responsible for any damage or loss to data or equipment that results directly or indirectly from use of this book.

Publisher
Lyn Blake

Publishing Manager
Melanie Rigney

Managing Editor
Lisa Wilson

Acquisitions Editor
Robyn Holtzman

Development Editor
Bront Davis

Copy/Production Editor
Michael Brumitt

Technical Editor
Richard Romano

Publishing Coordinator
Rachel Byers

Cover Designer
Jay Corpus

Book Designer
Gary Adair

Manufacturing Coordinator
Brook Farling

Production Team Supervisor
Laurie Casey

Production Team
Janelle Herber
Joe Millay
Laure Robinson
Christy Wagner

Indexer
Bront Davis

About the Author

Cynthia Baron is a designer, typographer, writer, educator, and technical director of computer graphics for the Department of Art & Architecture at Northeastern University in Boston. Along the way, she has picked up an MBA, been a contributing editor to *Computer Graphics World*, executive vice president of Serif & Sans, and partner in LeWinterBaron Graphics Multitasking. She fondly remembers her zippered portfolio binder.

Trademark Acknowledgments

All terms mentioned in this book that are known to be trademarks or service marks have been appropriately capitalized. Hayden Books cannot attest to the accuracy of this information. Use of a term in this book should not be regarded as affecting the validity of any trademark or service mark.

Dedication

To my parents, who have weathered much and given more.

And to Shai, who made it possible.

Acknowledgments and Permissions

If it's true that good company makes a journey seem shorter, my journey from the beginning of this project to its completion had good company indeed. This book had to come to fruition in a remarkably short period of time. To make that a possibility I relied heavily on the support, encouragement and time of a great many friends and colleagues.

First, I'd like to thank the book's contributors for their service above and beyond the call of duty. In some cases their decision to take part in the book was also a decision to redesign and recreate their presentations under a tight deadline. Their names and bios are listed in the Introduction. Between visits, interviews, flurries of email and packages, I received a tremendous amount of input, anecdotes, and encouragement from artists, designers and technical wizards, some of them contributors to the CD. I would particularly like to mention Kimberley Anderson of Los Angeles for creating the elegant portfolio seen in Figures 2.1 and 8.1, Bob Antia and the crew at The Left Bank Operation in Cambridge for their gracious use of their computers and work space, David Ibbetson of Toronto for sending me in the right direction on dot pitch, Flo Scott of the Electronic Imaging Center in Boston for the use of her studio on a very busy weekend, Michael McPherson for help in getting the process moving, and Mary Ann Kearns of the 911 Gallery for relocating to Boston and sharing her good taste, commitment, and connections.

In addition, some special thanks to Samuel Bishop, Seth Merriam, and Ofer Inbar for sharing their expertise, Elizabeth Calitri for her last minute edits and artwork, Robyn Holtzman and Bront Davis at Hayden Books for encouragement and good email, and Brian Dellascio, for being my hands (and occasionally my brain) for numerous screen captures, mockups, and graphics.

Permissions to reproduce from:

Corey & Co. (Web sites of the company and its three studios)

Larry Burks (Web site)

Allen Toney (portfolio slide shows and CD images Xmp 28, 29, 30)

Diane Fenster (Web sites for fine art and illustration)

Ark Studios (Web site)

Kimberley Anderson (traditional portfolio: two slides, Figures 2.1 and 8.1)

Holland Wilde, Designer, and Arthur Perry, Assistant Designer, of EastCoast Creative for permission to feature their videotape packaging.

Hayden Books

The staff of Hayden Books is committed to bringing you the best computer books. What our readers think of Hayden is important to our ability to serve our customers. If you have any comments, no matter how great or how small, we'd appreciate your taking the time to send us a note.

You can reach Hayden Books at the following:

Hayden Books
201 West 103rd Street
Indianapolis, IN 46290
317-581-3833

Email addresses:

America Online:	Hayden Bks
Internet:	hayden@hayden.com

Visit the Hayden Books Web site at http://www.hayden.com.

Contents at a Glance

vii

Table of Contents

Contents

xi

Contents

Contents

Creating a
Digital
Portfolio

Contents

xvii

Contents

What *IS* a Digital Portfolio?

Don't be nervous, don't be frightened, don't be scared...be prepared!
—Tom Lehrer

The phrase "digital portfolio" may be redundant in the near future. Today, it's still being defined. When I discuss a digital portfolio in this book, I am referring to a collection of personal visual material created and/or presented via digital media. This definition encompasses a wide range of forms: digitally-printed output, work on diskette, removable media or CD, work presented on portable computers, and work displayed on the Internet. This book should give you a good overview of all of these options, lead you through the concepts and issues they raise (from basic to complex), and help you determine whether a digital portfolio is right for you.

Current portfolio expectations vary from industry to industry, and even within industries, depending on the nature of the work you intend on showing and who will see it. Some artists and designers will continue to show a traditional portfolio. Others are moving their material to some form of digital media. The vast majority are somewhere in between. With so much variation in expectations, portfolio creation and maintenance are becoming more serious and detailed marketing issues than ever before.

Why Do You Need a Portfolio Now?

For most people, a portfolio describes the investments they own. Since those investments can mean the difference between financial security and dependence on the government, they are taken very seriously. As a result, there are hundreds of books and magazines offering advice on how to play the market, invest in real estate, or handle portfolio diversification.

For those of us whose livelihood is described in visual language, the word "portfolio" describes a different type of asset. If we think about it carefully, however, the two kinds of portfolios are not as different as they might seem. Both represent the fruits of hard labor. Both are the result of choices made to maximize potential, and both can spell the difference between long-term success or failure. But the visual portfolio is such a personal, unique asset, we are not inclined to approach it with the same cold eye and constant attention that we would if it held text-only information.

In fact, we tend to treat our portfolios with benign neglect. As long as we aren't actively looking for a job, most of us pack them away without a glance, even if our work has changed radically. People who have become involved in visual media through non-traditional routes, such as corporate publications, marketing divisions, programming, or a hobby that has become a vocation, may not even have one. Individuals or firms who do client presentations take their portfolio more seriously, but a lot of that concern can be lip service. Paying jobs and deadlines take precedence, sometimes for months or even years. No one wants to put in overtime *just* to overhaul a portfolio. Even students, for whom the portfolio looms as the single most important factor in their future, seldom begin to prepare one before graduation. The lucky ones attend a portfolio seminar or receive the quick blessing of a favorite teacher. Others follow their instincts or the recommendations of people who may know no more than they do.

Then, at some point, the portfolio issue becomes your focus. This can happen slowly as friends talk about the Web sites they're involved in, or come as a thunderbolt when

the communications department you've worked in for ten years is downsized. You look through your portfolio assets and realize that you've done the visual equivalent of running up credit card bills while your savings account earns 3%. "Where are those samples? What happened to the storyboard? How fast can I get this scanned? Why does this stuff look so rough? Do you know anyone who has FreeHand…I have to fix this!" You move into high gear, and there's no time to strategize.

The worst nightmare is having to apologize in an interview. "No, I don't have my installation on the Web. Oh, you wanted to see original art? I can leave you these laser prints, but I don't have extra copies of anything else. You don't have Photoshop on your machine? Well, I can see if one of my group members kept a copy of the Player." This is like telling a broker that you could have bought Microsoft when it was $4 a share.

Whatever else you may have on your To Do list, developing, maintaining, and upgrading your portfolio should never be off it for long, especially now. We are in the throws of a culture-wide shift in expectations as change (for good or ill) races to keep pace with baud rates. Ever since the Macintosh gave birth to the desktop concept, the computer has become a required tool for design students. Soon, no visual professional will be able to survive without making it part of his or her career, at least at the marketing level. That's where the digital portfolio comes in.

2

Using this Book

Before you can develop or update a portfolio of any kind, you need to clearly define yourself and understand your goals. A good analogy is to think of your portfolio as a carefully composed gourmet meal. Any chef will tell you that a good eating experience depends on four things: a good recipe, organized kitchen skills, the best ingredients, and good taste. Your recipe is your personal marketing goal; your skills are your process; your ingredients, your work; and your personal taste, the one thing left completely to the chef. A portfolio is not a leftovers stew, where you throw in everything you can find and hope it's edible.

My purpose in writing this book is to look at this portfolio process with a fresh eye, and in the context of the increasingly virtual world most art and design professionals are now exploring. Even if you've been "cooking" your portfolio for years, making it accessible in digital form demands new criteria, new technical skills, and maybe a fresh look at your work and your assumptions.

I admit to some biases in creating this book. The first is technical. Like many design professionals, I am more comfortable on a Macintosh than a Windows machine. Because of this, there are more hints, tricks, and suggestions for the Mac user than the Wintel one. I have, however, tried to be even-handed in exploring software for digital portfolio creation. Additionally,

I have concentrated some of my attention toward "translating" Macintosh-based files into Wintel format. Just as there are many Mac aficionados creating work, there are even more Windows users viewing it.

My second bias is more subtle. Many people who will read and use this book have presented their portfolios for years and have a very good sense of their profession, their skills and talents, and their local market. These professionals are most interested in the how-tos of digital portfolio creation, but a surprising number of digital portfolios are being created by recent entrants into the working world. These are people who have a sophisticated knowledge of software but have never wrestled with the issues of self-marketing and presentation. While emphasizing the how-tos, I have tried to present the digital portfolio process as part of a larger scheme. Whichever camp you pitch your tent in, using this book should make the process of developing your new portfolio a little less painful.

My third bias is one I hope to pass along to others—the understanding that a portfolio (digital or otherwise) is not your autobiography. It's a marketing tool that can help you improve the amount and type of work you do, the kinds of assignments you land, and the rate of response to your presentations. Treat your portfolio project like a paying job —because it is.

About the CD

The portfolios on CD which accompany this book are widely disparate in style and content. All the contributors, however, are siblings under the skin. Each, in their own way, is at the top of their form at this time. Their contributions reflect a passionate belief in themselves and their creative vision. Each approached their version of a digital portfolio not as a finished object frozen in time, but as an opportunity for self-definition. All of them attacked the project with a commitment to excellence and a sense of humor.

Most of the contributors expect that new material will be added to their portfolios even in the short time frame between the creation of the CD and the time you read this book. Visit their Web sites and check out how their work is evolving. Use their contributions not as templates for portfolio creation, but as examples of the possibilities inherent in a digital format. Throughout the book you are presented with dos and don'ts, which can be interpreted as rules. As all good artists and designers do, sometimes the contributors break these rules, but never without thought and a clear understanding of when and why it's necessary.

4

The CD Contributors

Ark Studios

Boston-based Ark Studios develops cross-platform digital animation, music and interface design for CD-ROMs, interactive museum/entertainment kiosks, and online destinations on the Internet. Ark Studios, Inc. began in 1994 when David Curtiss, David Clark, and Robert Odegard banded together to form a creative partnership for the development of interactive media. This endeavor has grown to include other talented artists, designers, musicians, and programmers who work in an open and collaborative environment known as the "Ark." Each partner contributes their skills and technical knowledge to formulate a humane design driven experience. The Ark Studios URL is http://www.arkstudios.com and their email address is stuart@arkstudios.com.

David Clark

David holds degrees from Dartmouth College and the Rhode Island School of Design. Trained as a Product Designer, he enjoys thinking through the user/tool/task relationship as it applies to graphically engaging interfaces. He currently teaches Multimedia at RISD in the Industrial Design program.

David Curtiss

David has studied video, electronic music, and studio art at Hampshire College and The Museum School. His varied interests meld in a uniquely integrated approach to developing interactive environments.

Robert Odegard

Robert holds a BFA in Fine Arts from the Minneapolis College of Art & Design and an MFA in Graphic Design from the Rhode Island School of Design. Prior to Ark, Robert cultivated his design experience through work in film and television production, museum exhibit fabrication, and graphic design. He currently teaches Multimedia as Product Design at RISD in the Industrial Design program and serves as a lecturer of Advanced Interactive Design in the Graduate Design program at Yale University.

Larry Burks

Larry, a native Texan, moved to Boston to study art and architecture at Northeastern University and is currently completing a graduate degree in Architecture at Harvard University's Graduate School of Design (GSD). Intensely interested in fusing architecture and digital media, he has worked at several architectural firms in Boston and New York on projects ranging from modeling and animation to application development. He received the Computer Graphics award at the GSD for his innovative use of GIS mapping systems and CAD

CAM technology in the design studio. Larry's thesis project, which was recently featured in a Japanese journal 10+1, will focus on the design of virtual environments for the World Wide Web.

Corey & Company, Inc.

Corey & Company, Inc. was founded in 1983 by Tom Corey and since then has grown to more than 50 people. To maintain their small firm spirit they expanded by spinning off studios rather than becoming one large organization. Today the company comprises the studios of Corey McPherson Nash, Big Blue Dot, and Hatmaker. Each one is unique in character and focus, but can draw on the resources and talents of the entire organization. The Corey & Company Web address is http://www.corey.com.

Corey McPherson Nash

In 1987, Tom Corey named Michael McPherson, Scott Nash, Susan Gilzow, and Beth Maynard as partners and the studio name was changed from Corey & Company: Designers to Corey McPherson Nash. In 1993, Phyllis Kido was also named a partner. Throughout its history the studio has worked with educational and corporate clients. As graphic design has assumed a critical role in corporate and brand identity, Corey McPherson Nash has developed and expanded its capabilities. While continuing to grow, the studio remains committed to providing clients with creative work of the highest quality. To achieve this goal, Corey

5

McPherson Nash approaches each job from a strategic perspective. The client's needs, market, and resources are all examined and challenged to produce a fully-evolved identity. Corey McPherson Nash's current clients include Hewlett-Packard, Agfa, HBO, Harvard University, Wellesley College, and the Boston Pops. You can reach them by phone at 617-924-6050 or by email at `jalexander@corey.com` (Jason Alexander).

Big Blue Dot

In June 1992, Tom Corey, Scott Nash, and Susan Gilzow formed Big Blue Dot, a print, new media, and broadcast design studio dedicated to creating promotions and products for kids. In addition, Big Blue Dot's "trend tracker" conducts research to provide up-to-the-minute information on trends in the children's market. This information is gathered, analyzed, and presented in *BIG BLUE BOX*, the publication that delivers the ever-changing world of kid trends and products in one handy box. Along with written information, *BIG BLUE BOX* is chock-full of the trends being written about, everything from candy to software products. Big Blue Dot's clients include Y-TV in Toronto, HandsOnToys, Silver Burdett Ginn, Nickelodeon, Children's Television Workshop, Microsoft, ABC, Viacom, TBS, and PBS. Their email address is `mokeefe@corey.com` (Maureen O'Keefe).

Hatmaker

Formed in 1995, Hatmaker split off of Corey McPherson Nash when it became evident that the practice would benefit from the establishment of a smaller group with a single focus: broadcast design. Hatmaker is comprised of a team of writers, producers and designers who provide positioning, strategy, and visual identity for such notable clients as Warner Brothers International Channels, TNT, TBS, MTV, Comedy Central, and The Cartoon Network. Over the years, they have developed ideas for both themselves and their clients. Our calendar, our trend tracking publication, *BIG BLUE BOX*, and interstitial programming for Nickelodeon called NICKDAYS are just a few examples of some of the ideas we've conceived, developed, and produced. Other projects are in the works. The Hatmaker email address is `shorrigan@corey.com` (Sean Horrigan) and their phone number is 617-924-2700.

Diane Fenster

In addition to being a Computer Graphics Illustrator and fine artist, Diane Fenster is an internationally exhibited digital artist. Her style is an innovative combination of her own 35mm photography, video, still video, and scanned imagery. Her images appear in numerous publications and CDs on digital art including the APERTURE monograph, METAMORPHOSES: PHOTOGRAPHY IN THE ELECTRONIC AGE. She is a guest

6

lecturer at many seminars and conferences including Macworld Expo and her work was exhibited at the SIGGRAPH 95 Art & Design show and FISEA. Her illustration style is an outgrowth of the explorations she has taken with her personal work and her commissions range from editorial to advertising to Web. Diane's clients include Apple, IBM, Dell, Adobe Systems, Inc., IDG, Ziff Davis, and Fractal Design Software. Diane maintains two Web sites where she presents her work. Her fine art is featured at `http://www.art.net/Studios/Visual/Fenster/riotfab_Home/fenstr.html` and Diane's illustration portfolio can be seen at `http://www.sirius.com/~fenster/`. She can be reached through email at `fenster@sfsu.edu` or by phone at 415-355-5007.

Allen Toney

After beginning his career as an oil painter/printmaker at Marshall University in the late '80s, Allen is now a Computer Graphics artist. Since 1990, he has worked exclusively with "electronic painting," using a graphics computer and electronic drawing tablet to produce his imagery. Allen's work weds liquid, sensual, neo-classical forms with mystical, mathematical, and surreal sensibilities. In so doing he forms a new hybrid visionary style which is unique to the computer medium.

Since 1992, Allen has been in seven one man shows as well as over 45 group and juried exhibitions throughout the US. He is considered one of the premiere figures in the field of computer fine art. His work has also appeared in international shows in Europe and Japan, as well as in numerous publications such as *Mac World* (3/92), *Wired* (1/94), *Verbum* (5/91), *Computer Artist* (5/93, 8/94), *Creativity* (3/94), Fractal Design's "Painter" advertisements (93/94), and numerous interactive multimedia CDs (93, 94, 95). Allen's URL is `http://www.marshall.edu/~jtoney`. He can be reached via email at `jtoney@marshall.edu`.

Conclusion

In addition to the portfolio contributions, the CD contains illustrations for the imaging tutorials in Chapters 4, 5, and 6, and a Netscape 216-color palette for Photoshop import.

CHAPTER ONE

Developing a Good Portfolio for Any Medium

"To be happy you must have taken the measure of your powers, tasted the fruits of your passion, and learned your place in the world."
—Santayana

Who Are You?

Defining who you are in the marketplace is more difficult than it used to be, particularly since "the marketplace" is both broader and more fragmented than it was a decade ago. To add to the potential confusion, one job description can have dozens of different titles, each of which puts a slightly different slant on the type of experience, talents, and skills the position demands. Inhouse, this leads to job position documents that sound like a shopping list. For freelance positions, it can breed a lot of frustration and dissatisfaction on both sides of the desk.

What, for example, do you call someone who creates Web sites? A Web designer? This job is becoming popular, despite the fact that many graphic designers, who also are involved in Web design, see it as unnecessarily narrow. How about graphic designer? This is certainly the umbrella term. For many non-designers, however, graphic design equals print design or is too vague a term for

what is becoming a design specialty. An interface designer? Interface design is needed to really do justice to a commercial Web site, but it gets confused too frequently with interactive design. A Webmaster? Besides the dramatic role-playing tone, this frequently means corporate Information Services and has little or nothing to do with visual issues.

Does this seem like splitting hairs? Not when the appropriate definition can make the difference between $30,000 and $60,000 a year. And not when you are trying to position yourself for the type of work you'd like to be doing or studying. You must be confident of what your strengths are, know how they might be applied in a position, and provide hard visual evidence that you have the necessary chops to handle the task. This can be a problem if you are transitioning between two areas, as many visual artists and design professionals are. When there are gaps between your experience, your goals, and the marketplace, it is up to you to build the bridges between them.

It's difficult, however, to build a bridge without surveying the site first. In this case, the first step in portfolio construction begins with a quick overview of different market-places and their current approaches to portfolios. You will notice that some jobs require that you present yourself in a time-tested, specific way. Other job descriptions are so new that every time a portfolio is created to meet them, it sets a standard for future expectations.

The Four Elements of a Portfolio

All portfolios have underlying elements that when combined in the right proportion can speak effectively to its intended audience. A portfolio can emphasize creativity and variety, but ignore process and treat tech-nique as a lesser issue. Although this mix is a very personal and specific thing, many disciplines have unspoken assumptions about how the following elements should be expressed and their relative importance.

Variety

Should you show the full range of your capabilities, or should you focus on one aspect? Some professions offer more opportunities to answer that question than others. Even within an artistic discipline

with general guidelines about how homog-enous your work should be, how you answer this question will depend partially on where you are in your career. For example, young freelance designers often have a more varied portfolio than those who have been long-time employees at one firm or corporation. This variety can prove flexibility and showcase a freewheeling creative spirit to an interested creative director. On the other hand, the type of audience and the market's general expectations could view variety as a negative. Some clients have difficulty making the jump between what they see in a book and what they think they should see. A portfolio focused to a specific client or addressing the appropriate niche lets one know you understand his needs.

Creativity and Technique

There are arguments that these two catego-ries should be seen as separate portfolio elements. The reality of how portfolios are evaluated in different disciplines makes complete separation problematic. In some circles, creativity and technique are seen as polar opposites, as in the fine art debates about formal versus visceral art. In graphic design, they are seen as mutually dependent but separate. In 3-D modeling and anima-tion, techinque and creativity are seen as inseparable parts of the same thing. How much technical expertise should be show-cased will depend on the discipline, the specific requirements of a position, and the stage in the artist/designer's career. Although creating a portfolio should always be done with care and attention, the work and the feel of the packaging (organically developed or carefully organized) can effect how a reviewer relates to it.

Process

Most portfolios only contain finished or printed work, but showing design process can be a tremendous plus in a professional's career. Work in process, or work about your process, can give a sense of how your ideas evolve. For a young professional whose clientele is a budget-conscious crew, it offers the opportunity to show creative capabilities without being tempted to apologize for the finished work. For portfolios where post-production costs are high and work can be tied up in proprietary issues, process work and prototypes can serve as the basis for a capabilities portfolio.

Purpose

Your purpose should affect how you develop your portfolio. You might develop and present your portfolio for the following:

 Sale to potential buyers or gallery owners

 Admission into academic programs

 Work in a freelance or full-time job

 Show to curators or for academic positions

A student applying for a graduate degree, for example, will develop a creative portfolio highlighting his or her unique talents and emphasizing concept work. Semiotics, video, or photography could all play a part. A student looking for work will want to develop a portfolio based on skills and structure with creative experimentation grounded in practical production.

Note

A cautionary note before moving on: The usefulness of these elements lies in their potential to help you unify your portfolio and emphasize your strengths in relation to your market's needs. The profiles can't, and shouldn't, represent the state of the profession for everyone at every point in his or her career. When an individual moves upward professionally, guidelines fall apart and expectations change to meet reputations. An architect might be maintaining both a professional practice and a university post. His or her portfolio elements would lean toward creativity, such as building ideas, and work for show, such as competitions, which would join client-centered material. Conversely, an established artist might explore paints and pastels after years in monoprints and charcoal, adding variety to his or her portfolio.

Keep these issues in mind as you reconsider who you are—or who you'd like to be perceived as. The thumbnail descriptions throughout this chapter will reference the portfolio elements for each group of practitioners and function as a reality check. Does your work, your market, and your portfolio match these descriptions?

Different Markets, Different Portfolios

In describing the following disciplines, I have stuck to the descriptive names that are most common but provided examples of related categories of artists and designers for whom the guidelines might apply. Technology is blurring the boundaries between photography, painting, and illustration; between sculpture, animation, and architecture; and even between fine art and computer programming. It's therefore impossible to try to cover all the new job descriptions being created.

Students

Undergraduate student portfolios usually display a range of work that enables reviewers to determine general strengths and weaknesses, the student's level of preparation, and his or her artistic commitment. Although craft is not irrelevant, technique, which is taught, takes a back seat to potential. The exception to this is a portfolio that has clearly been treated in an off-hand manner. It takes some exciting visual thinking to dispel a reviewer's sense that a

student is indifferent to craft and not simply ignorant of it.

A much higher standard of presentation is expected of a graduate-level portfolio. Anyone who is sufficiently committed to his art so much that he wishes to refine his knowledge and, perhaps, teach it to others, should expect to treat his portfolio as one of his most important projects.

The Portfolio

A lot of variation exists in the student portfolio, although its format is almost always dictated by the specific requirements of the institution. With very few exceptions, the prospective student will be given guidelines for portfolio submission. If the institution is familiar with and willing to accept digital portfolios, this is usually stated explicitly. As a general rule, most art institutes or other fine art-oriented programs expect to receive 35mm slides. Some architecture programs expect a designed portfolio in some combination of print or slide form. Graphic design programs vary greatly. Graduate programs are usually more comfortable with digital work, although not usually to the exclusion of more traditional material.

Figure 1.1
The elements of a student portfolio displayed on slide bars.

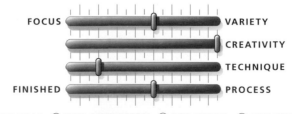

12

Fine Artists

Fine artists include painters, sculptors, photographers, performance artists, videographers, and animators.

Surprising as it may seem to a young artist, diversity in a professional portfolio is not necessarily good. Most of the elements that make up a student portfolio are irrelevant to gallery owners, agents, or dealers who are looking for a consistent style. They want to be able to state authoritatively, "This is a Judy X work," when they see one. If Judy X is both a photographer and a watercolorist, she must not only maintain two portfolio books but show them separately. Only after showing regularly and successfully can these interests be recombined in one portfolio.

The Portfolio

An artist's portfolio generally takes the form of 35mm slides or some other photographic image, yet lately artists have been experimenting with other options, from transparencies to brochures.

Digital artist portfolios still represent a small percentage of these experiments, but their numbers have been growing as the volume of galleries and museums online has exploded. Not surprisingly, artists working with the computer constitute the largest group online. But artists working in more traditional media are using their online presence to create mock-ups of proposed work and are beginning to scan their slides or reshoot their work for a digital audience.

Alan Tomey, whose Web-site-as-art-space can be found on the accompanying CD, says of his fine art portfolio, "Fewer traditional galleries are online and thus need to be approached with more traditional tools. To galleries, I send a sleeve of 35mm slides, two diskettes, one formatted as IBM, the other MAC. On each disk is a self-running JPEG slide show. I also include a bio, a resume, an artist statement, tear sheets, color reproductions, and so on. If the initial contact is successful, an actual print is usually sent to the gallery for inspection."

Architects

This section includes architects, landscape architects, interior designers, furniture designers, industrial designers, and VRML designer/engineers.

Architectural portfolio requirements change as an architect's career matures. Recent

13

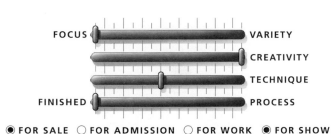

FOCUS — VARIETY
— CREATIVITY
— TECHNIQUE
FINISHED — PROCESS

● FOR SALE ○ FOR ADMISSION ○ FOR WORK ● FOR SHOW

Figure 1.2
The elements of a fine artist's portfolio displayed.

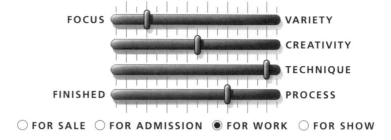

Figure 1.3
*The architect's
portfolio elements
displayed.*

FOCUS ———————— VARIETY

———————— CREATIVITY

———————— TECHNIQUE

FINISHED ———————— PROCESS

○ FOR SALE   ○ FOR ADMISSION   ◉ FOR WORK   ○ FOR SHOW

graduates discover that interviewers are more interested in their drafting expertise or facility with AutoCAD than the creativity of their student projects. A portfolio that doesn't display the highest possible professional craft with the widest variety of tools will go to the bottom of the pile.

This doesn't mean that conceptual projects are worthless. In a market full of aspiring practitioners, conceptual projects are how a firm recognizes long term potential. Architecture, however, as a profession has a strong commitment to apprenticeship. A vanishingly small percentage of architects go right from school to a full design partnership. Later, as the architect enters competitions, lands commissions, publishes, and completes projects, more emphasis is put on documenting existing work than on production issues, which are handed off to the next crop of new graduates.

The Portfolio

Unlike most other design professions, even established professionals often show unbuilt projects in their portfolios. Ideas about designing a space always outnumber the actual commissions to do so. Unbuilt work,

if strongly conceptual, can be a real portfolio addition and is readily accepted.

On the other hand, the architectural profession is very split on the subject of digital portfolios. Some firms and individuals have embraced them enthusiastically. On the other extreme are architects who insist on seeing even the most dry and technical elevations on paper. Even architects with a well-developed digital presence will frequently have a traditional bound portfolio of elevations, plans, renderings, and photographs. A creative example of a promising new architect with a strong interest in digital technology can be found on the accompanying CD.

Photographers

Although working for *National Geographic* might be a life goal, most photographers do specialized advertising or promotional work. Product shots are handled by one person, building shots by another, and portraiture by someone else entirely.

The in-house photographer is practically extinct. Most professional photo work is done for hire, on assignment, on contract, or

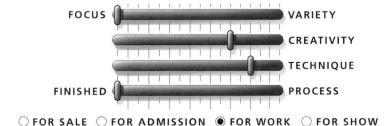

Figure 1.4
*The photo-
grapher's portfolio
elements displayed.*

on speculation. This adds to the pressure for a narrow focus, because prospective clients only want to see work that relates to the job at hand. Many accomplished photographers also work in technical positions—commercial photo labs or as assistants in large photo studios—to maintain a consistent cash flow.

Variety in subject, style, or tone exists in the portfolios of photojournalists and stock photographers; however, of the two, only the Photojournalist is likely to have an actual portfolio book. A stock photographer is more likely to maintain a large collection of slides or a computerized image database.

The Portfolio

The traditional photographer's portfolio is in 35mm slide form. Occasionally, prints or color transparencies will be shown as well. Photojournalists generally have more latitude in their format. Slides, prints, or even laser prints can be shown. Because of the rapid computerization of the print media, photojournalist's portfolios have been on the forefront of the move to a digital form. Additionally, photographers' portfolios are being packaged and marketed as royalty-free art on CDs. The need for imagery in

corporate documents and Web sites is turning this digital field into a growing opportunity.

Illustrators

This category includes architectural model makers, textile designers, computer artist/ illustrators, and commercial animators.

Like fine artists and commercial photographers, there is substantial pressure to specialize in an identifiable illustration style. Illustrators are usually hired for a specific assignment or series of related pieces. Although there is a market for click art (the illustrator's parallel to stock photography), most illustrations are unique to their project. This requires a successful illustrator to be both market-savvy and good at self-assessment. Illustration portfolios should reflect this awareness in their variety of form and presentation.

The Portfolio

An illustration portfolio format is dependent on whether the work itself is traditional or computer-based. For a professional in transition, a mixed approach is possible.

15

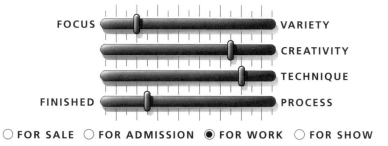

Figure 1.5
An illustrator's portfolio elements displayed.

FOCUS ——————— VARIETY
——————— CREATIVITY
——————— TECHNIQUE
FINISHED ——————— PROCESS

○ FOR SALE ○ FOR ADMISSION ⦿ FOR WORK ○ FOR SHOW

Non-computer pieces can be scanned and shown with digitally-crafted ones, or a traditional portfolio book of prints can be augmented with a digital component. Ilustrators working in traditional media sometimes show original artwork to emphasize their drawing skills, especially if the work was scanned and modified in final production. Computer-based illustrators, particularly those whose market is in a major city, are moving rapidly to the digital portfolio format, primarily in the form of sample diskettes and Web presentations. As Diane Fenster (see accompanying CD) says, "There are still some ADs who want to see a printed piece. I send them tear sheets, but most of them are thrilled when I ask them to look at my Web site. Usually that's enough."

Graphic Design

This section includes graphic designers, art directors, creative directors, broadcast designers, multimedia or Web specialists, industrial designers, and some animators.

The graphic design profession and the portfolios of its designers have changed so rapidly that defining either one is impossible. As a result of computer technology, graphic design has undergone a massive upheaval. Designers create Web sites, design 3-D broadcast logos, develop prototypes for interactive CDs, design annual reports, or any combination of the above. Most of these roles involve computer expertise and production skills.

Many designers work in-house for other designers, for advertising agencies, or in corporate publishing or communication departments. Designers often begin their careers as freelancers, either doing work for hire or as independent contractors on a project basis. This freelance work is an opportunity to build a professional portfolio and gain production experience, both of which are a requirement for moving up the ladder of project complexity.

The Portfolio

Technical presentation, flair, and attention to detail are particularly crucial for the design portfolio. The traditional portfolio is usually a combination of printed pieces and process work that is shown as a way of indicating the designer's approach to client needs. A portfolio on disk, however, dispenses with process samples and concentrates on a slide

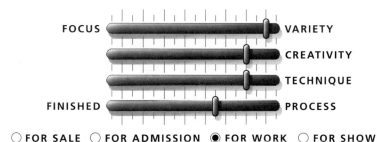

Figure 1.6
Elements of the graphic design portfolio displayed.

show or interactive presentation of finished work. This presentation is often a portfolio piece in itself. Digital graphic design portfolios are becoming so common that they may become a standard expectation within the next few years. Web sites in particular are becoming designers' main presentation medium.

Designer/Programmer

This category includes multimedia producers, interactive designers, interface designers, game designers, Webmasters, computer graphics artists, and most animators.

Art and programming are a recent marriage. No traditional career path or presentation standards have been set in stone, but many of the criteria for a design or illustration portfolio apply. After all, many interactive designers were educated as graphic

designers, industrial designers, and animators. Most interactive media designers picked up their programming skills on the job, cutting their teeth on Macromedia Director's Lingo or launching into HTML coding and CGI scripting. Many people in multimedia today also have some background with a CAD or modeling program.

17

The Portfolio

Interactive design demands a digital portfolio, and the more sophisticated, conceptually and technically, the better. Given the likelihood though that many projects might be in production at any given time, showing prototypes or work in process is a necessity. Craft, in the form of programming expertise, is also highly regarded but might be less of an issue if the person is more involved in the design of the project than the implementation.

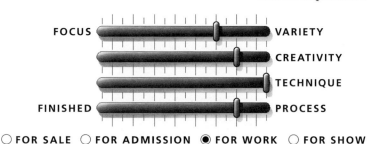

Figure 1.7
A designer/programmer's portfolio elements displayed.

Production Specialist

This category includes production artists or assistants, desktop publishers, desktop video specialists, and Web technicians.

Production can be temporary for a junior designer, or a means for an illustrator to hold an on-staff position. Most frequently, however, the production artist is a skilled practitioner who has all or some of the skills once divided among typographers, editors, paste-up artists, and printing strippers.

The Portfolio

The production portfolio usually comes in a portfolio binder because it must accommodate printed pieces. Before and after technical examples, such as a raw scanned photo with its retouched final for example, are other good ways to show expertise and lend themselves nicely to a digital presentation.

Figure 1.8
The elements of a production specialist's portfolio displayed

18

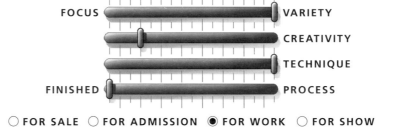

Production is also one of the few art- and design-related professions that is as likely to be held by a permanent as a contract employee.

A production artist's portfolio will be radically different from most designers' or artists' books. For one thing, it's likely to have wide stylistic variety, because it represents design execution, not development. This portfolio should be filled with challenging technical exercises in a variety of software programs. It also doesn't hurt to show design sense and typographic sensitivity.

Group Portfolios

There are three types of "group" portfolios with digital counterparts. The first is in the traditional gallery mold, where one person organizes the work of many individuals. The second is the corporate or design firm portfolio, where a highly crafted unit is created that merges different individual pieces into a presentational whole. The third can barely be called a group portfolio—it's more like a visual source book.

The Gallery

Although some artists share space, show together, or even work collaboratively, they still maintain their own portfolios. In the real world, galleries can be expensive to run and time-consuming to maintain. Rent on appropriate space alone can be prohibitive and seldom comes with adequate storage space. With the advent of the World Wide Web, a director can operate a visual site for comparatively low overhead. The 911 Gallery (http://www.911gallery.org/911/), one of the first online galleries of digital fine art, is an excellent example of a curated space with regular shows. Some of the artists also have their own Web spaces linked to their gallery "room."

The Presentation

Portfolios representing design, architectural, or multimedia firms are by nature the result of collaboration, occassionally on a very high level. These portfolios may be stylistically parallel or wildly different from project to project. Because of the clear marketing plus a digital presence these firms offer, owning and promoting some form of digital portfolio is fast becoming a requirement for a design firm to be taken seriously as a full-service house. This portfolio presentation can be anything from a formal presentation on a laptop to a multi-layered Web site. Excellent examples of these forms can be found in the Corey & Co. Web site and the Big Blue Dot presentations. Corey & Co.'s

work can be found on the accompanying CD.

At the other end of the spectrum, these group displays take more care and maintenance by the host of the site than the individual artists because the host has the task of coding and designing the area. Logistics and consistency are important because a real incentive for the Web host is to keep maintenance costs down. The individuals have no control over the context of their work and there is no curator to exercise quality control over the participants. DesignLink is a site that offers a fee-for-service space for illustrators, photographers, and designers to show their work.

Who Is Your Audience?

You don't serve steak to a vegetarian or waste time carefully creating sushi for a fast-food junkie. Most design professionals know the value of focusing on their strengths and targeting their work to a specific audience. On the other hand, it's easy to believe we know our audience when we actually only know who they *were*.

For the first time in history, we can work in Wisconsin for a company in Connecticut without leaving our homes. We can live in Boston and show our work in a Japanese gallery. This doesn't mean there are no regional differences. Quite the contrary. It does mean that people tend to take for granted that you are familiar with their criteria without taking these differences into account.

Awareness of what's going on in our corner of the universe does not necessarily mean that we are prepared to present at different locations, levels, formats, or even to a different category of client. For example, traditional portfolios on the East Coast usually contain matted boards or printed samples, and on the West Coast a portfolio might be a light box and sheets of 4×5 or 8×10 chromes.

Multi-World Networking

But how do you get target audience and regional information? Two solutions are personal contacts and information research. Both of these have been enriched by current online technology and should be mined to the fullest.

A personal network is the obvious starting point, beginning small and radiating outward. Creative professionals in related areas are good contacts, as are supplier companies and their representatives. Sharing information with your peers can let you know who in your city is busy and might be interested in hiring new talent. Getting to know your printing representatives and service bureau technicians can often give you another view of your local marketplace.

If there is a professional association in your field, join it. Most national associations have regional chapters, whether it be AIGA (American Institute of Graphic Artists), AIA (American Institute of Architects) or ACM (Association for Computing Machinery, the parent organization of the SIGGRAPH group). People are more likely to answer questions for someone they've met than to respond to a phone call from out of the blue. In addition, most of these organizations have statistics and surveys about your profession, from pricing structures to presentation standards. Although some of this material may be published for general use, other parts of it may be for members only. Contact information for a good selection of art and design organizations can be found in Appendix B.

Newsgroups = Instant Community

What if you're relocating? How can you find out what to expect in a new area when you have no personal network? The Internet can be a tremendous help. It's alive with special interest groups that share problems, suggestions, philosophies, and tips. Some of them are very specialized indeed while some are more general in scope. People go online for many different reasons, but artists and designers in particular can lead deadline-intensive lives with irregular hours. Newsgroups and mailing lists are a wonderful way to stay in touch with a world-wide community who share the same interests.

To find the newsgroups specific to your career, you have two methods. Anyone with a Unix shell account (universities, many BBSs, ISP budget accounts) can go to their newsreader and search on a subject, subscribing to groups that have the right focus. The other alternative, if you have Web access, is the search index Deja News, which enables you to search by subject matter, rather than the name of the group. An example of a simple Deja News search session can be found in Appendix A. Given the fact that some newsgroups are not named intuitively, this can be an easier way to zero in on your community. You can always go back later to the Usenet group menu and, armed with knowledge, select the few groups that really interest you.

The same purpose can be served if you subscribe to an online service. America Online and CompuServe both have lively special interest groups, particularly on graphic design and desktop publishing issues.

Email Lists and Chat Rooms

Another method of finding a network is the subscription mailing list. It operates somewhat like an open forum and does not require Web access. You send messages to the list as if you were sending regular email. You receive messages, either as individual email or an entire day's conversations in a digest. Because you have to subscribe to the list to read it and since a list can fill up your mailbox quickly, these lists have a more

selective community than the typical Usenet newsgroup. A page of art and design-related discussion lists can be found in Appendix A.

A fairly new phenomenon on the Web is the chat room. Some sites sponsor online discussions organized around a specific topic, and some are simply treated like a free-form mingling space. You're asked to register at these sites, but in most cases, they can be accessed on the spot. To see a lively example in action, visit the Advertising Age site (`http://www.adage.com`).

In all of these conversational environments, there are rules of etiquette and protocol, just as there are in a face-to-face get together. It's possible that the group has created an FAQ (Frequently Asked Questions) document that gives you the rules of the road and will help you determine whether it is indeed the right newsgroup for you. If there isn't one, read and listen first before posting   first impressesions count. People on line hate "seagull" posters—unknowns who fly into a newsgroup, make a lot of noisy demands, then fly out with the words, "I don't usually read this newsgroup. Can you email me your answers?" You are joining these groups to glean information, share experiences, and make contacts with people you might meet later in a new city, at a conference, or in an interview. If you become a responsible member of the online community, you may end up in offline private conversations, which could lead to invaluable advice, critiques, or job leads.

Research for Job Hunting

Remember that information is a form of power. It certainly can decrease trips to the library and rounds of phone calls. While you're exploring personal resources, you also can research other information: backgrounds on potential clients, gallery spaces, names of design firms or advertisers in different areas, the types of work they specialize in, and even specific people to contact.

22

You can also find a tremendous amount of misinformation on the Web. There are just too many sites for anyone to police content. Make sure that you treat what you find as opinion until verified from colleagues or traditional research references. "Why should I bother to search it on the Internet when I'll have to go to the library anyway?" you might ask. You don't have to contend with missing references, books out on loan to someone else, and limited open hours. Besides, the Internet is better on time-sensitive information than a library, or even a magazine or newspaper. If the specific information you need is available, the Net is a much faster means of accessing it and opinions are not valueless. You simply want to sprinkle uncorroborated material with some salt before swallowing it, especially if it could be the basis for crucial decisions on your part.

Some areas of information are more fully developed than others. Generally, the longer a category of industries or users has had access to the Internet, the broader the searchable options. If you don't find anything on a specific subject after trying several indexes or search engines, don't just assume it's you. Cut your losses and go the traditional route before you chalk up emiles on a wild goose chase.

Research for Job Hunting

Almost everyone knows that you can find job postings on the Internet. Some services advertise on radio and TV, but few general sites are equally good for all professions. The ideal site not only allows you to search for appropriate positions but enables you to compare other professional's résumés and portfolios to what you have to offer. Sites that carry advertisements for artists and designers can be found in Appendix A, followed by sites whose listings are specifically oriented to the art and design community.

Education

It's easy to find information about educational institutions. Every library has an extensive compilation of books in their reference sections. In addition, universities and colleges are charter members of the Internet community. They have online catalogues complete with admissions requirements (including what form your portfolio should take for each institution), separate sites for their faculty, and documentation on different programs of study. Simply searching under the educational institution's name should bring you to their Web site.

Don't forget that education is also a source of employment opportunities. Tenure-track teaching positions are generally the product of a formal search through established journals and other academic channels, but often part-time teaching positions are available. Many colleges and universities post these and other staff openings on their Web pages.

Corporations

Corporate information hunting is more of a hodge-podge process. Not all companies are represented on the Web and those which appear are not always represented well. Sometimes this is a Catch 22: you really need information on a corporation because they are a potential client, but they really need you because they're a start-up and information on them is not widely available. Companies involved in information as a product are more likely to be reachable—and searchable—through online sources than manufacturing firms or traditional service industries. You'll find a small book publisher on the Web faster than a law firm.

This doesn't mean that information on more traditional industries is not available, it just means that you may have to keep your inquiries general. The exception to this, of course, is government information. Public corporations in the US must register with the SEC (Securities and Exchange Commission), which means that annual report information can be easily searched. Online business magazines and newspapers are another source. *The Wall Street Journal's* site at http://bis.dowjones.com is a gateway to a substantial database of industries and individual corporations, both in the US and around the world.

23

Business Profile Research

How do you go about a serious profile search? This depends on whether you just need some background information or a complete work-up on a specific issue. For example, let's assume that you work for a design firm that takes on projects from an advertising agency. The agency has been contacted by a potential client for a rework of the client's Web site. You've done a few Web sites before, but you know nothing about the company and don't want to show them irrelevant material when you present your work and ideas.

A slew of questions comes up. What does their Web site look like now? Who created it originally, and what don't they like about it?

What is their industry? How does their site compare to other sites in their industry? What's wrong with it now? Where is the company located and will its cultural origin make any difference? What about budget? You're going into this presentation blind and you could use every shred of information you can find to give you an edge on the other design firms who will be presenting their work.

Believe it or not, answers to most if not all of these questions can be found simply by using available Internet search engines. In Appendix A, you can follow the actual search path taken to find source material for this hypothetical client profile.

As you try the links and discover those of your own, remember to make *bookmarks* so you can return to them later, and organize your bookmarks into categories. Half of the battle in making your way through research issues is knowing where to look for answers, and if you have to reconstruct your sources every time you have a problem to solve, the process will take much longer.

Next...

Now you know who you are in the context of the marketplace you move in, you've checked out available jobs and their requirements, and you know how to go about finding information to help target your portfolio and its presentations. Now let's deal with choosing your portfolio medium next.

CHAPTER TWO

Choosing Your Portfolio Medium

Unlike happy families, happy portfolios are not all alike. Even within the common formats, there is plenty of room to personalize your presentation. The goal of this chapter is not an encyclopedic description of every possible choice, but an examination of the pros and cons of the different formats so you can find the best medium for the story of your portfolio to unfold.

Traditional Media

Although this book is about digital portfolios, more familiar ways of presenting work cannot be neglected. In fact, a large percentage of individuals and companies who maintain portfolios do so in more than one form. These should be viewed as complementary rather than competing options. Never forget that the digital portfolio forms are very new, and that some clients or potential employers will expect to see physical finished pieces in a face-to-face presentation.

Portfolio Binder

This is the most familiar form for designers, illustrators, and production artists. The archetypal portfolio binder is a zippered leather case with interior side pockets and plastic protected sleeves. Ranging from simple three-ring binders to four-foot long cases, they can be purchased from most art supply stores.

It's fairly obvious when a portfolio binder is your best choice. More useful is to realize when it's the wrong one. Don't carry a big portfolio just to accommodate one large piece. Negative space on a page is good, but too much of it can make your other pieces seem lost. Unless you have to shoot your work down to such a small percentage that important details disappear, it's always better to keep your presentation as compact as possible. Size according to the majority of your work, then consider other ways of showing an off-size piece.

Saddlewire or vello bound items are usually too thick to sit in binder sleeves. They always slide to the bottom of the plastic, forcing you to readjust them as you present. Attaching them limits you to showing the cover or one inside spread. If you have only a few booklets, they can be placed in a separate folder which you can slip spine-in into the side pocket, but a large group will shift in transit, slowly becoming damaged. Storyboards are also too thick if mounted properly, as well as awkward to pull out for examination. Corners tend to catch.

A good alternative in these situations is the carrying case, which is available in a nice range of sizes, materials, and colors, ranging from clear flexible to black hard shell (see Figure 2.1). They're much better for thick or irregular shaped pieces, and are more graceful for presenting one board at a time. It's true that they hold less, but being forced to choose carefully can improve the overall effect of your work.

Slides

Artists and photographers usually fill 3-ring binders with slides of their work. This is a much more satisfactory system for photography than it is for other media, but because there is such an experiential gap between viewing real work and shining light through a tiny piece of film, this is still often a compromise. It can also be expensive, if you are sending out multiple duplicates of your slides as samples. It's also harder to break format to distinguish your portfolio book.

Three-ring binders are easy to carry around and are nicely expandable, but they are mediocre protection off the shelf, and have little stylistic variety (see Figure 2.2). Particularly if you are mailing your work, consider velcro-tab, string-tie or elastic closed folders instead. Not only are they fairly inexpensive, but they immediately set your work apart.

Figure 2.1
Open carrying case with mounted boards.

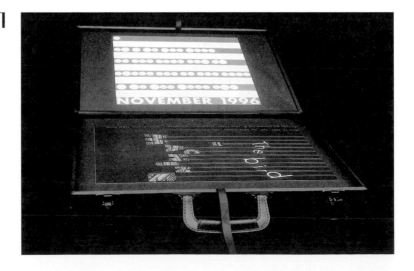

Figure 2.2
Examples of a portfolio binder, case, and mailing folder.

These folders are inefficient if you need to show a large body of work, but there are very few occasions where that is really advisable. Because one standard slide sheet seems so small and thin, it's easy to forget that it holds 20 slides—20 different examples of your work. Unless someone has specifically requested your entire oeuvre, you need to ask yourself how many examples you can legitimately show without dipping into the second string, or back into an earlier style.

Being selective about your work has financial and process benefits. With fewer slides to label, you can spend more time making sure you've handled their details well. Slides should always be correctly and legibly captioned, their viewing orientation marked on the slide and reinforced by standardizing the way they're placed in the sheet. You know exactly how your work should be oriented. Unless it's strongly

representational, most people glancing at it will not, and will be irritated at being corrected if you are presenting in person.

Contrary to popular belief, expensive black cardboard mounts are not always welcome. Although there are some situations where this level of formality can make a difference, in most situations the person looking at your work would rather not fuss with it. A clean, new slide sheet properly oriented can be laid on a light table and all slides viewed at once, reducing wear and tear on your materials.

Alternatives to Slides: Transparencies and Brochures

Although there are many circumstances where slides are a required format, there are two good "non-digital" alternatives. One possibility is to substitute 4×5 color transparencies, particularly for your large-format, detailed or three-dimensional pieces.

Although more expensive, this is a considerably more satisfying alternative for all photographic presentations. A growing alternative is to invest in a printed brochure with additional samples of your work. This avenue is particularly cost effective if your work emphasizes form over color, because a run of high-quality laser brochures on good paper stock is a fraction of the cost of duplicating slides. If you already do work in a digital medium, creating the brochures yourself may cost some time and a learning curve, but are worth the investment as a supplement to both a traditional and a digital portfolio.

Video Cassettes

Video can be the only reasonable medium for showing installations, 3-D art, or broadcast material (see Figure 2.3). This is true regardless of whether a computer is involved in the process, but it's particularly useful if your work is computer-based but the people you need to present it to are not. Even if your intended audience does have access to the right kind of computer to view your work, there is no guarantee that their computer's processor speed will be the same as yours. A video tape insures that your work will be seen exactly as it was designed when you recorded it.

Good video requires several things: either a threshold of prior experience in video creation and editing as well as access to the right equipment, or a substantial amount of money. It will not benefit your portfolio to create a substandard video. On the other hand, your computer-based video portfolio does not necessarily have to be a broadcast-standard effort, as long as the information you show is cleanly presented and edited.

Figure 2.3
Example of a finished videotape package.

Most noncomputer-savvy people in the United States who might be viewing your video presentation will need it in standard VHS format, which means that videos you may be creating in Hi-8 for desktop purposes would need to be time-coded and transferred. Additionally, outside the US the standard format is the PAL system, an important consideration if you wish to show your work overseas. Every time a video is rerecorded it loses quality, so you may have to plan your logistics carefully.

If you are shipping or showing videotapes, remember to label them attractively both on the tape itself and on its outside case, as well as clearly title the tape itself at both the beginning and end of your presentation. Your labels should include your name, your representative's name (if applicable) and contact address, a simple title for the tape (Demo Installation, White Heat Project, Sculptures in Situ, and so on) and the tape length in minutes. Because videotapes are linear, no one will play them through—or rewind them—just to find out whose work they're seeing.

Digital Media

One of the convenient things above developing a digitally based portfolio is the capability to move up in quality and presentation sophistication using much of the same content. You can begin very simply with a small group of files on diskette, and graduate to a true interactive presentation as your technical knowledge broadens and your body of work increases.

Diskettes

The simple diskette needs no introduction and its usefulness is underestimated by people developing their digital portfolio (see Figure 2.4). Diskettes come in a wide range of colors, and blank, laser-ready labels can be purchased to personalize them. They're small, relatively sturdy, and extremely inexpensive, especially if purchased in bulk. For protection and to add another presentation layer, you can find compact 2-disk carrying cases. Assuming you make the right choices in file formats and compression, these can be ideal cross-platform leave-behinds or bulk-mailing promotional materials.

Removable Cartridges

I have noticed a growing trend toward using removable media in presentations. Many files are simply too large to fit on a diskette, and with the recent shift in removable technology to diskette-sized cartridges, this change seems as natural as moving from low density $5^{1}/_{4}$" floppy disks to our now familiar $3^{1}/_{2}$" hard-case diskettes. The new breed of cartridges are much less fragile than the old SyQuests or Bernoullis, and are considerably cheaper megabyte-for-megabyte. Although at $20 to $30 each they are still too costly for a leave-behind, prices are dropping so quickly as third-party licensees

Figure 2.4
Examples of diskette portfolios.

30

begin to offer the formatted cartridges in bulk that these prices could be halved by the time this book reaches print.

One of the longest-running arguments against cartridges no longer exists. As recently as mid-1995, bringing a cartridge meant verifying in advance not only the brand of drive the client or prospective employer had available, but also its capacity. How many of us have (at least once) asked about SyQuest capability and been told yes, only to discover that the available drive was an 88—or a 3.5" SyQuest—and our cartridge a 200MB? The new drives are tiny, and thoughtfully equipped with guest software functions, so we can carry the drive as well as the cartridge.

There are a few downsides to this strategy. First, the convenience of the cartridge can make you lazy, with potentially serious consequences. Cartridges are still sensitive to heat, and magnetic fields have the same

effect on them as kryptonite on Superman. How easy to stop on the way to or from a presentation at a store with a security gate! This could happen to a diskette, but the effect is not equally serious. If you lose 1.4 MB of compressed, duplicated work, you can always send another copy of it to your presentee. But the cartridge will not only take longer to replace, it may have been your only portfolio copy. After all, it was so "EZ" to pick up and carry, but not a "Zip" to duplicate on your old Centris 650!

Even if your backup strategies are models of caution, there are some other technical issues to consider if your digital portfolio will live on a removable. First, Mac and PC formatted cartridges are not always usable nor readable on the other platform, even if you have the right connectors to adapt the drive. You may have to carry two cartridges, along with your cables and the appropriate software. Second, since you may have live programs being executed on the computer, run speed for animation or video could be variable. Test first!

Compact Disc

In most situations where you have enough material to justify carrying a removable to presentations, you could benefit from transferring that material to CD (see Figure 2.5). Blank CDs for recording can be purchased individually, or in bulk, from most computer supply stores and mail order houses. They range in price from $5 to $10, are manufactured by all the major suppliers of standard computer disk media, and currently come in two flavors: 550MB/63 minutes and 650MB/74 minutes. The price gap between the two formats is so minimal (.40–.50 on the average) that, if your service bureau's recorder can handle them and your volume is low, you might as well use the 650s.

CDs, besides solving most of the problems inherent in the direct use of computer disk media, are a fairly familiar technology to most people. They are easy to integrate into a traditional portfolio, are impervious to magnetic fields, and their jewel boxes lend themselves to attractive customization. Best yet, you never have to expose original art to loss, damage, or unexpected appropriation.

Laptop

For a group or a company with a serious budget and an extensive portfolio, the best presentation strategy is to move your show to a portable computer. Besides being an extremely compact and elegant way of transporting large volumes of work, the dedicated laptop gives you ultimate control of your presentation. You never have to worry about platform issues, or whether the people you are presenting to can tell the difference between a diskette and a coaster.

31

Figure 2.5
CD portfolio package.

You can show in an intimate setting, or hook the computer to a projection system and present to a filled room. There are no surprises in animation speed and image color, and you're less likely to be plagued by technical gremlins because your environment has been controlled and pretested.

A laptop, however, is usually overkill for an individual, except in industries like entertainment or in special circumstances like seminar presentations. It demands a large hardware expenditure dedicated to a single purpose and sets up a very high expectation of quality and technical expertise that might lead to unrealistic assumptions and deadlines.

32

Web Site

The Web version of a digital portfolio might look like other digital formats, but is physically (and should be conceptually) very different. We will discuss the concept and implementation in the chapter dedicated to Web sites, but some quick format considerations are worth addressing here.

Your Web site, when all is said and done, is nothing more than a collection of files and images residing on a computer that has been dedicated as a Web server. For it to perform well as a marketing tool, it must reflect well on you. The most successful sites are those that provide material tailored to the Web's opportunities and limitations.

If you are considering putting your work on the Web, remember that it is closer in concept to a leave-behind than it is to a presentation. Being a truly interactive, real-time experience, portfolio presentation allows you to adjust your tone, emphasis, and pacing to the listener's reaction. If you make a minor error or an awkward gesture, no one remembers it. The Web, however, enables the infinite and exhaustive replay of both your strengths and weaknesses. You no longer have control over pacing, the order of presentation, or the opportunity to engage in ice-breaking repartee. Your objective, therefore, in fielding a Web site is not to eliminate the need to present, but to broaden the base of people who will ask you to do so. For most people, the Web page is not a substitute for other media.

When NOT to Digitize

Obviously, if you're reading a book titled *Creating a Digital Portfolio*, the assumption is that you're interested in developing one. Especially if this is your first foray into displaying your work digitally, you'll want to make sure that you've chosen the right medium at the right time. It's equally important to know your audience and consider where they might stand on experiencing your work a new way.

Audience Preconceptions

Unfortunately, technophobia is still with us, more in some areas of art and design than others, and it can surface in the most unexpected of surroundings. I vividly remember attending a panel discussion at a computer graphics conference five or six years ago. One of the panelists was a well-known art critic, who used her appearance on the panel as an unexpected opportunity to state that no computer-based art had yet shown artistic merit, and that furthermore, none would or even should. Many curators of contemporary art disagree with her assessment, but not all.

Some areas of expertise, such as interactive design or 3-D animation and modeling, fully expect a digital presentation. Others are open to a Web site, but frown on digital output. Still others accept only grudgingly their profession's use of computer tools, and will only consider working with people who can show training in more traditional methods. Before you put the energy and time into creating a digital portfolio, be prepared to deal in advance with the questions that might arise. If you don't know the standards of presentation in your discipline or you've recently moved to a new locale, don't assume that what you've seen or done before fits your current criteria. Turn to Appendix A and exercise your networking options first.

Hardware Barriers

Attitude isn't the only barrier. Sometimes it's access—yours, theirs, or both. Museums of all sizes have been rushing to develop a Web presence, and many curators have become interested in digitally-generated work. Universities, too, have become much more open to disk-based presentations. On the other hand, most gallery owners operate on such a small margin that a computer purchase is a major capital expense. Diskettes or CDs bulk-mailed to galleries are certain to end up shown frequently—as coasters and paperweights.

Who will They Show it to?

In many cases, the digital portion of your portfolio will be a leave-behind. Samples and diskettes can be very powerful reminders of what you can do, especially to a busy creative director or editor who runs back through their files two months later to fill an assignment. Be careful, however, if you are shopping for a new job while working full-time for another company. Unlike printed samples, which usually stay with a candidate's résumé in a folder or office file, digital samples are almost always copied to a hard drive for future viewing. Files are very easy to duplicate and move, and many local art and design communities are small. If this fits your local description and you don't want everyone in your office to know about your job search, think very carefully before digitizing.

33

Is Your Work Ready to go Digital?

Not all work is appropriate to show digitally. Before you begin the process, you should look at the nature and current form of the work you want to show. In the rush to reformat, you could be decreasing your marketability! The following categories of work should at least raise red flags:

Complex or Large-Format Work

Artwork meant to be seen large seldom looks right on the monitor screen, particularly if it is in portrait orientation. If your piece can't be viewed without scrolling, the image is too large. If scaling it to fit a 17" screen makes the work hard to distinguish, it's probably not worth showing on disk, and even less likely to work on a Web site. Smaller work with complex finishes, such as die-cuts, pockets, pop-ups, and fold-outs, is also hard to translate effectively. There are work-arounds for some of these types of pieces that I will discuss later in the book, but none of them are completely satisfactory.

Work That Looks "Unfinished" On-Screen

AutoCAD drawings, which are generally created on a black field with a limited pen palette, should always be printed for

portfolio showing. The same is true for any desktop work which has pixelated FPO (for position only) art. This doesn't mean that production artists could not show their work on disk to show their expertise, only that a printed version should be shown first, and the actual file brought out only if the interviewer has technical questions.

When Your Best Decisions Get Lost in the Bytes

If you are a graphic designer who has worked extensively in print production, you should apply a very strict criteria for your on-disk or online decisions. An experienced designer knows all too well how paper quality decisions can make or break a design. Although it is possible to incorporate the appearance of the paper, usually there is no substitute for the actual piece. Some of the most disappointing designer Web pages happen when displaying what the maker obviously believes to be tour de force work.

In the rush to *webify* a portfolio, it's easy to be misled by a professional photo's detail, not realizing how much it will lose in the translation. Subtle touches, like blind embossing, disappear or flatten when scanned. Spot varnish, depending on the nature of the scanner used, either disappears or translates into a textured hot spot. At the very least, you should look at ways of reshooting large pieces or scanning details to minimize turning an expensive, elegant design into just another printed piece.

The Perils of 3-D

Unless your 3-D is already virtual, sculpture and installations can be very difficult to present on-screen. Scanning a still photograph removes the viewer two steps from the original, and frequently demands a deft touch with the virtual brush to be useful. Video capture is the best solution, but requires massive processing power for decent resolution. Additionally, current technology leaves most inexpensive video capture in a Lilliputian viewing window. For almost every presenting situation except the Internet, traditional analog video is probably still the best method of giving a sense of mass, proportion, and space to a 3-D environment. From there, a good video deck and an off-line editing program (depending on your quality needs and general access, anything from Adobe Premiere to a Media 100 board with its software) can enable you to grab relevant pieces to incorporate into an on-screen presentation.

Why Digital?

A growing number of artists and designers have added the digital palette to their list of art-making tools, either as their exclusive expression, or as a natural outgrowth of more traditional work. For these people, an on-screen portfolio is an obvious next step. But the computer can be an effective portfolio tool for existing work as well.

Easier to "Leave" as a Visual Résumé

Résumés are very nice, but they don't show what you can do. Many potential clients request that you leave portfolio examples with them. This can be expensive, not to mention that it can eat into your samples cache. Leaving a diskette, CD, or Web address, on the other hand, is inexpensive and painless. It also offers follow-up opportunities you would not consider in a traditional setting.

Flexibility/Updateability

Work shown digitally is work that can always be current. After you've developed a portfolio and begun archiving your work as you go, updating a Web site is often as simple as editing a page, renaming it, and converting a new image to the right format. Leave-behinds that simply involve substituting one piece for another are equally straightforward. If you tend to do more than one kind of work, or for a variety of industries, you can maintain a number of carefully targeted portfolio versions. Each version can have most of the same material, with different modules inserted as needed.

Portability

Have you ever had to carry a portfolio on a plane, sandwiching it behind the last seat before the bathrooms and dreading the trip to the baggage carousel? Portfolios on disk can be packed into a carry-on bag. Even if you have a traditional portfolio as well, chances are you'll be able to compact portions of this work, transfer some to a digital format, and end up with a smaller, lighter binder.

Note

All it takes is one bad experience to bring home the need to maintain a spare collection of your work. A graduating design student, for example, was carrying her portfolio from one interview to another and left it on her back seat while she made a quick stop. When she returned, she had a pile of shattered glass and no portfolio book. No one responded to her flyers asking for its return. Some pieces were irretrievable, but fortunately she had a backup disk of all her computer-based work, and some scanned photography. It wasn't everything, but it was enough to allow her to continue interviewing. No matter what form your portfolio ultimately takes, you should always have it totally backed up so you can recreate it quickly. Going digital, in whole or in part, can save you from disaster, because files are so much easier to protect and archive.

Long Term Cost-Effectiveness

Between slide duplication, high-end digital output, case, and mounting materials, it can cost a designer or artist over a week's pay to create a traditional portfolio. If the work needs to be sent out for evaluation, the outlay is an ongoing drain, and not everyone who sees your work will end up calling you. If you can only afford to send your package to 50 contacts per year, a mere fraction of

these people will result in an assignment or job. Obviously, minimizing costs can mean more possible contacts. It's not that creating a digital portfolio is free, but it can be a much more efficient use of money and time.

Larger Potential Audience

Not only will a digital portfolio help you in your direct mail efforts, but a Web site can offer multiple possibilities to extend your reach. This is particularly tempting now that geography has begun to count so little in contract work. Many artists, photographers and designers seldom or never meet with the people who buy their work or offer them assignments.

It's not surprising that many artists are creating digital galleries to broaden the chances of people seeing their work. Web sites are relatively inexpensive, allow additional creative expression, and lend themselves to "group shows" and other collaborative innovations. They also can be useful as "teasers" for a traditional show, especially if you can convince established sites to link to your page.

Enables You to Show Your Design Thinking

Everyone has to make compromises at some stage in their career. Sometimes these compromises are made up-front and are called design constraints. Good design accepts these constraints and incorporates them as part of design problem-solving. Other compromises come in response to client input during the process. Sometimes these compromises work beautifully, other times they leave a designer wishing for just one project where their own creativity could have free reign—at least within the problem's constraints. Web sites are particularly useful for designers, because a good page is more than a vehicle for showing previous work. The design Web site should be viewed as a project equal to the firm's corporate identity package. It is one of the best ways of making a self-promotion part of your portfolio without the piece being seen as "make work."

A Better Medium for Traditional Work

Artwork comes in many sizes, shapes, colors and media. Some of it—performance and installation art—is ephemeral. Yet the standard way of showing art is to reduce it to a flat framed film about the size of a thumb. This might be acceptable if this slide was seen as intended—projected large in a darkened room. Most frequently it's held up to the light, squinted at quickly, and judged in the space of a minute. Transparencies offer one way around this, but they're relatively expensive and not nearly as compact.

On the other hand, the brightness of the computer screen is a natural substitute for light through film, and even a 15" color screen will display an image larger than a

6"×4" transparency. A computer takes up less space than some light tables. Disks are easy to handle and store, cheap to duplicate, and comparatively insensitive to heat, cold, humidity, and light. As art and design sites become more common on the Internet, more artwork will be previewed on-screen.

When Technology Belongs Center Stage

Animators, videographers, and broadcast designers have often been frustrated by the limitations of a standard portfolio. Storyboards can only show so much, and videotapes must be completely redone to add or subtract even a frame. Even worse, stills from many animations show nothing of what the animator does best: the mastery of motion. This can be particularly frustrating if the animator is a graphic designer who has created a logo to be used in both broadcast and print. In such situations, the digital portfolio might be the only reasonable way of presenting this work.

Creative Compromise

The digital portfolio concept is still evolving. During this transition period, design professionals and artists might still need to maintain a traditional portfolio. Holding a combination portfolio offers the best of both worlds: the immediacy and tactile satisfaction of work in print with the computer color and format flexibility of the digital world.

There are as many different ways of creating a multimedia portfolio as there are combinations of individual media. The three major ways of approaching the problem are *duplicating*, *dividing*, and *developing*.

Duplicating

A duplicated portfolio assumes that its owner has a single body of work viewable through a variety of means. In this case, you would develop your portfolio themes, choose the best pieces to illustrate them, and create one portfolio version—either the easier to create, or the one needed immediately—first. After this new portfolio has been tested, presented, and, if necessary, refined, it is duplicated in either the digital or the traditional version. If the volume of work seems to warrant it, you might pull out a few elements to be duplicated as a leave-behind. The plus of this approach is the simplicity of presentation and the speed with which you can accomplish the task. Updates happen in tandem, and you never have to remember who saw which version of your work. The minus is that you may be showing some work in a medium which compromises its effectiveness, or weakening one version with a piece that plays very well in a different format, but seems redundant in the other.

Dividing

The divided portfolio is a compromise position, and demands more thought and preparation than the duplicated one. Having sorted through your work, you need to determine which elements will translate effectively to a digital presentation, and which would be better seen traditionally.

The next step is to see how these decisions affect the way you've been developing your portfolio themes. It's possible to jump back and forth between a traditional binder and a computer screen, but logistics can be tricky. You frequently don't know what kind of space you'll be given in which to present, or even whether you'll be given the opportunity to show in both media. Sometimes the solution is to concentrate the "story" in a traditional portfolio set-up, and choose specific digital examples for your leave-behinds or promotional materials or for presentation emphasis. This approach can bear some resemblance to the concept of movie trailers, where you show "highlights" of the themes you will develop further in person. The rewards for this approach can be very satisfying. Done well, it displays your understanding of your own work and is a wonderful example of design problem solving. The negative is how easy it can be to lose track of where you are, or lose your audience's interest if you are bouncing back and forth too much.

A divided portfolio is particularly useful if you do more than one thing well. Fine artists who also actively solicit commercial illustration commissions often change media to suit their sense of audience. Alan Toney (see CD) says of his Web site, "I feel it functions as a portfolio only in a select target group. In other areas I use it as an adjunct to a more formal presentation. My main thrust is in the area of fine art. There, oddly enough, I believe the Web site has less relevance, even though a large part of the site contains a fine art print catalog. I also actively solicit commissions in the record/book/magazine publishing industries. Here, I feel the site has greater value as a quick, cheap, first approach tool."

Developing

Developing is both easier and more difficult than the other two options. When you develop new materials, you are solving a design problem from scratch. This allows you to optimize your work for the new medium. One of the nasty surprises we all discover with our first digital portfolio is how difficult it is to shoehorn some of our work into a new format. If we are committed to developing a book specifically for a digital presentation, we only have to use older material when it's relevant and will play well. In fact, when freed from the work-as-it-was, we can revisit ideas and show precisely how we translate the concept with new constraints. An interior designer, for example, could develop a walk-through with different solutions for a space. An animator can translate a complex 3-D piece's ideas into a Shockwave or GIF animated "trailer." A design firm can create a mock-up of a Web page based on a previously-completed corporate identity.

It's important not to treat this—or get suckered into doing it—as "work on spec."

These should not be potential design solutions for a real job on the horizon. If you get the job it will be hard to charge appropriately for it, and if you don't, it will be hard to show the work as a viable, independent design solution.

The negatives of developing new work come down to two little words with big impact: money and time. A successful firm can usually afford to throw money at what is clearly perceived as a marketing issue. An artist or independent professional can't spare the money, but usually has periods of feast and famine even during good economic times. The quiet periods are ideal for expending time and effort on developing new material, which will hopefully help to minimize the down times in the future. Each individual firm or practitioner must survey their own resources against what they have to gain in determining realistically what form of digital portfolio to create.

Next...

We've come a long way through the preparation phase. In fact, we seem to have covered all the basics and now we can start massaging the work. Well, not quite. Hiding in the wings are organization and preparation. Those tedious and boring words are more critical to your portfolio than you might think. We also have to develop a successful approach which will link your audience and their expectations to your format and your work. Let's deal with these issues next.

CHAPTER THREE

Pre-Portfolio Considerations

I have yet to see any problem, however complicated, which, when you looked at it in the right way, did not become still more complicated.
—*Poul Anderson*

By this time, you have a good idea of what type of portfolio you want to produce. You might have all the right ingredients on hand. Possibly, you'll have realized that you could use something specific and need to create it, re-create it, or find it. With the growing variety of considerations for creating and maintaining a portfolio, preparation—often weeks to months ahead—can spell the difference between a mediocre presentation and a successful one. This chapter deals with organizing your work and preserving your materials so that you can count on everything coming together at the right time.

Does Organization Matter?

It's very tempting to just pull together the things you've always used, add a few newer pieces, and send out your resume. Maybe you could scan them in and give out a disk, too. This approach works fine if nothing in your life and practice has changed over time—and you don't want it to. But the more technology encroaches on creativity, the less likely it is that your digital portfolio should be a clone of your traditional one. Creating a digital portfolio is a license to invent, to refocus your view of yourself, and to project a new image to others. It's easier to take full advantage of that opportunity if you have prepared for it in advance. This requires being able to look at your body of work in its entirety so that you can evaluate its condition and relevance to your current needs.

Let's take one of the many examples of how personal interests and practice can slowly change over time. Imagine an architect with a small studio. His primary focus is his architectural practice. He's been using a computer to render digital walkthroughs to help his clients visualize unbuilt spaces as well as handle routine CAD drawings.

Now let's imagine that this same architect is practicing in a city where the market for new architectural design is soft. Lately he's been getting calls from some established architectural design firms that have heard about his walkthroughs and might be interested in subcontracting with him. They want him to come in and show them samples. In all honesty, he really enjoys this end of his business, but he doesn't want to stop creating new work. He wants to take advantage of the opportunity but wants to make sure they recognize his creative potential, too.

42

So our architect looks through his materials. He has one walkthrough for a house he recently finished. Should he include scanned photographs of the completed building as part of the presentation? He has some conceptual work he did purely as an exploration, but he'd really like to show it because it combines his talents. OK, where is it? The Pentium drive is full and it's not there…wait! He moved it off to make space. Now which disk is it on? What about the walkthrough animations? He usually presents them to his clients here in the office. They're too big to fit on a diskette and he doesn't have a portable computer. What about those glossy prints he made from the stills? Oh no! The best one was pinned up on the wall and it's beginning to fade. Now what about that conceptual work? He roots through a pile of unlabeled removable cartridges, realizing that he'll have to check each one.

It's not that our architect doesn't have a perfectly good design portfolio. It's just that almost none of the work in his case is relevant to this new opportunity. He's about to spend a significant amount of time and some money pulling together something that might have been right at his fingertips.

Quick Start for the Organizationally Challenged

Portfolios are dynamic documents. As we've seen, some people need more than one version, yet others need one body of work in multiple formats. But no matter what the form, excellent portfolios are not created the night before you need them. They require the kind of planning many creative people avoid. This has always been true, but in preparing a digital portfolio lack of organization is more than a personal creative quirk. In the worst case, it can damage your reputation and it's guaranteed to make the creation process a nightmare. So what can you do right now if you strongly identify with our architect?

If you're like most of us, the last thing you want to do is RTFM (Read The Fabulous Manual). Of course, you want to do things the right way, but you're in a hurry, and you can always catch up later. If you absolutely must have a digital portfolio *right now*, follow these short tips for cut-rate organization.

Print out all your disk directories, including subdirectories, and keep them with your disks. This way you'll at least know what's on each one without having to waste time swapping disks in and out. This is a trivial process in the Mac OS, an irritating but manageable one in DOS/Windows 3.1 (many utility programs are for printing directory trees), and an admittedly tedious one in Windows 95 but worth the effort. Using a highlighter, mark each file that you think could be useful as a portfolio element.

 If your samples are not all in one place, bring them together. If you have a file drawer in your desk, make folders for all samples that are small enough to fit inside them. Dedicate one flat file drawer or storage shelf for anything that's too big for the file drawer.

 Look over your current portfolio. Make a list of those pieces that you feel might be relevant to your revised version. Find a second copy of all of these items. You don't want to compromise your existing portfolio while you are preparing a new one. If you don't have a second copy, note that on your list.

 Skip to Portfolio and Proprietary Issues later in this chapter and continue reading. Take the time to read how to organize as you work. After all,

there's a distinct possibility that you will need to make a new portfolio again. Why create work for yourself multiple times? Bear in mind that being organized is only hard at the beginning. Once you get used to it, you don't even notice the process.

Proactive Organization: Doing It Right

The best way to create a digital portfolio is to anticipate the event. Whenever you begin a new project, in the back of your mind you should be asking yourself if this piece might be a keeper. This is especially critical if you are doing something you enjoy and would like to do more of. After all, the enjoyment is why you're in a creative profession, rather than influence peddling on Wall Street. Every project, job, personal exploration, or visual document is a potential player in the final production. As such, you'll want to approach your normal working process with the idea of making a digital file and its final form "portfolio ready."

Begin with Your Digital Work

Organizing traditional materials is a piece of cake compared to dealing with computer files. Computer files are hard to recognize on sight, even harder to find than a buried piece of scrap paper, and all too easy to throw away. And there's no question that having to go back months later and

43

reorganize work is tedious and pointless. Starting with your next job, optimize your process.

 Name uniquely. Avoid generic folder and filenames. Be concise but as descriptive as you can. If your work is computer-based, versions of your original idea, development, and concept refinement take place onscreen. This digital idea trail can be a wonderful resource if you can find the files! Filling a disk with multiple versions named "image1," "myproject3," or "brochure" can be almost as useless as deleting them.

44

 Name descriptively. Avoid numbers in filenames. Use them only as "save as" devices for purely chronological stages of a working session (see Figure 3.1). If your current project is to create the background image for a new Web site, HomeBgd might work. At the end of the session, you'll know that HomeBgd2, HomeBgd3, HomeBgd4, and HomeBgd5 can be deleted and HomeBgd6 can be renamed without the last digit. If you create a different version of a file, *don't* number it. Describe what's different. HomeBkgdGara, HomeBkgdRed, or HomeBkgdTxture are good examples of documenting variations in typestyle, color, or style.

Note

Special circumstances will arise in which you may need to break our anti-number rule. This is likely if you are a member of a production team or a freelancer on an ongoing project. If so, create a log in a spreadsheet program, a template in a page-layout program, or even a simple word processed document with columns. Add a date ("front.11.5") or sequence ("back.v5.2") to your root name and log a simple description in the document. This will help you remember the version's look or format and allows someone else to find an important file in your absence. Remember, too, that some kinds of programs—Premiere comes immediately to mind— import images according to a numerical naming scheme. Taking advantage of this can save you hours of renaming if you plan to create animation clips of your work.

 Don't get long winded. Try not to exceed 22 characters. Yes, the Macintosh OS and some versions of Windows let you use long filenames, but these names truncate in directory displays and will be too busy and confusing in icon form. Not only is your creative time too valuable to waste, remember that your service bureau's clock is running while you open multiple files searching for the right one to output.

Figure 3.1
Open window with sliced file names.

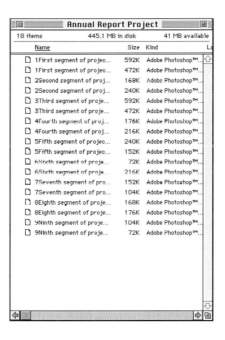

 Group your projects. If you have multiple projects for a client, class, or publication, dedicate a removable cartridge to the group. Cartridges have become so inexpensive and small that this should be quite practical for ongoing clients. Create a new folder on the cartridge for each project you do for the client and make sure you use it. Before you shut down for the day, print a disk directory and keep it with the drive. Label your removable drives and your drive cases.

 Alias everything. If your operating system supports them, make aliases of your major folders so that you can jump directly into them. Put one set of aliases directly on the desktop, but don't stop there. Make multiple aliases

of each folder, and put them inside each of the other folders of live jobs (see Figure 3.2). You'll be able to reach any folder almost immediately and you won't be tempted to put files in the current directory to "save time."

 Avoid platform partisan errors. You may need to show your digital portfolio on a different platform than the one you created it on. Whenever possible, use naming conventions that are legal on all likely operating systems. This may limit you almost exclusively to letters and numbers, but it's probably worthwhile. See Appendix C for a list of appropriate naming symbols and procedures for different operating systems.

Figure 3.2
*Two open folders,
each with the alias
of the other.*

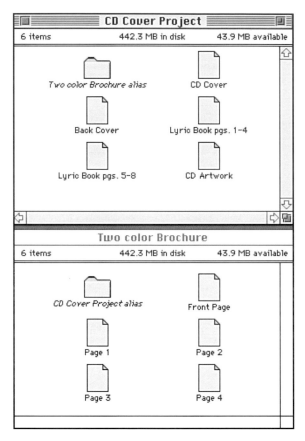

 Consider a visual database. If your work depends on image volume (product catalogs, multiple scanned photos, video clips) you should consider investing in an image database program like Claris FileMaker Pro where you can reference the work visually and define the information you need to access about it. This is particularly important for photographers and photojournalists who hope to sell rights to existing images.

 Beware of image previews. By all means create image previews for work in process because they're an invaluable shorthand for identifying files, but don't depend on them. Not only are they too small to show subtle changes, but they give you a false sense of security. They vanish if you resave in another format and it's all too easy to confuse images that look the same but have radically different resolutions or sizes.

Clean up before your store. Ongoing file management will help you stay organized, but a few endgame strategies can painlessly help you develop your portfolio.

Remember that craft is not concept. Even if your portfolio is production focused, no one really cares how long it took you to get your developing times right, your images to output properly, or your Lingo code to work. Any material that merely displays your learning curve belongs in the circular file. When you're certain your project is finished and no documentation will be needed for billing purposes, review your project folder and disk. Throw out the errors while the project is fresh in your mind, and use the opportunity to make sure that the important work exists in whatever form you'll need it.

Make folder icons. On the Macintosh, using images as folder icons can be a clever move. Note: you will need an image editing program for this hint. Although any program with the right capabilities will do, the following instruction uses Adobe Photoshop.

1. Save the image you want to use in a format that Photoshop can read. It's easier to list formats that Photoshop can't read.

2. Launch Photoshop and open your image in it (see Figure 3.3).

3. Select the entire image or a portion of it, and copy the image to the Clipboard. Square chunks are better to avoid distortion.

4. Return to the Finder. Select your folder (see Figure 3.4).

47

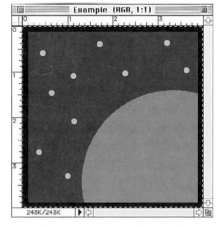

Figure 3.3
Photoshop window with image selected.

Figure 3.4
Folder before icon.

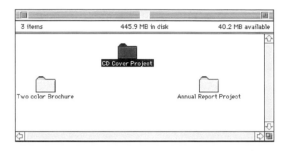

5. While your folder is selected, go to "Get Info" under the File menu (see Figure 3.5).

6. In the upper left of the Get Info box is a generic folder icon. Click it once to select it. A box will appear around it.

7. While the icon is selected, Paste the Clipboard image. A small thumbnail will take the place of the generic folder icon (see Figure 3.6). You now not only have a descriptive name, but a visual reminder.

Beware that desktop icons use the Macintosh's System palette. Images that use colors not in this palette may appear ragged. To avoid this, before you copy your image to the Clipboard, change the color Mode to Indexed Color (see Figure 3.7). Then, in the dialog box, choose the System palette and a Diffusion or Pattern dither (see Figure 3.8). Your colors may shift slightly to accommodate the System palette, but your image drop-outs should be gone.

Figure 3.5
Get Info box open.

Figure 3.6
Folder with icon applied.

Figure 3.7
Mode bar with Indexed Color checked.

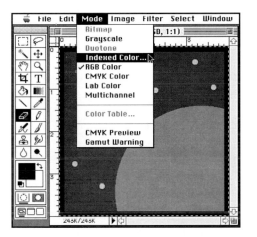

Figure 3.8
Indexed Color dialog box.

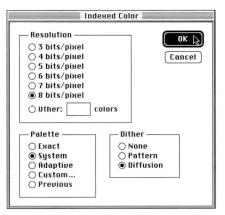

Note

You can use a similar strategy in Windows, although it's more time consuming. Make a .BMP file in an image editing program. (Even Windows Paintbrush will do.) Save the file and open an icon-editing Windows utility program like the Windows Resource Kit. (There are several icon editing programs, and none is an industry standard.) Make sure you save the file with an .ICO extension.

Now go to the Program Manager. Highlight the generic icon you want to personalize. Go to the menu bar and click on File > Select Properties > Change Icon. Choose Browse and locate your customized icon. Highlight this file in the file directory window. Select OK to return to the Properties window. Select OK again. Your new icon will now be attached to your file.

50

 Update files to final form. When a job is printed, sometimes last minute changes are made at the print house, not by the designer or illustrator. It's very tempting to shrug your shoulders and simply celebrate the end of the project. Don't give in to temptation. Unless the correction is something that is unlikely to effect some future version of the piece, or is work that was not your responsibility, take the time to make the edit in the original file. You will not remember the change if you need to output the file again.

 Backup to a portfolio disk. No one needs to tell you that you should have backups of your work. You can take this good advice one step further by dedicating a removable cartridge or other storage space specifically to your portfolio. When your project is finished, copy the final version onto the dedicated space. If you have to create your portfolio in a hurry, everything you need will be in one place, ready to be output, moved into a presentation format or converted for the Web.

 Eliminate thumbnails. Many software programs create automatic thumbnail files. Some of these are just simple PICT resources and will be ignored by any software program you import the files into. Others, like Adobe Illustrator 6.0 EPS thumbnails, can actually cause problems when you try to place them in non-Adobe programs. If you are planning to import files into a slideshow or interactive program, resave these files on your dedicated portfolio disk without the thumbnails.

Make Sure You Have Everything

You never know when you may be asked to show a portfolio of your work. Much as you feel you've earned that break, you haven't finished a project until you've archived it for your book. Although sometimes it's most cost-effective and efficient to do this all at once—scanning batched photos, or hiring someone to shoot your work—it's better to do it in smaller clumps than to be caught empty-handed.

Unlike people in other lines of work, everything you do results in a unique creative product. This means that if you complete something you're satisfied with, it should remain in your possession in some form: original, sample, slide, print, or disk. This may seem obvious, but it's a rule that's frequently violated in the breach.

■ **Retrieve your graded work.** A no brainer? Unfortunately not. Between summer break, coop stints, and requests by faculty to document student work for their own needs, student pieces often fall into limbo.

■ **Photograph your work.** Most artwork is one-of-a-kind. Even computer art is often output in large scale in a variety of individual forms or on special materials. As soon as the piece is dry, shoot it, even if you plan to hire a professional later. If the worst happens and your artwork is stolen, damaged, fades, or is sold to someone you can't find later, you still have a portfolio record. You can always replace your initial pictures with more formal documentation.

Shooting your finished pieces is not just for fine artists or architects. Unless your work is flat, very compact, or fairly small, it will need to be converted to be displayed. Packaging design, posters, or billboards need to be photographed while they're still in decent condition.

If you have a good camera, a tripod, and a cable release, excellent Internet guides to shooting your own work are listed in Appendix A. Here are a few basic guidelines if you have to move fast:

1. Hang flat work to shoot it unless it's very small.

2. Shoot against a clean, untextured, solid-colored background. Avoid glossy, reflective surfaces.

3. Don't shoot work framed under glass or reflective plastic.

4. Unless you have appropriate filters or are willing to do color correction in Photoshop, don't shoot your work under fluorescent or incandescent lights. Use natural but indirect light whenever possible.

5. The bigger your artwork, the harder it will be to shoot. Try to avoid the temptation of a wide-angle lens. If you are good with Photoshop and are shooting your work for digital purposes, take several shots in quick succession to visually "tile" your photographs. Scan them in at the highest practical resolution, and then merge them in the software.

51

Keep process materials safely filed. Most artists and designers give birth to ideas in the real world, not the virtual world. From quick pencil sketches to detailed storyboards, the first stages of creativity are seldom found on disk. Set aside a sketchbook or folder to keep these non-computer project materials together. Keep the folder materials off your working surface. Maintaining your initial concepts and their evolution can be a powerful tool to help you understand and illustrate your creative process—a real plus at the presentation stage.

 Keep backups of computer work. If your work consists of on-screen art, try to keep original uncompiled code, not just player versions of your work. Not only can files be easily lost, but you may want to change frame rate later for new output. If your final product is a printed piece, don't assume that's all you need, especially if the work is product packaging or oversized flat material like a poster. You'll discover in a later chapter how useful original art can be if you're creating a digital portfolio or a Web site.

Ask for samples. Once a piece is printed, pressed or otherwise completed, make sure you get as many copies as you can. (If you're asked to specify a number, ask for more than you think you need. You can never be too rich, or have too many samples.) If the client is handling his own printing, make sure in advance that he knows your needs. Speak to the printer yourself if you're dealing with them directly. Print runs are not an exact science and most jobs result in more finished impressions than the quote specified. If you're doing work for hire, don't be shy about asking your employer about sample copies. Even if you are not retaining copyright, in most situations you're entitled to add a sample to your portfolio.

Portfolio and Proprietary Issues

There are some occasions where you must proceed with care before blithely assuming that work is yours to display. Although a more detailed exploration of copyright and intellectual property issues appears in Chapter 6, some proprietary issues are worth mentioning here.

Imagine a situation where you are employed by an firm to create computer renderings and presentations for a contractual bid. The design is a tightly guarded secret, pending the final client presentation. Your portion of the project, however, is finished. You get a phone call from a prospective new client who wants to see examples of your work. She's not in the same line of business as the other firm. Can you show the renderings?

If you're a "hired gun," you may already have signed some form of trade secret or non-compete agreement that bars you from displaying this work in any form without a release from the hiring party. If you're a full-time employee of the company, you probably don't have any copyright to the work. Either way, you must depend on the firm's willingness to grant you a release, or provide you with a sign-off letter in its stead saying that you have completed the work satisfactorily and outlining its scope.

Acting in any other way is not only clearly unethical, it's also terrifically dangerous. In the preceding example, simply counting on the difference in industries isn't enough. Imagine that you go ahead and show the work without requesting permission. Your potential client is suitably impressed—and recognizes the logo in the corner as belonging to her spouse's company's major competitor. She goes home and tells all. You have not only violated your written agreement but can look forward to a series of unpleasant court dates for industrial espionage, particularly if the illicit presentation won you an assignment.

This is one of those situations that you must try to anticipate, bearing in mind that samples are your lifeblood. Deal with the problem when you first negotiate the contract. Explicitly ask what rights you can

retain to show the work. Make it clear that you are not asking for copyright, only for the opportunity to have a copy for portfolio purposes. Try to negotiate a date or ask them to specify the circumstances under which you might be free to use the material. Maybe there are elements of the job that are not critical, and you can negotiate to show only a specific image or group of images from the project. Always be willing to compromise.

Once you have signed the contract, even if your client has agreed to your request, you must *still* ask permission before you exercise your option. Take nothing in your contract for granted. If your client agrees to let you show the work, get his dated permission in writing, on his corporate letterhead, and signed by someone who is a responsible officer, not a freelancer or consultant. Keep this release in a safe place with your other legal documents. No matter how desperately you want to show the work, the stakes are too high to make assumptions.

Storing Critical Portfolio Elements

Great work can easily turn into useless trash. Most artists know that mounted boards curve, glues lift and yellow, and prints badly framed will bubble with moisture. These lessons are learned in school and sometimes from miserable first-hand experience. Yet the same people who are very craft-conscious in traditional media can be remarkably careless with digital output and

53

printed samples. Because digital material is more "mechanical" and can be exactly reproduced, people make the mistake of thinking it's more durable. Yet how many designers can afford to reprint a poster or replace a set of dye sublimation prints? If you are keeping material for portfolio use, store a library of samples and pieces to create a portfolio later.

The Truth About Digital Output

Most student and some professional work is only output on a digital printer, not professionally offset or chemically developed. The quality may look almost the same initially, but the inks, toners, dyes, and even the papers are unstable. Some forms of digital output chemically react to the plastic holders used for portfolio books. Copier and laser prints can stick to the inside of vinyl, ruining the sample and the portfolio page at the same time. Heat-based color printer output—and this means all wax and many ink jet printers—not only stick but may also crack, split, and bleed, particularly if carried in a nice black portfolio case in the summer! And almost all output—even the very best—will fade. The difference between good output and the very cheapest desktop printer is frequently measured in weeks or months, not years.

It's hard to lay this at the door of the manufacturers. Very few design professionals put archivability on the top of their list of features when shopping for a printer. Until

recently, only fine artists who were experimenting with the computer used the output as a final form. With the advent of cheaper, high-quality printers and the growth of digital imaging, more companies are attempting to stabilize their materials and processes, but no one can boast unqualified success. Of course, ideally we would print or chemically develop everything, or show it only onscreen. Since this isn't always practical, we need to optimize the digital alternative.

Testing Your Output

The easiest way to discover how well your printer's output will hold up is to test it. To check for fading, run a simple CMYK bar test (a full page of output with each of the four printing primary colors running vertically) on the paper you'll use. Cut the output in thirds so that each portion has all four ink colors. Pin one up on a sunlit wall. Put one in a flat box with a lid and put the box someplace dark. Leave the third out of direct light but uncovered. A month later, run the CMYK test again.

Now pull out all three pieces and look at them closely, using the newly printed copy as a guide. In most cases, there will be clear color degradation in the print that was hung in bright light. Has there also been a shift in the other two pieces? One month is not a particularly long period of time to archive a print. If you can also see color problems in the third piece, you should find an alternate printer for your portfolio work. If you see any change in the copy you held in the dark, the inks are chemically degrading without the benefit of light and your printer shouldn't be used for anything other than quick proofing.

Strategies for Storing

Always store your potential portfolio work flat, between acid free paper, and out of direct light in a cool place. If you must roll the work, store it in a closable tube with as large a diameter as you can find. If you have a portfolio case full of work, store it on a shelf without any bulky items or additional folders inserted, and never place anything on top of it.

Multiple printing is another useful strategy. Once the job has been processed in the printer's RIP, duplicates often print very quickly, and many service bureaus discount additional editions run at the same time. Recognize that this is an expensive suggestion if you're operating at the high end or in large format. You have to weigh the pros and cons carefully. Many people will argue that, because digital images are infinitely duplicable and are much cheaper to store on disk, this is a waste of time and an even bigger waste of money.

On the other hand, set-up time can be critical for an artist outputting for a show, especially if the printer is not around the corner. It can often take several tries to get a digital print's color to match the saturation level and color gamut the artist requires. Once that's been accomplished, the piece is usually framed and hung. The longer it hangs, the more likely it is that the color will fade. If the work will be displayed for any length of time, have it framed under UV-blocking plastic. Not even Iris prints, which are the high-end standard for digital color output, match the archival quality of any of the traditional processes, even when kept safe from direct light. If the stakes are high enough, a second identical print preserved in the dark can provide short-term insurance against fading, loss, or a botched framing job.

Laminating

For the right kind of output or printed piece, lamination is a terrific way to preserve your work. Because it insulates your material from direct contact with other paper or plastic, it's a good solution for laser or photocopy prints. Color prints that are output on lightweight paper gain mass and substance. Additionally, it keeps fingerprints off work that will be picked up and handled, prevents edges from getting dog-eared, and as a bonus, saturates color.

Unfortunately, not all pieces lend themselves to lamination. Original art, besides being too precious to handle this way, can simply look tacky. Textured work loses its tactile charm. You're also limited to one, or at most two, layers of material. More than that will not lay perfectly flat during the process, which could lead to a bumpy plastic pocket rather than a tight, clean seal. If you have any

55

questions about whether a piece will work well, test the process with something similar first.

Reworking Your Material

There are many reasons why you might want to rework material, even if you have a "finished" piece. Pulling out an older piece and updating it, scanning an old watercolor and using it to create a digital collage, reprinting a file originally output at 300 dpi on a better quality printer, scanning a series of photographs and improving their contrast or color—all of these are examples of freshening old work.

It's never too late to improve an existing piece's level of professionalism. This is particularly true for graduating students who are still in the process of learning how to manage production issues. All too frequently, students maim what could be a wonderful portfolio piece because they have a poor sense of time management, have had little or no prior experience with service bureaus, or don't know enough about materials. Most entry-level design and architecture positions involve a substantial amount of production, and poor craft in a portfolio sends a bad message to a prospective employer.

Reworking is also in order if you've had to make compromises based on client decisions or financial resources. While many rejected concepts deserve their fate, some end up on the cutting room floor for purely pragmatic reasons. As long as doing so does not violate any prior agreements with the original client, developing an alternative solution to a project can be very satisfying, as well as being an excellent way to explore a new technique or technology.

Reprinting Your Work

Some reworks are relatively inexpensive and simple but give ample payback. Is your identity package just getting laser printed until the client has enough cash? Is your package design on hold? Color printing from the computer has become so affordable that it's hard to come up with a reason not to show a version of the project the way you designed it.

Make sure to choose the right printer for your project and take the reprint all the way to its finished design. If your work is photographically based, use dye sublimation, Iris ink jet, or at least an Epson XL Pro. Don't settle for a 300 dpi PostScript printer designed for spot color. Find a duplex printer for a tabloid project that prints both sides. For a 3-D object, make the die-cuts and assemble the piece if possible. Don't leave it in sheet form.

Showing Versatility

Some ideas come to you in a blinding light of creativity—the corporate brainstorm, the sculpture that builds itself, the photograph taken in ideal light at the perfect moment—but far more work is the result of hours of development. In the context of exploring specific portfolios, we've already discussed how useful development material can be in helping others see how you approach problem solving. It's also potentially helpful in upgrading your portfolio.

Sometimes it can pay to rethink and totally redesign an idea from your alternate versions. The printed piece may be full of design compromises, or represent a less-accomplished stage of your creative or technical skills. If so, you're in good company. Most professionals can point to projects they wish they could go back and redesign. If you've sketched several solutions for a problem but only brought one to completion, reexamine the others. Showing radically different designs for the same problem shows initiative and flexibility.

You may discover that you are deficient in a specific category of material that might be critical to your portfolio. If so, you may keep altering your constraints instead of rigorously working within them. If you're in this boat, Paula Scher's *The Graphic Design Portfolio: How To Make a Good One* is a book of design problems from which you can develop new solutions.

Finally the Good Stuff: Expressing Relationships in Your Work

The last stage in the pre-portfolio process is the most fun but the most difficult. You need to make connections between your individual pieces that will make your portfolio, and ultimately your presentation, flow smoothly. Hopefully, you've been a

dedicated collector and careful archiver, and can now pull out your work and look at it as a whole.

Keeping Your Eyes Open

You read trade magazines, pour over award-winning advertising, and visit galleries. You study older work in your discipline for ideas. You talk shop—constantly. This search for source material and creative sparks should extend to your portfolio. Take every opportunity you can to look at other people's portfolios, not just to see what type of work they've done, but how they've chosen to display it. Has someone figured out a totally cool solution to a display problem? Is their portfolio unique or unusually effective? Notice what you don't like as well as what you do. Is the book too large for the work? Is the presentation awkward? Do you find yourself getting impatient?

One of the best ways to develop ideas is to look at portfolios outside your own area. It's easy to make assumptions about what a portfolio should be if you only see those of the people around you. If you're an architect, look at a multimedia developer's CD. If you're in industrial design, examine a print designer's work. Since your work is so different, you'll be less inclined to compare the projects to yours and more likely to notice what they've done to enhance them.

Quality versus Quantity

You might think from all the archiving suggestions that your digital portfolio will

57

have more material in it than your traditional portfolio. That's possible. Don't confuse the benefits of holding on to your work with trying to show it all. Keeping material clean and easy to find makes it easier to create and customize your book for your potential audience or medium. It also gives you the widest possible range of projects, artwork, and images from which to choose. Just remember that most people have a finite amount of time and disk space to devote to viewing your projects. They won't thank you for cramming in more images, particularly if the additional work is inferior. Your pack rat tendencies should be in full force as you collect, but ruthlessly suppressed as you actually create your portfolio.

Be Prepared to Change

Many people decide on a format for their portfolio first, then try to fit their pieces into it. They buy a multi-ring binder case the same size as those they've seen, or borrow another person's basic layout for a Web site, or mount all their work on black matte board. When things don't fit the format they've chosen, they compromise or try not to notice because they've already invested so much time and money in the process.

There is a particular temptation to follow form if you're a working professional with an existing portfolio. But if your current portfolio is perfect and complete, why are you reading this book? A digital portfolio that is an exact duplicate of your physical portfolio probably won't be as successful as

the original. Look at the new format as an opportunity to do something fresh. Let your work drive the form, not the other way around.

If you are in transition between types of work, don't just sigh and pull out the best of what you used to do. If you want to be doing interactive media but almost all your work is traditional print production, ask yourself how you can frame this work to show a talent for sequencing and organizing information. Plan to make your portfolio an interactive project. You might even go so far as to create full-fledged storyboards for your digital portfolio, include them as a portfolio element, then implement them. The most important thing to remember about your portfolio is that it only seems to be a record of what you've done. It's really a tool to get the future work you want.

Plot and the Personal Portfolio

Begin with the general proposition that you are telling a story. You need a good opening to grab attention. Then you'll need a plot, a real page turner that holds your viewer's interest. The ending must be strong so that you'll be remembered. And let's not forget that people often buy their books because of the cover. What are your absolute best pieces and how can you connect them sequentially?

When you think of your work as connected material rather than a random group of jobs, you should notice your strengths, and perhaps a few weaknesses, that you never paid attention to while moving from project to project. Analyze these strengths and note how the work you've created highlights them. Some projects will make you smile because they were particularly satisfying experiences. Perhaps you'll discover that you've been carrying others around simply for the prestige of having worked for a specific client, not because you find the work indicative of who you are as an artist. With a lot of the latter and not enough of the former, it's time for a reality check. How long have you been in the business and what do you really want to be doing now?

Look at your work for themes. Unless there's a thematic point involved or a major change in style or outlook that can only be seen in sequence, don't make the mistake of just showing your work chronologically. Your portfolio is not a history text. Maybe your theme could be variety; your ability to handle work in a wide range of media. Maybe you've been exploring new processes and want to emphasize your experimental side. Perhaps your objective is to emphasize your special understanding of a vertical market. Links can be forged in many ways: in subject matter, through format, typographically, or using color progressions.

Don't forget to consider visual pacing in your portfolio. Some pieces will require more examination than others. You may want to show one item briefly, or flip between two related elements. Digital images can be superimposed on each other to show the stages of a project's development. If you're showing a booklet, you might want to alter the speed that pages "turn."

Once you've planned your work and begun the design process, it's time to compare your concept to the different potentials offered by a "firm media" delivery—disk or CD—or the purely electronic Web site. Despite the fact that they are all digital portfolios, they offer different possibilities. In the next two chapters, you'll explore the creation of the disk and CD types of portfolio, discuss pluses and minuses, and work through some of the stickiest technical issues in transferring your portfolio work to these media.

CHAPTER FOUR

Preparing Work for Disk

Technical skill is mastery of complexity while creativity is mastery of simplicity.
—*E. Christopher Zeeman*

In this chapter, we tackle the process and issues involved in transferring and homogenizing your existing material into a digital portfolio. To create usable images, we are forced to grapple with some serious technical issues. This is unavoidable, since perfection is an illusive thing. For example, I once designed a poster and asked for samples from the printer. Despite my request for unfolded copies, every one of the samples came to me sharply folded that when scanned showed the crease every time. Also, results from a photo shoot can suffer from allowing too much ambient light, too little skill in the developing room, or work mishandled in framing, hanging, or storing. Given the number of things which can go wrong, simply saying, "Scan in your work, copy your digital files, and put them in a presentation" would be as useful to you as, "Get copies of your work, put them in a binder, and send out your résumé." For a portfolio—your digital representative to the world—you don't want to settle for second best.

First Steps to a Disk-Based Portfolio

Not all portfolios will require all the following steps. In fact, for some projects the process can be simplified enormously. But if you have a complex story to tell and a reasonably large body of work, you could be involved in any or all of these stages.

1. Decide what non-digital material can be digitized effectively.

2. Digitize or scan the appropriate work into the computer.

3. Edit the work as necessary.

4. Transfer any digital work from its native formats into a usable format for on-screen display.

5. Integrate scanned and digital material visually for size and color issues.

Digital Craft

If you bought a book about creating a portfolio in 1960, it would still be eminently usable in 1990. Since then, every year has brought us farther from the world of maylines and drafting tables. There are people with years of professional experience who have never cut a rubylith to make a mask or run imagesetter output through a waxer to paste it on a board. Soon there will be photographers who will barely remember the smell of chemistry and the problems of clogging airbrushes. On the other hand, these specialized traditional skills have their counterparts in the virtual world. A badly created mask in Photoshop will result in stray jagged pixels on the edges of silhouettes. Type can still be improperly aligned in a QuarkXPress document, and retouching is still an art even when the tools are cloning and histograms. These are all examples of digital craft at work.

A good digital portfolio displays its owner's understanding of his or her craft as well as their creative side. Nowhere can this be more clearly exhibited than in the care and attention you pay to transferring your work from its tradtional roots to its digital flower. You'll need to choose the right medium for

transferring your work, consider your raw materials carefully to see if they are good candidates for a digital conversion, and then optimize the scans to bring out as much of the original material's quality as possible.

Do it Yourself, or Send it Out?

At this point you may be asking yourself if you should scan your own work. It does involve a fair amount of sweat equity, but if you have access to a decent scanner, it's by far the cheapest way to go and offers the most control. On the other hand, there are viable alternatives which might meet your needs.

If you want to scan flat art you can't beat a good drum scanner. In most cases it will give even better results than the Photo CD. However, unless you happen to moonlight at a pre-press facility or have considered buying a scanner instead of a Lexus, you're probably going to work with a lower-level piece of hardware. This matters, of course, but not as much for on-screen imaging as it would for work that you intend to print. High-end scanners sell in the neighborhood of $25,000–$80,000, depending upon image size, resolution, and speed.

Flatbed Scanners

These are the ubiquitous tools on the desktop that are remarkably inexpensive. If you have reason to need regular scanning (for Web page creation, FPO for print production, and so on) you may own a flatbed scanner already. A color scanner that handles 30-bit scanning at 300 spi (samples per inch) optical resolution is usually adequate for work that will remain on-screen.

If you want to scan your work but are thinking of sending it out because you don't have scanning access, rent a flatbed from a service bureau. Depending on the quality of the machine, your mileage may vary, but something in the range of $25–$30 a day is reasonable. As they become more popular, prices will probably continue to drop.

Slide Scanners

If your work exists on slides, don't try to scan them on a typical flatbed scanner. Some flatbeds come with transparency attachments, but the quality is not equivalent to a dedicated slide scanner. Using a silde or transparency attachment on a flatbed scanner may not result in enough information being captured to provide a very good on-screen image. Slide scanners aren't as easy to find as flatbeds and are more expensive for equivalent resolution. Given the quality of Photo CD, I recommend that you take the slide scanner route for scanning 35mm slides. Kodak's film scanner technology, despite its tendency toward soft images, is a much more versatile method than the simple slide scan.

Digital Cameras and 3-D Objects

Scanning anything that began as a 3-D object, not 2-D art, can be frustrating. High-quality digital cameras are excellent alternatives for industrial designs, sculptures, and many architectural applications. The best ones, unfortunately, are expensive for anyone but a professional photographer, which means that you will probably have to pay for a photo shoot. Of course, working with a professional is always the recommended method of shooting artwork for slides, so having to spend the money for a digital version of the porfolio should be equivalent. Any pictures taken with a digital camera should also be usable in most traditional formats, too. (Most of the black-and-white photographs in this book were taken with a digital camera.)

The world of 3-D digitization is a moving target. A growing number of VR (virtual reality) tools enable you to merge photographs of real spaces or PICT files of virtual environments into a seamless space. Although the possibilities are intriguing, the solutions are currently on the expensive side for someone who merely wants to capture their actual environment or interactive space for a personal portfolio. If you are willing to spend about $500 to explore the possibilities, you have two competing cross-platform options: Apple's QuickTime VR (you buy the software) and Omniview's PhotoBubble (you buy the hardware, they keep the

63

software). Omniview charges an additional fee for post-processing. In both of these new technologies, digital images made of the same object from different angles and rotations are digitally "pasted" together. The result is something between a movie and a stereogram, and can be very effective.

Photo CD

Why not transfer your work to a digital medium while it's still in it's truest form? Kodak Photo CD master discs can be made from existing slides, as well as film negatives of various sizes. They hold about 100 images, each in a variety of resolutions. For on-screen work, you don't need the high-quality versions, but you may want to print some of the images for another purpose. Having a variety of resolutions to work with ensures that you will not have to re-scan. Costs for each image vary from about $4 to as little as $.50 each, depending on the service bureau, whether you want them to do image correction, and the form of film you bring. It's cheaper to digitize an entire roll of film than it is to print from strips of film negatives or individual slides. You also don't need to keep buying CDs when you have new material to scan. You pay once for the CD media itself but can continue to append image pacs (what Kodak calls their group of multi-resolution images) until the disc is full.

In addition, Photo CDs come in a Portfolio format, which is becoming popular with

professional photographers. The wide range of detail that is difficult to maintain with other methods is beautifully captured on a Photo CD. Because these discs also can support PICT and TIFF files, as well as sound information, some people are using them as a medium for their digital portfolios, not just as storage for raw material.

Photo CDs are not perfect, although they are better than any standard slide scanner. They do tend to err on the soft side, guaranteeing that you will have to do some sharpening on your images. They also faithfully reproduce everything that's wrong with your originals, complete with color casts. You will be charged for every image that's converted, even if you would not have used them because they were substandard. If you are planning on converting many images, you might have prints made beforehand so you can judge for yourself.

Service Bureaus

If you don't have access to a scanner and you're dealing with existing flat art or photos of your work, you can have your work scanned at a service bureau. Provide them with removable media, specify the scanning resolution you need, make sure that your material is clean, and you can usually count on a competent job. Beware, though. Sometimes it takes some shopping around to find a service bureau with compatible external drives. There is also a wide pricing variety on scanning. High-end service bureaus catering to professional pre-press needs will correct and optimize your work, but will charge you top dollar. If you don't intend on printing out the work, this may be overkill.

Note

Removable Media and Service Bureaus

"Where's the SyQuest drive so I can scan my work?"

"Oh, we don't usually have it hooked up to this scanner. Wait a minute and I'll get it." Sound of footsteps retreating and returning.

"But that's not a SyQuest 200! It's an 88! I called up and specifically asked for a SyQuest 200!"

"We don't have a 200. We've never had one of those. Everyone's using Zips these days!"

"I spoke with Sandy."

"Sandy who? Oh, the night receptionist?"

Although Zip cartridges have been my personal salvation, I know many people with perfectly good four-year-old SyQuest drives who refuse to buy a new format when the old one still works. It doesn't really matter what removable media format you use until you hit the service bureau. Make phone calls in advance, be specific about your needs, and don't assume anything. Instead of asking "Can you take a SyQuest?" ask "What forms of removable cartridges do you support?" For many years, the SyQuest large-format drives were the service bureau standard and king of the Macintosh platform. Iomega Bernoulli drives were a distant second. Not long after the smaller format SyQuest drives made their appearance and service bureaus began to support them, the Iomega Zip drive was

introduced. It has taken both platforms by storm and is heading for the low-capacity removable standard. (Do you remember when 100MB storage was considered high-capacity?) SyQuest countered with the EZ135, but not effectively. With the introduction of the Jaz drive, however, service bureaus have a dilemma; which one to buy and how many? Many service bureaus are waiting to see how much traffic in Jaz cartridges they'll see, while taking advantage of the Zip drive's Guest function that enables a client to bring in their own drive and connect it without a real installation. What this means for you is a round of phone calls. Before you book time for scanning at a service bureau, verify *very specifically* that they can accommodate your needs.

Outside of the high end, scanning is affordable, and there are price breaks for volume. A price break on $10, however, (which is too much if they are not offering color correction or other image tweaking) is very different from one on $1 (which usually means they've got an assembly line approach). Sometimes you get what you pay for, sometimes not. There are fly-by-night operations, particularly on the Net, which have a nice side business in adult BBSs and copyright violations.

Besides asking for recommendations from friends and associates, try to find out how long a company has been in business and whether they handle work for the trade or for the consumer. Don't buy work whose quality will actually cost you in time.

Scanning: Guide to a Good Portfolio Image

Assuming the material you want to scan meets minimum standards and you haven't managed to bypass the task through Photo CD or professional help, we move to scanning itself. With the exception of Photoshop, which is a ubiquitous image editing tool on both platforms, I have tried to stay away from suggestions which relate only to one program or scanner. There are so many levels of technical expertise and variations in software that trying to go through every possible variation would be impossible.

The actual process of putting a flat image on the glass and running a scanner plug-in is not exactly brain surgery. On the other hand, it's hard to scan your work successfully without a working knowledge of resolution. Fortunately, many of the most complicated issues involving this thorny topic simply don't arise when scanning for on-screen display. We simply need to insure that your scan resolution will be appropriate to what you plan on doing with the file.

Resolution: The Cliff Notes Version

What is resolution? Like the metric system or the Fahrenheit temperature scale, it's a method of measuring something, in this case the number of visual units in an inch or centimeter. Like distance and temperature though, there are different resolution units which, when confused, can lead to error. For example, let's say you're planning on visiting Italy and you call and ask about the weather. "Oh, it's close to 30 right now, but that is a little unusual for the season." You hang up and gulp. "Wow! Gotta replace those bathing suits and linens with some heavy gear!" Won't you be surprised when you walk off the plane to sweltering heat—because 30 degrees Celsius (European scale) equals about 85 degrees Fahrenheit (USA scale). Similar misunderstandings about resolution abound. The only thing all units of resolution have in common is that larger numbers mean better quality (although not necessarily the best choice for every purpose).

To a traditional pressman, the most important resolution unit is lines per inch (lpi). It measures the number of linear divisions per inch in a half-tone screen. To a desktop publisher or digitally-savvy printer, dots per inch (dpi) is equally critical. Both of these resolution measurements are specific to printed output. They have nothing to do with on-screen resolution, although they will certainly be affected by it. On-screen resolution is defined by pixels per inch (dpi), not dots. Dots are variable shaped printing units; pixels are usually square on-screen ones. They do have a mathematical correspondence, just like Fahrenheit and Celsius do, but they are no more equal than is 1°F versus 1°C.

Scanning resolution is another crucial resolution step, measured in samples per inch (spi). This one is more difficult to separate, because dpi and spi are the same scale at different times in the process. A scan per inch unit determines the image's depth of information when it's first digitized. If the scanned image is cropped, scaled, or resampled, it's the dpi which will change because you're adding to or throwing out samples.

Anyone who has worked with Photoshop has seen the on-screen effect of changing dpi resolution, although they have not necessarily understood it. Let's say that you've scanned an image at 150 spi.

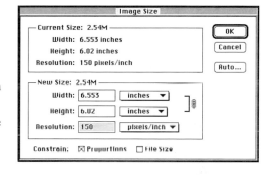

Figure 4.2
Image Size dialog box with File Size box unchecked.

Change your resolution to 75 dpi. Notice how your file size changes immediately. Click OK.

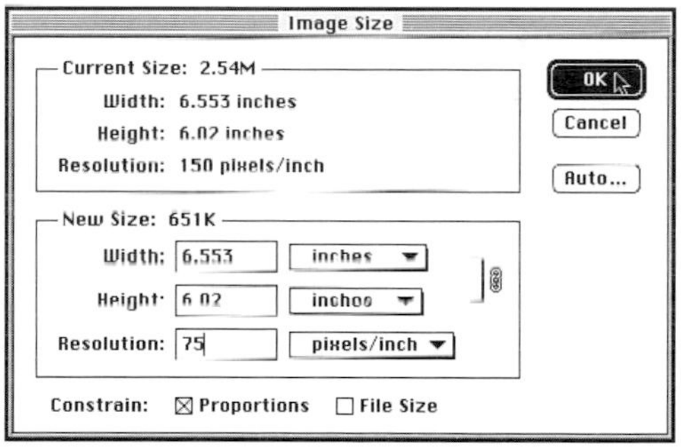

Figure 4.1
Scanned image at 150 dpi.

You decide to take its resolution down to 75 dpi (50%), but change nothing else. In Photoshop, go to the pull-down menu Image > Image Size. You'll get the Image Size dialog box. Be sure to uncheck the Constrain: File Size box here, or you won't get the benefit of bringing down the resolution.

Figure 4.3
Image Size dialog box with new resolution.

The image window scales down to 50% of its previous size, and the image goes with it.

Why does this happen? Imagine you have a balloon, and you let out half of the air in it. Because the balloon's physical size is a reflection of how much air is inside it, it shrinks. Your file has done the same thing.

Figure 4.4
Scanned image at 75 dpi, with file size noted, at 1:1 scale.

When you took down the image resolution, you threw out half of the samples. In technical terms, you have *downsampled* the image. If you zoom the image up to 200% so it takes up as much space on your monitor as it did before, you'll see that it is much coarser. Formerly smooth areas have been replaced with jagged edges.

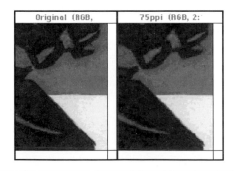

Figure 4.5
75 dpi image at 2:1 scale.

Notice something else that's peculiar. Although you've reduced the resolution to 50%, the file size is 25% of the original. This isn't really peculiar at all since the area of a rectangle is equal to the height times the width ($4W \times 5H = 20$). If you cut the length of the sides in half, the resulting product will be $\frac{1}{4}$ the size ($2W \times 2.5H = 5$).

What if you want to take an image that you've downsampled and put information into, like reinflating the balloon? Choose Save As from the File menu and save the downsampled image under a different name so that our original file remains untouched. Now, with the downsampled file active, go to Image>Image Size and return the resolution of our downsampled image to the original 150 dpi.

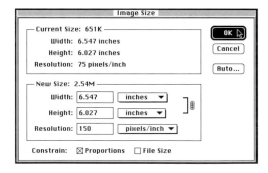

Figure 4.6
Image Size dialog box at 150spi.

Click OK. Save the file under a different name, and then open the 75 dpi, the new 150 dpi, and the original images at the same time.

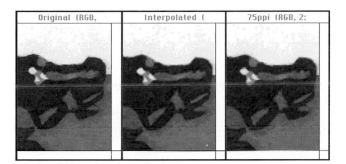

Figure 4.7
Three images: the original at 100%, the interpolated version at 100%, and the 75 dpi at 200%.

If you compare the original and this new upsampled, or interpolated, file, you'll see that the new version looks smoother than the downsampled one but does not equal the quality in the original. You can blow it back up to the same size, but just as with the balloon, it won't have the same content. After you throw out information by decreasing resolution, it's impossible to get it back.

However, there's one more thing to try. Take your three sample files and zoom the two higher-resolution versions down to 1:2 proportion. Leave the 75 dpi version as 1:1. Now compare the way they look on-screen. Although the differences are there—mostly with varying degrees of apparent image sharpness—the three files look surprisingly similar. A little sharpening of the 75 dpi image and it will probably be indistinguishable from the original but much, much smaller.

Good Things Come in Small Packages

For most digital portfolios, size really counts. The smaller you can get your files without on-screen degradation, the more you can do with them, the more images you can show, and the faster any interactive players you make with them will run. So if the only reason you are scanning your pieces is to incorporate them in an on-screen presentation, you need to have a good reason to scan

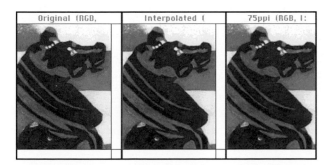

Figure 4.8
Three images: the original at 50%, the interpolated version at 50%, and the 75 dpi at 100%.

your work at any spi larger than monitor resolution. For your portfolio project, you'll only do so if you will have to make repairs and alterations in the post-scanned image, or if you are unsure as to what size you will eventually be displaying the artwork. No portfolio work scanned at screen resolution should ever be scaled up. If you miscalculated and you've scanned too small, re-scan at the correct percentage.

"…But will it print?" you ask. Not well, but that's OK. Scanning for on-screen work is not the same as scanning for print output. That's why Kodak, in its infinite wisdom, offers so many variations in resolution in their Photo CD format. It is pure luck if a scan you've taken for on-screen use is also acceptable print quality. Scanning for good print reproduction not only requires a scanner with a good dynamic range, it must be done at a high enough resolution not to pixelate or posterize. Instead of svelte little low-res files, you're looking at megabyte monsters. Additionally, effective scanning for print applications involves a fair amount of arithmetic to match the dpi and/or lpi of the output process.

You might be wondering why you can't scan at a higher resolution, then downsample to the appropriate lower one. You can, but if the original scan's resolution is too much larger than what you'll ultimately need, downsampling will soften it to such a degree that you may find the result unacceptable. Your touch-up work will definitely expand. Since anything that lengthens the time it takes to

create your portfolio decreases the likelihood that you'll actually finish it, starting from scratch for on-screen display can really make sense if the work you're scanning won't otherwise need imaging repair.

There is only one situation where high-res image display can make sense. As we saw above, zooming into a low-resolution image makes all its defects come to the forefront. If you absolutely must show fine detail in your portfolio, or you have designed something that will require an actual zoom into an image rather than a jump to another one, you must work with higher-density images. Even here, never work with a resolution higher than what you absolutely need to do the job. After a point, extra information doesn't result in better quality, just in overfed file sizes.

Scanning the Scanner

Having graduated from Resolution 101, we're ready to turn to our scanner and give it a cold, hard look. There are several things you can do to improve the likelihood that your scans will not need to be repeated, and many of them are fairly low-tech in nature.

The first is obvious, but often forgotten. Is the glass on the scanner clean? Every speck of dirt, dust, or other leftover will be reproduced on your scan. Some specks are inevitable, but cleaning minimizes your touch-up time. To check how clean your scanner board is, scan a clean flat black matte sheet. White specs on screen mean it's time to clean.

Is your scanner itself going to make your work harder? Try scanning a clean black and white piece of line art in RGB color mode. When you zoom in to the file, black should still be the predominant component of your lines. Some color breakup is inevitable, but if they look like they were painted with gummy bears, your scanner is out of registration. Mis-registration is responsible for fuzzy scans and unwanted color artifacts, which will make it harder for you to convert your files to different file formats for interactive and Web use.

Scanning Printed Pieces

There are some special issues in scanning printed artwork for a digital portfolio. Unlike photographs, printed pieces are often the combination of several media working in concert with each other. With a wide variety of material, inks, and screens, it's easy to decrease their quality when scanned. Badly scanned printed work can suffer from broken or pixelated type, from indifferent preparation, or simply from the interaction of the printing process with the digital scanner.

Squaring Up Your Art

If you are scanning photographs or the printed material, make sure that you have done a good job of squaring up your art before scanning. In general, it is very

distracting to look at a portfolio piece on-screen which is not aligned in its frame. I once saw the Web site of a design firm where the Web perpetrator cut a brochure apart, scanned one of the pieces at a slight angle, and then tried to make them fit back together. Of course, you can rotate an image in Photoshop to make it square, but remember that Photoshop does not have a snap grid function. It can take a little work to change an image's angle. Each time you rotate to adjust, you lose just a little sharpness and image clarity. If your image is slightly soft to begin with, you will make it harder to clean it up later. One low-tech way of making sure your scanning is square is to align your work using a small plastic triangle as follows:

1. Attach double-sided or artist's masking tape to the face of the triangle, with the 90° angle of it on the right.

2. With the artwork face-up, align the bottom and right edge of the piece to the 90° angle of the triangle.

3. Press down lightly to hold the piece against the triangle.

4. Gently flip the work and triangle over and square the triangle to the bottom left of your scannable area.

5. Do a prescan to adjust your marquee.

This method is also useful in situations where your artwork itself is easy to square up, but the image inside it was not aligned on the horizontal. You can simply attach the

71

image with the new horizon aligned on the base of the triangle, making sure to leave enough room against the triangle's flat vertical edge to prevent the image from being inadvertently cut off.

Moire Is Less

What's a moire? Alas, not the Italian word for love, but one of the least lovely and most obvious problems with scanning printed work. You probably know that color printing depends on fine-screened overlays of dots to mimic continuous tone color. Unfortunately, the dots that blend smoothly to the human eye are the product of screens, and as mentioned above, these printing screens do not have a one-to-one correspondence to pixels. Because scans per inch are based on the pixel as a basic unit, when the two resolutions collide, we get ugly, distracting patterns. These patterns will be particularly obvious if you want to show details of printed work on-screen.

Fortunately, there are some strategies for minimizing moire as you scan, and for eliminating most of what remains in Photoshop afterwards. Some of these strategies are quite complex, but are geared toward situations where you will need to output the image afterward. In our case, we can use the following simplified process.

First we'll violate all our earlier guidelines and scan the piece in at least double the ultimate dpi, rounding up to the nearest number that is a divisor of your scanner's optical resolution. Avoid a number that's

evenly divisible by your final resolution, however, or the moire will come back when you scale. This would mean 150 dpi for an image that will end up at 72 dpi ("standard" Macintosh), or 225 for one that will end up at 95 dpi ("average" PC). Once you've done this, downsample to your target monitor resolution. This will radically soften the image, which is exactly what you want. By itself, this general blurring should abolish most if not all moire effects. If there is still a general mottling, examine each of the three channels. Find the one with the worst mottling, and highlight it so it will be the only one effected by the next step. Go to Filters > Blur > Gaussian Blur.

Figure 4.9
Gaussian Blur filter dialog box.

The exact setting here will vary, but you will need little additional blurring at such a low resolution—a pixel setting of one or two should do it. Now the entire image should be moire free, but somewhat blurry. Follow the instructions below for Unsharp Mask, and you should end up with an image that appears crisp without ugly color patterns.

When to Overscan

There are circumstances besides printing moires where you will want to scan your artwork at a higher resolution than your target screen. For example, line art never looks right directly scanned. It gets jagged and very pixelated. If your ultimate goal is screen resolution, you'll need to scan at 300 spi at the very least. Make sure to scan in greyscale mode, not in bitmap, because you'll need the extra levels of information not to lose line detail. Open the image in Photoshop and go to Image>Adjust> Brightness/Contrast.

Move the slider back and forth in the dialog box until you get the line thickness that most closely resembles your original art.

Go to Filter>Sharpen and apply the Sharpen Edges filter to your scan. This will reinforce the changes you made in your line weight and make the line edges feel crisper.

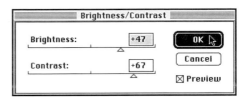

Figure 4.11
Brightness/Contrast dialog box.

Last but not least, you can finally change your mode to bitmap, choosing the Diffusion Dither option in the Mode change box.

If there are any stray points, use the pencil tool to delete them. Then scale your image down to the size you need.

Scanned Type

Type will give you problems, too, since you're rasterizing outlines when you scan it. In essence, you're giving up all those crisp rounded PostScript edges and settling for

73

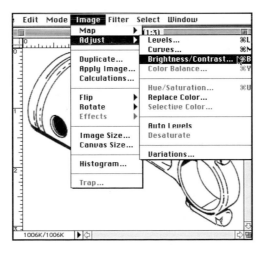

Figure 4.10
Brightness/ Contrast pull-down menu.

Figure 4.12
Sharpen Edges pull-down menu.

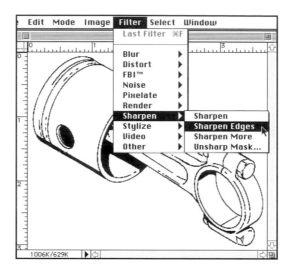

Figure 4.13
Mode change dialog box.

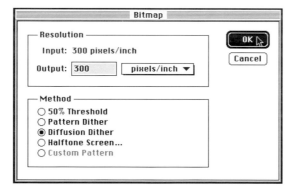

anti-aliased bitmaps. (And you know what that looks like when you go from Illustrator to Photoshop!) Always scan type at least double the resolution you'll need to show on-screen, then scale it to 50%. This will help to clean up the look of the edges. Another solution for simple black and white work is to shoot it up on a copier machine before scanning it. Then you can scan at 100% and scale to 50%. This often gives better results than scanning the original,

especially if the original is on textured paper.

Scanning Photographic Prints

We've already noted that there are better scanning methods for photography than a flatbed scanner, namely the traditional drum scanner or the Kodak Photo CD process. However, there are occasions when you have no choice. You may have done extensive airbrushing or chemistry-based changes in developing the print. The print may be on a special photographic substrate. You may have lost the original negative. You may be too tight on funds to pay for a drum scan and you know you only need the work for your digital portfolio.

Under these circumstances, you'll spend more time than you want attempting to adjust for the difference between what you can see in the print and what the scanner can capture in its dynamic range. If so, there are a few useful hints for maintaining your sanity.

First, we've mentioned that scanners have problems with detail in deep shadows. They have even more problems with images with a very broad value range: bright, clear highlights as well as the deep shadows. If you scan to hold one, you'll lose the other, and vice versa, leading to a very flat piece. The best work-around is to just accept the limitations and minimize their effect. Take two different versions of the scan. Everything about these two scans should be exactly the same—image size, resolution, color mode—except their tonal balance. For the first, use your scanning software to adjust tonal values to maximize detail in the shadows (see below for how to do this with levels if you are acquiring your scanned art into Photoshop). Don't worry about the highlights getting washed out as long as you are picking up the maximum quality in dark areas. For the second, follow the same

process but go for a wide range of detail in the highlights, allowing the shadows to fill. Save them both. Open the two images and make the darker of the two a layer of the lighter. Adjust transparency, and blend the two images together.

Editing Scanned Art

The process of transferring your printed or photographed work gives ample opportunity for you to display craft and knowledge. If you do it well, no one will notice anything. If you do it wrong, you can trivialize your body of work and negate the effort you've expended.

It is an unfortunate fact that some of your portfolio material will transfer poorly to the digital medium. Be prepared to evaluate your work twice: before you scan it and when you see the images themselves. If you're afraid it will be too hard for you to be objective, ask a trusted colleague to go over the scans with you. No matter how much you want a digital portfolio, you will regret wasting time trying to doctor the terminally ill file. By the time you're done, you could have chosen the Develop route and crafted a capabilities portfolio with new material.

On the other hand, don't do a detail-for-detail comparison, or you'll never use any pre-digital work! On-screen imagery always flattens in comparison to the real thing, or to a good analog image. Evaluate based on how

you feel about presenting this material to someone who has never seen the original piece. Remember that your goal is to prompt the viewer to call you, which will give you the opportunity to show original work if you wish.

Saving Yourself Headaches: When Not to Scan

How can you tell what's appropriate material, or at least salvagable, if you've never done this before? As anyone who has ever been involved in production knows, there are times when you have to analyze a situation and recognize that you haven't the time (or expertise) to waste on a lost cause. You reshoot, redesign, or adjust the work so the problem element is either eliminated or used so that its problems are minimized. Remember, the issue is not whether an image can be fixed (given time, patience and experience, almost anything can be repaired), but whether the result will be worth the sweat. You won't want to show everything you've ever done in your portfolio anyway. Anything that you can't rework to display it in a positive light should be put aside unless it's a centerpiece of your portfolio idea. If you absolutely must work with images that are seriously substandard, attend a seminar in Photoshop photo-retouching first.

Is the Image Second-Generation?

Non-digital imagery is degraded each time it's processed. To some degree, if you've shot a piece of art, printed matter, or a 3-D object, your intended viewer is already one generation removed from it simply by the process of translating it to film. If in addition the material you're working with has been processed twice—an analog videotape that's a copy of a copy, for example—you will always have lost some image definition. If so, don't weaken your presentation by using it.

Is the Photo Overall Too Dark?

Flatbed scanners tend to make things darker, and even decent scanners can have problems holding shadow detail. If your photo has deep shadows, subtleties in them will disappear when you scan. Photoshop is a miraculous program, but it can't manipulate material that isn't there. If you're working with a photograph and the detail exists in the negative, reprocess the shot and rescan, or have the negative made into a Photo CD image.

Can You See Color Halo Outlines Around Objects?

Halo outlines may indicate that the video camera a capture was done with was not in registration. It can also happen when the scanner itself needs calibration. You will tend to see faint blue and yellow shadow images at major changes in value. If the halos are not too prominent and you don't need or want the background, you can protect the vital objects by masking them, then apply a massive Gaussian Blur in the rest of the image to bring the background to a neutral continuous tone. You can see a before (XMP41.jpg) and after (XMP42.jpg) example of this repair on the CD. If, on the other hand, the background is not expendible, you have no choice but to go back and recapture with better equipment, or drop the item.

How Much Contrast Is In Your Photograph?

Photographers sometimes increase the contrast of images for dramatic effect or underexpose them slightly to produce more saturation. This can be a problem for flatbed scanners, which actually scan flat, low contrast images far better than they do high contrast ones. This is because low contrast images usually have more overall image detail in the midtones and fewer deep shadows. There are several methods for increasing contrast in an image, and none for grabbing back completely posterized detail.

If the scanned image still has identifiable details in the dark areas, sometimes you can emphasize them by Unsharp Masking (see below) the channel which has retained the most detail. You must apply this stage with care, or your image will develop weird color

shifts around the edges of objects. If you don't mind a slight desaturation of the image and want even more overlay of subtle differences, export the channel you've sharpened to a new file, change its mode to greyscale and then to rgb, and re-import it as a layer into the original file. Set the layer to a transparency level of about 15–20%, and your details should be emphasized.

If You're Scanning from Original Line Art, What's Its Condition?

Scanned line art pixelates. There are strategies for dealing with this problem, but they either involve scanning your image in chunks, then tiling them together in Photoshop, or enlarging the original before scanning, usually on a copier for pen and ink or charcoal work.

In general, if your original art is too big to fit on the scanning bed, you may have to shoot it first, unless you are very good with overlapping tiled imagery. Photographing original art is also wise if you want to capture texture, or if the original image is damaged from storage or handling problems like sharp folds or dogeared edges. Then you can bring the negatives in to be converted to Photo CD.

If there is any overriding theme to watch for here, it's the well-known programming GIGO acronym: Garbage In = Garbage Out. Whether you're digitizing video, capturing a 3-D object, or scanning a printed piece, imperfections mean extra time and the possibility of making the situation worse. Always digitize the cleanest, crispest, closest-to-original material.

Editable Sins: Fixable Images

Well, we've dealt with the bad news. The good news is that most common image problems are eminently fixable in Photoshop. Obviously, simply recropping an image or editing out distracting background detail can be done on any scan. But in addition to the obvious, Photoshop makes faults that would have been terribly difficult to handle in the past surprisingly easy to resolve. We'll deal with the following common problems here:

 Muddy-looking or flat images. Images with too little contrast will flourish in Photoshop.

 Color casts. Fluorescents, for example, give everything a blue-green cast. Other forms of indoor lighting will also shift the image's spectrum. We don't tend to notice these things because after we've acclimated to a lighting situation, our eyes adjust to it. Film, however, does not. Photoshop offers several possible ways of attacking global color problems.

 Fuzzy or soft pictures. This is one of the most common problems with

photographic artwork, and a surprisingly easy one to address.

We'll discuss these solutions below.

To show these image edits, I use Adobe Photoshop. Don't take these explanations, however, as the be-all and end-all of Photoshop editing. They are, in fact, some of the most basic and straightforward tricks. I am concentrating only on the functions you are most likely to need to optimize your scanned portfolio art.

One important thing to keep in mind is everytime you do a color or tonal correction, or scale an image, you are effecting the original scanned information. Once you've made a change and gone past your single undo, there's no return. If this is your first serious foray into image correction, make sure to keep copies of your work in stages, and always keep a copy of the image before you try something radical, especially if you're applying changes in a series. It's all too easy to hit the Save rather than the Save As…, especially if you're working with a drawing palette rather than a mouse.

Adjusting Tonal Values

Always fix tone before you attack color issues or other image problems because you may discover that your color issues were really a symptom of squashed tones. If the image looks muddy, with no strong highlights or shadows, you've probably got a problem that's calling out for tonal correction. Such images are simply not using the entire greyscale value range.

The simplest and easiest way of doing this in Photoshop is through Levels. Professional retouchers will recommend Curves instead, and for print applications they are absolutely right. Careful Curve adjustment will beat Levels any day because Curves has an infinite number of tweakable points, whereas Levels only provide you with three. Your objective though is to get the most effective, easiest image repair with the shallowest learning curve. Levels will correct about 80% of what's wrong with an image, and for on-screen viewing that's probably enough.

You can follow this process in a sequence of changes made in a sample photograph (Xmp43.eps) on the book's CD. Make sure you are viewing all layers and channels, and that RGB is highlighted in the Channels Palette. Go to Image > Adjust>Levels…

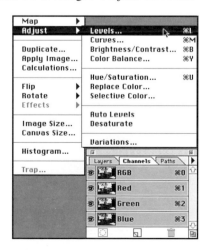

Figure 4.14
Levels pull-down menu.

You will be at the Levels dialog box. First, make sure the Preview Box is checked. Then click on the Auto Button.

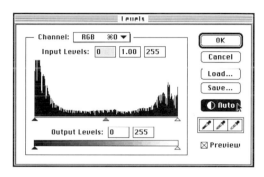

Figure 4.15
Cloosing Auto Level in the Levels dialog box.

79

If you're lucky, Photoshop will automatically repair your tonal problems. Your image will both brighten and appear to have additional depth. Unfortunately, sometimes this is not enough (see CD, Xmp44.eps). Your image could have some areas which you want to be much brighter, but the computer can't judge what they are. If so, Undo your Auto setting, and return to the Levels box.

You will see three small Eyedropper boxes on the lower right. The one on the far right sets the white point, which is the brightest place on your image—a place that you want to define as pure white. The one on the far left sets the black point, the place of deepest shadow. Used together, they have the effect of taking a rubber band and stretching it out in both directions, forcing the image to use the entire value range.

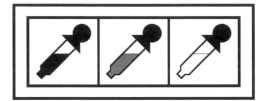

Figure 4.16
*The Eyedroppers in Levels for setting
highlights, shadows, and midtones.*

To watch them in action, click the white
point Eyedropper, then click your image. If
you clicked one of the places which are
already light, the effect will be to brighten
your image, increasing the strength of the
highlights. If you clicked someplace dark,
you will wash the image out, since everything brighter than the place you chose will
be reset to white.

Try the same test with the black point
Eyedropper, and the result will reverse. The

lighter you define the black point, the fewer
highlights you will retain. The center
Eyedropper is for midtones, but this is much
harder to see and control on your first few
outings and is best avoided when beginning.

Find the area on your image that you would
like reset to white, and using the white point
Eyedropper, choose it. Do the same for the
black point. With luck, you will have an
infinitely better image (See Xmp45.EPS). If
most of your image looks much better but a
small portion is washed out or too dark,
probably that section was at a correct tonal
value to begin with. If so, undo your Levels
work. Select those areas which should not
have been changed, save the selection and
go to Select>Inverse to protect them from
Levels change.

Return to the Levels dialog box and try it
again. Chances are you'll now be much
more satisfied with your results.

Figure 4.17
*Inverse under the
Select menu.*

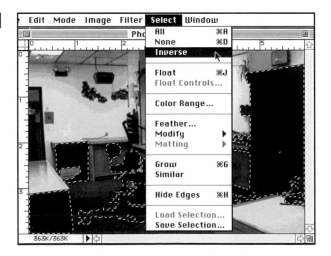

Adjusting Color

How can you tell if your image has a color cast? First, adjust the tonal values in Levels. You may be pleasantly surprised. However, if you still think the colors are off in the image and you can't tell exactly how, go to Image>Adjust>Variations…

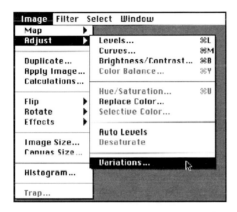

Figure 4.18
Variations pull-down menu.

Variations is a useful "cheat sheet" for helping you figure out the next direction. Make sure to check all three possibilities: highlights, shadows, and midtones. You may discover that your color cast is not a problem overall but is stronger in the darker or lighter areas. Although you can choose a variation from the menu choices here, it's somewhat like doing a drive-through fast-food lunch rather than sitting down for a real meal. It's fast, but you won't be completely satisfied.

Although they're a little complicated to work with, Levels can help with color casts too. You may remember that there were more options in Levels than just the eyedroppers. Let's assume that you looked at Variations and discovered that your image would look much more like the original if it had more blue in the midtones. Return to

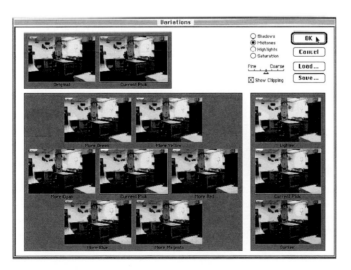

Figure 4.19
Variations dialog box with images showing.

Levels, go to the pull-down menu, and choose the Blue channel.

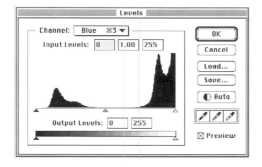

Figure 4.20
Levels dialog box, with the Blue channel chosen.

You'll notice that there is a histogram of the Blue channel below the pulldown menu labeled Input Levels. It shows you the gamma of this channel. Like the eyedropper, the left arrow slider is for black, the right is for white, and the grey is for midtones. Move the gamma slider left. As you move it farther into the darker areas, the image increases in blue (See xmp46.eps).

Figure 4.21
Histogram in Levels, indicating the slider arrows for white, midtone, and black points.

After you've finished this process, there may still be minor problems with color and value in the midtones. If so, move to the midtone Eyedropper and locate a medium value in your image. This may take some hunting at first, but as you click the midtone Eyedropper over these areas, you will be able to see the result of your search. Look in particular for a midtone in your problem hue. In our original photograph, we had too much red, so this was our target. You can see the results in the final image in our sequence, Xmp47.eps.

Looking Sharp: Repairing Soft Images

Image editing can be awfully counter-intuitive. When our images have ugly stairstepping, or aliasing, we solve the problem with anti-aliasing, a process that makes things look sharper by blurring them. To successfully sharpen and clarify a soft image, we blur it too. The trick lies in the process.

Images that are too soft, that have been scaled down, or which suffer from moire mottling can be repaired, often very successfully. However, if you don't have a tremendous amount of experience, it's easy to overcompensate. Beginners try to sharpen their scans using Photoshop's Sharpen filter, which can work nicely in color images if the change required is minor. Everything will seem to come back into focus. If a quick pass with Sharpen doesn't work, there's a tendency to reach for Sharpen More. This is a great way to introduce rough-looking texture to a file but a terrible way to clean up a scan. Every minor change in pixel color will get highlighted. Flesh will mottle, making people in a photo look like they have measles.

The Sharpen filter does have the solution to soft images, and it's found in the strangely named Unsharp Mask. The name alone tends to scare away beginners, which is a shame considering how effective it is. Just like anti-aliasing, it works by blurring under controlled conditions. Since soft scans are the most frequent problem with otherwise usable artwork, let's walk through this in detail.

Imagine we have two pixels next to each other. They represent the visual edge of a face and its lighter background. To help us visualize how these pixels will be affected by the filter, we'll assign the predominant value of the face the arbitary number of 20, indicating that it's at the dark end of our

photograph's value range. We'll give the background a value number of 11—it's light but not white. (Note that this is an arbitrary number range, chosen to illustrate the point simply.) If you were to zoom the file up to see the transition between the two colors, it might look something like Figure 4.22 below.

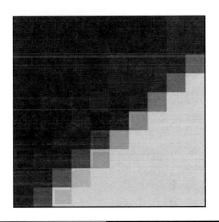

Figure 4.22
A zoom into the image at 16:1.

If you assign numbers to a horizontal row of these colors 10 pixels across, you might have a grid which looks like this:

11	11	11	11	11	16	18	20	20	20

Figure 4.23
A horizontal band of pixels 10 units across.

Now let's assume that the image we're looking at is somewhat soft and fuzzy. We go to Filter > Sharpen > Unsharp Mask….

Figure 4.24
Menu choice in Unsharp Mask.

We choose an amount of 100%, a radius of .8, and a threshold of 5. Our original image suddenly looks clearer. Let's look at a zoom of the newly sharpened area. Notice that there is more contrast at the edges where the light and dark areas meet. What happened?

Figure 4.25
A zoom into the image at 16:1 after using Unsharp Mask.

The key to the filter is hidden in its name. It works by taking a blurred copy of the image and using it as a pixel mask. Remember that blurring is anti-aliasing. Graduated changes in value replace abrupt changes to give the appearance of a smooth transition. Our 10-pixel blurred bar might look something like Figure 4.26 below. Notice the smooth sequence of numbers which has taken the place of the big jumps in the original Figure 4.23.

Figure 4.26
A horizontal band of pixels 10 units across, repre-sented as a smooth progres-sion of values from blurring the darkest to lightest pixel.

But how does combining this ramp make for such a sharp definition in the final piece? The filter compares each pixel with its blurred mask. Pixels without changes (because they are not at the edges of areas) are untouched, or masked out. Instead, the filter pays special attention to areas where abrupt color or value changes indicate edges. Then it determines mathematically what to change and how much.

This complicated algorithm has been simplified in Figure 4.27 below.

Essentially, the two pixels from the same position in the color bars in Figure 23 and Figure 26 are compared. The value in the first box in both figures is 11 so no changes in the pixel are made. In the next pixel comparison to the right, the shade in the blurred bar is one value level lighter than the original image. The computer filter inverts that difference, subtracting one level of value from the second pixel to give it a value of 10. This makes the color in that pixel slightly darker. This process continues for the first five boxes, each one getting progressively darker.

While this is happening, the filter is working its magic on the right side's color also. Note that the three boxes on the right are getting progressively lighter, as the filter adds brightness rather than subtracting it. Only one of the anti-aliased pixels in the middle is changed, going slightly lighter. The overall effect is to heighten the contrast between the two areas, as the darker background gets even darker as it approaches the edge, and the lighter area gets brighter, without compromising the anti-aliasing where the two areas meet.

Seeing the explanation, it's easy to see how too much sharpening could be applied, since the edges where colors meet would be more contrasted. How do you know what variables to put in the dialog box to prevent this from happening? Let's look quickly at what each of the variables controls.

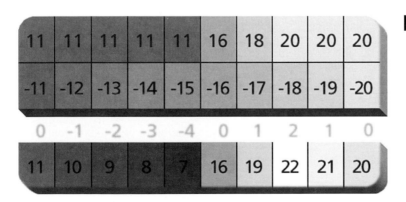

Figure 4.27
The process of altering the light and dark edges of an image shown graphically.

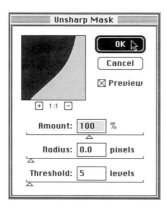

Figure 4.28
Unsharp Mask dialog box.

The Radius variable determines how many pixels on either side of the edge will be changed and is the setting most likely to effect your image. The larger the number you use, the more pixels will be involved. This number should increase as your resolution increases, since you need to effect more pixels to handle the same visual area. If you have been scanning at screen resolution, your pixel radius should be between .3 and 1.0 pixels, with .5 to .8 usually giving optimal results without oversharpening. If you have scanned larger because you plan on collaging or image editing, your radius will also be larger. At 150 dpi, for example, a good setting for the pixel radius is between 1.0 and 1.5.

Amount is the next most critical setting. It sets the actual value of change to be added to or subtracted from your effected pixels. In the example above, I simply incremented the blurred image by a factor of one along the 10-pixel line. Imagine how much more dramatic, and possibly bizarre, the effect would be if each increment equalled 2 instead. Once again, the bigger the number, the larger the amount of change. I tend to start at a default of 75% and move up to 175%, checking the Preview box for harsh lines indicating I've gone too far.

Threshold is the easiest setting to understand. It determines what constitutes an edge and enables you to block the filter from some of the worst blotching and outlining effects in an artifact-laden scan. Threshold also protects color and value ramps. The higher the setting, the more different two adjoining pixels have to be before the filter treats them as edges. You'll need to judge the Threshold number on an individual image basis, but a Threshold of 3 to 5 will take care of almost any normal sharpening situation at screen resolution. If you are working at a higher resolution, your threshold number will decrease.

Normal flatbed scanners often distribute unequal amounts of noise in the three channels as they interpolate scans at different percentages and spi values. Noise is what creates odd bits of new color in a file. Sharpening these noise-created pixels causes unexpected posterization and artifacts in an image. Therefore, if you have images which seem to develop unacceptable outlined edges even when you use Unsharp Mask, your best strategy can be to work on each channel of the image separately, sharpening the noisiest channel (usually blue) the least, and the cleanest channel (usually green) the most. But be careful—this solution has its down side. Sharpening one channel at a much higher percentage than the others can lead to color shifts.

Always make Unsharp Mask the last image edit you do in a file. Adjust tone, color, and scale first. If you work in a different order you could be blurring and sharpening several times, leading to color shifts, loss of detail, and weird artifacts in what should be masked areas.

Transferring Existing Digital Work

The plus of working with digital files is that you don't have to go through the tedious process of scanning and correcting them. However, not all work that exists in digital files can be used as is. They usually live in proprietary file formats that require a specific program to open and view the work. They come in a variety of page sizes, color palettes, and scales. All of these variations must to some degree be minimized or eliminated for portfolio viewing. Finally, all artwork will have to be transferred to the same file format for smooth and seamless viewing by others.

Your Rosetta Stone for translating and homogenizing files will vary. You'll need a file format converter, like Photoshop, to

process frames for slide shows, animations, or interactive presentations. You'll need a document translator, like Acrobat, for a portfolio of publication design. Analog animations and videos may need to be digitized and integrated with computer-based work. Let's take the general categories one at a time.

Importing Vector Files

Files created in Illustrator, FreeHand, CorelDRAW!, and so on are known as vector files. If you have plans to create an image slide show or interactive presentation using vector files, you will have to *rasterize* them first. Photoshop is the best way of handling this on both Mac and Windows platforms. Be sure to create a checklist to prepare your vector files beforehand. Not all vector drawing programs will require all of these actions, but check your manual before you assume anything!

87

- Transfer your fonts to outline form.

- Deal with placed or embedded raster images in vector files—some programs or versions of programs will not rasterize well or at all with placed art included.

- Crop or resize your image area to the correct dimensions or aspect ratio. You want the rasterized file to be as crisp and clean as possible.

- Delete hidden objects or elements which could slow down the rasterizing process. Even if something is hidden from view by other objects, it has to be processed if it's in the file as data.

 Save your rasterized files in the format you'll next need them in, and with the correct naming convention. Not only is naming consistency a virtue, but if you are working with Adobe products exclusively, it can allow you to import whole folders of images in sequence into Premiere.

Publications and Page-Based Documents

EPS may be cross-platform for print applications, but it is not ideal for digital portfolios. The files are too big and slow to read. If your work is exclusively print based and tends to be text heavy, consider transferring all of it to Adobe Acrobat (or a similar cross-platform document solution). Acrobat creates files from existing documents which display almost exactly as originally designed, including typographic decisions. Any EPS file can be run through the Acrobat Distiller to create a .pdf file. This solution is also useful when applied to the Web, where you are confronted with no typographic control and your documents can suffer mightily under normal preparation. Adobe has been evangelistic in shipping Acrobat Reader software with most of its other products, so chances are very good that most people will have access to it. For insurance, you can always include it on a CD, because

the Reader can be distributed freely. Acrobat also allows you to zoom into the page while maintaining readability, which is not something you can count on with a typical rasterized file. On the other hand, if your portfolio is more eclectic and varied, the PDF format will lock you into a fairly static and sequential presentation. Some things to watch for:

 If you are using Acrobat, don't plan on creating a diskette-based portfolio. The Acrobat Reader software is 800K and can get even larger with add-on files.

 Font problems can still creep into your work. Everything is fine, for example, if you've exclusively used Adobe PostScript fonts and are porting your work to Acrobat. If you've been working with fonts from other founderies, Acrobat will chose its nearest font equivalent when it translates the information. Kerning, spacing, and line breaks can change when that happens.

 If you are rasterizing print document work, plan on scaling portions of your work before you rasterize so you can show detail. Portrait format work with lots of type can get pretty small and uninteresting on a 640×480 default screen.

 Annual reports and other text-heavy, highly grid-intensive material frequenty translates poorly into a static slide show presentation. Consider using covers, or abstract elements drawn from the material and reconfiguring them as individual animation elements. This way, you can get across the volume of print material you've designed without forcing people to view it in an uncomplimentary format.

Downsizing Raster Files

Resolution is important when you first scan your files since you need to hold as much scan information as possible. Anything displayed on-screen, however, is merely some form of bitmapped graphic, not a sharp outline. If you do a careful job of down-sampling your files, you can fill a 17 inch monitor edge to edge with a file only 96K in size. It will look basically the same there as the 70MB wonder you may have started with. Things to watch for:

 If your file has been rasterized from another program, try to do all size changes or cropping either before you rasterize or as part of the same process. This will keep your on-screen display as sharp as screen-resolution allows.

 Avoid multiple rescales of files. Crop only once, and check your image carefully aftewards. You may have inadvertently cropped to a size that

unevenly divides your pixels. This will slightly stretch and blur the work. If you're not satisfied with the results, undo and try again. Don't try to correct the work unless you have no choice.

Color Fidelity

Not a problem digital to digital, right? Wrong. Take a color file in Illustrator and make a copy of it. Leave the original open on the screen. Then open the copy of the file in Photoshop and compare the two windows. Chances are good that the colors will look slightly different, particularly if your Illustrator file had custom colors in it. Because they were designed for print production uses, vector drawing files are usually based in CMYK. When they are rasterized, their colors are mapped to the screen's RGB mode. Not all software uses the same color space, and not all screens display at the same gamma or with the same system palette, so even though the PostScript interpretation would be consistent in printing, screen color may not. This only becomes a real problem if for some reason you need to show portions of the same project at different stages of completion. If you have a scanned printed piece, a raster image, and an illustration in FreeHand or Illustrator, you may need to make color adjustments in Photoshop to make the group of images feel consistent.

89

Integrating Images Pre-Presentation

After your material is on the computer, the next step is determining whether printed work will be shown separately from existing digital material, or if it will be integrated into one presentation. Stylistic and textural considerations will come into this decision, as well as your original sequencing and portfolio "story" decisions. Additionally, technical issues should be kept to a minimum, both for yourself and for your viewer.

Consistent File Formats

If your portfolio items will be organized into some form of presentation, you will want them in the same format. PICTs, JPEGs and QuickTime movies are the standard building blocks for interactive work using the Macintosh. Windows is not nearly as standardized, but you're probably safe using .TIFs, JPEGs (.JPG), .AVI (Microsoft Video for Windows), and .MOV (QuickTime for Windows) files. The less variation in file format for each type of material, the easier it is for you to organize your presentation and to solve any problems.

Consistent Size

Despite the fact that most designers have 16, 17, or even 21-inch screens, there are many good reasons to plan your display for the standard 640×480 screen dimensions—the basic 13–14 inch monitor. The first is to allow for the possibility that your

presentation will be viewed on this smaller screen. There's nothing more awful than to transfer all your work to a CD, then find that all the windows are falling out of the monitor frame. The second is that setting up a presentation larger than this will take up a tremendous amount of memory—more than you can afford in diskette storage. Even if you are using the 640×480 screen, you probably won't be filling that image area with a full-color image. (Uncompressed and unaltered, a 24-bit 640×480 screen will gobble around a megabyte of memory.) Lastly, the 640×480 dimension is the closest thing to a universal page size we have on the computer. Just as $8^1/_2 \times 11$ is the standard paper size for print, so is the 4:3 aspect ratio (horizontal to vertical) the standard for video, TV, and monitor screens.

Most animation and video software programs will provide you with a set of image size choices when you begin a new project, most of which will be preset to some variation of the 4:3 ratio. Although you can certainly design to a different shape if the program allows a custom dimension, for your first foray into this process, you might find it easier to minimize your variables and accept the defaults. Use your stage size as a determining factor when designing your presentation, scanning your artwork, and resizing it to be displayed.

Consistent Scale

If you vary image scale between your portfolio elements, do it purposefully, not just because pre-existing digital art isat a certain size. Visual variety can be a strong design element, but haphazard changes will confuse your audience. For example, if the cover of an annual report is scanned to display at 50% with no background or border, don't sandwich it between two full-screen illustrations. Not only will the annual report cover (already at a disadvantage from being scanned) seem like an afterthought, but it will break the flow of the illustrations. Each time viewers will have to readjust their focal point on the screen.

Consistent Palettes

If you have 7 small 24-bit images that average about 300K each, you are already well over the diskette limit. An interactive or animated diskette portfolio will increase dramatically in size compared to your original artwork. So how does everyone manage to present all those images, plus add a framing interactive inteface, animation and sound? The key is to think small. Really small. We've already talked about moving all your images down to screen resolution, and rescaling to fit within a 640×480 image area. Now we have to deal with minimizing image palettes.

You will not want to change the image palette of all your images. As you will discover in Chapter 6, "Work on the Web," photographic images reduce poorly when their color palette is minimized. You'll probably want to simply convert such material to JPEG files for viewing. In most cases, a medium level of compression will retain enough information for portfolio viewing while shrinking your file sizes enormously. A 1000K, 72 dpi image will end up around 80K in size (about 8–10% of the original) and be adequate for viewing at 100%. Beware: this approach is most effective in slide show situations. You will discover it tends to collide with color requirements in more complexly orchestrated material.

Vector graphics, created interface material, or any animations you may create in QuickTime will need to be even smaller than that. Since most computers simply can't handle a 16 or 24-bit animation, processor restrictions have made 8-bit graphics the standard for most interactive portfolios. In 8-bit, you can only display 256 different colors on a monitor screen at a time. In practical terms, you will have to make a strategic choice before proceding:

1. **Create everything from scratch.**
   Work primarily in flat color, using a palette you create. Make each individual element from as few palette colors as possible to keep them small and fast. Pros: no nasty unexpected color shifts later and you have the smallest possible finished portfolio file size. Cons: no solution for displaying existing portfolio work and any photographic imagery or video clips are blocked unless the colors are very carefully chosen.

91

2. **Convert existing graphics to 8-bit or JPEG files.** If you take this route, you've basically chosen not to show your portfolio graphics with any other elements unless those elements are compatible with the colors in the current on-screen image. Create additional interface material separately, and don't mix the two visually. Pros: allows you to show best-quality visual representation of each existing image. Makes it easier for a relative novice to create a simple clickable interface. Cons: limits creativity, can compartmentalize artwork.

3. **Convert all existing graphics to 8-bit, then apply the System Palette.** In this case, you just assume that the System Palette on your chosen platform has enough color variety to do an adequate job of translating your images. Pros: every computer OS has a standard palette, with a wide enough variety of colors in it to guarantee decent if not stellar imagery. Excellent solution for QuickTime movie imagery—avoids color shifts that can arise with custom palettes. Cons: images that have a narrow range of hues but a wide value range will suffer banding and artifacting. Not the most exciting palette to use for custom-created interactive imagery—limits blends.

4. **Create a custom "super palette."** This is a palette optimized for your range of imagery, which you then apply to everything and dither your images. The super palette is created by opening a large new file in Photoshop or other imaging program, copying images into it, then creating a compromise color table from those images. Pros: gets around the system palette limitations, and insures that everything will look at least adequate on-screen. Very effective for a small collection or images, or a group of images that share color and hue decisions. Cons: can lead to unexpected false spot color in graphics that weren't used as part of the palette creation process.

Note

Making a Super Palette in Photoshop

Go to Mode > Index and create an 8-bit adaptive palette. Dithering can be set to anything, because this large file is just an expendible tool to help you develop your palette. After the Mode change, go to Mode > Color Table and Save the palette you see there. Next, open one of your images in Photoshop. Go to Mode > Index and create an 8-bit Custom image with diffusion dithering. You will get a Color Table dialog box showing the last palette created. Click OK. Your individual image will be dithered to your super palette. If you leave this process in the middle, simply choose Load at the Color Table dialog box, find your saved palette, and click OK.

5. **Create several custom palettes.** If your multimedia application supports multiple consecutive palettes, switch them in and out as you need them.

This requires that graphics needing different color palettes not be on screen at the same time. Pros: enables the widest variety of colors in a presentation and limits overall compromise. Cons: complicated and difficult to implement. Not all software supports multiple palettes.

Note

Equilibrium's DeBabelizer (see Chapter 6 for a detailed introduction to DeBabelizer) is a great application for shrinking image palettes and applying them to multiple images. It's impossible to do a professional job of cross-platform multimedia creation without it.

Windows and Indexed Palettes

If you are creating your portfolio on a Wintel computer, it is more complicated creating custom palettes than on the Mac OS, even if Photoshop is your imaging application. The Mac OS does not really care what colors you use in your individual applications, but Windows does. In an 8-bit, 256-color palette, the first and last ten color positions belong to the system itself. If you change them, any portion of the Windows screen not dedicated to your portfolio application, like the menu bar, will display false colors and may be unrecognizable. Even worse, Windows "locks" white into the first color position and black into the last. They cannot be changed no matter what. So instead of 256 definable colors, you actually have only 236.

Next...

Thus ends the artwork preparation phase of our project. By this time, all your material should be digitized, corrected, and rephotographed if needed. All source material should have one type of file format and art used in an animation or interactive work should be scaled and have its palette homogenized.

From here, you have two possible paths. The first and most direct is to complete a disk- or CD-ROM-based portfolio. This involves organizing material, choosing a specific delivery format that suits your needs, designing and creating additional art and typography, and moving the material to its final resting place. The second possibility is to invade the World Wide Web. These two paths are by no means mutually exclusive, although I would not recommend trying to do both at the same time. Let's tackle the disk/CD format first.

93

CHAPTER FIVE

Portfolio to Go: Disk-Based Presentations

Twenty years from now you will be more disappointed by the things you didn't do than by the ones you did do. So throw off the bowlines. Sail away from the safe harbor. Catch the trade winds in your sails. Explore. Dream. Discover.
—Mark Twain

After you've brought all your work onto the computer and transferred it to an appropriate file format, it's time to determine what to do with it. Before you begin this process, become familiar with the tools you will need. There are a multitude of resources for free demonstrations. Imaging equipment dealers and user groups are constantly sponsoring seminars to familiarize people with new products. These seminars almost always involve examples and demonstrations, and sometimes short hands-on periods. Even a visit to the vendor's floor of a trade convention will involve basic demonstrations and the opportunity to ask questions. Check out your area's college and university continuing education programs for an introduction to some of the commercial software before you buy it to make sure you'll be comfortable operating at the level of complexity you've chosen.

Then, if appropriate to your needs and the nature of your material:

1. Bring the material into some form of display package.

2. Create a stand-alone player version of your show.

3. Transfer it to diskette or CD.

Finally, labels, cases, wrapping, or other packaging issues must be addressed before the portfolio is ready for prime time.

You have four basic options for an on-disk portfolio presentation. These are dealt with here in order of increasing technical and design complexity:

 Individual files in a "universal" file format

 Simple slide shows

Presentation slide shows

 Interactive presentations with animation

Each category will be explored below to help you determine which method is the most appropriate to your needs. Hints will be offered to avoid the most typical problems of each form of digital portfolio method. Note that suggestions and guidelines for these options are cumulative in nature. Anything mentioned as a consideration in a less-complex format will also apply to later, more sophisticated options. Be sure to read them all.

Warning

Everyone seems to approach this process thinking that their on-disk portfolio must be interactive. In fact, it's probably the wrong decision for most people, because the learning curve—technical and conceptual—is very steep. The desks of design directors are littered with amateurish attempts at multimedia. It's true that you won't be considered for certain jobs without showing your facility with moving images or your understanding of interactivity, but if you have no prior background or education in video, animation, broadcast, or interface design, you might be better off starting small and learning as you go, rather than trying for a position that's beyond your current development. There are several good books to help you make this transition, such as the *Multimedia Starter Kit* or *Adobe Press's Premiere book*. See Appendix D for some recommendations. What

is important is to show your work in a favorable light and to use the highest presentation form that you can handle successfully.

Individual Files in a "Universal" File Format

This is the simplest method for the artist to move his or her portfolio to disk. All it demands is that all scanned or digital work be saved in one file format and organized by project. A short text document can accompany each project if desired. Résumé or contact information can be left in a document on the root directory.

Although this was the first expression of the digital portfolio, it is infrequently seen today. Most of the time, simple viewers have taken the place of loose files on disk. The exceptions to this trend are portfolios where it is critical that the work be viewable cross-platform, but where the creator is not interested in learning or applying the intricacies of interactivity. Files and clips are much more sensible for simple gallery presentations, photographic stills on CD, or collections of video clips and animations. Otherwise, you should seek out slide show software to package your work. Given the rising level of presentation sophistication, a simple file on disk presentation will look amateurish or sloppy when viewed at the same time as more polished portfolios.

If you can't use a slide package or interactive software, be careful to ensure that your disk's file management and presentation are impeccable:

 Matte and position your digital artwork on a solid background.

 Trim any extraneous material from screen grabs. No one needs to be distracted by the menu bar or rulers from the software you grabbed the image from.

 Number your files or folders in the order they should be viewed.

 Always include a ReadMe document on your disk with your name and contact information. Specify if your work requires a 16- or 24-bit color monitor, and recommend a monitor size if you have screen-grabbed from anything larger than the standard 640×480 display. If you are providing complex video material, provide a plain-text table of contents, too.

 Make sure your ReadMe is in a non-proprietary file format. On the Mac, this means SimpleText. In DOS or a flavor of Windows, a .DOC or .TXT extension should insure your file's readability. Despite its ubiquity, *don't* create a ReadMe in Microsoft Word.

 Change your disk's name label to your first initial and last name, and edit its image icon to personalize it. (See Chapter 3 on icon editing for how to do this.)

 If any of your work depends on specific fonts to be viewed, make sure that they are available on your disk. Even if your viewer has ATM on his or her machine, your work will not be shown to best effect and lines may break differently than they did before. Even worse, if you have used a non-Adobe typeface, your font choices may be completely lost.

97

Simple Slide Shows

Simple slide shows are a clean and easy way to present portfolio work. They proliferate on both the Mac OS and DOS/Windows, and several good shareware options exist, many of which can be downloaded from the providers' Web sites. Almost any piece of software which is labeled an image viewer will also enable you to export a simple slide show presentation, including JPEGview. Although there are some general trends for different professions and purposes, portfolios on disk are still new enough that no one will be disconcerted by your choice of delivery software. Any that offer the options you need and allow you to produce a player application will be fine. A resource guide to slide show players can be found in Appendix A.

These presentations are essentially computer versions of the traditional slide carousel. They are created by software which generates a player or projector application from the art. These applications are completely self-contained and not editable after being created, nor is it usually possible to extract the images which comprise them by normal means. The user can generate the sequential slide show by choosing files in a specific order, or by batch processing an entire folder of work. Any text for introduction or titling must be made in a separate program and is treated like just another image in the tray. Most of these simple programs enable the viewer to choose between a hands-off timed display or the use of a simple mouse click to advance the presentation.

Simple slide show players demand few or no design decisions other than sequencing. They're also small and easy to create. What's particularly nice about the simple slide show is that there is no temptation to confuse the work with the presentation; the emphasis is clearly on the portfolio work. Fine artists and photographers generally tend to prefer this approach since they are not forced to learn a new piece of software or deal with interface issues. Given how easy to use and inexpensive they are to own, it makes sense to move a static collection of images into this format.

 All of the earlier guidelines for a simple file presentation apply as well to the simple slide show. A few additional issues arise as well.

98

 To make your slide shows manageable, keep the number of files to a minimum. If you have created a corporate identity, show its basic components in one frame. Group related components of a brochure series together. The people who will be evaluating your work are usually busy and can recognize filler when they see it.

 The order of your images is important. Always lead and end with your best work. Mark D'Oliviera of Hatmaker, a broadcast design studio featured on the accompanying CD, draws this analogy. "You know how they used to organize LPs? The big songs were the first song and the last song, and the first song on the other side. And the other stuff the record company figured was filler. I think that's how people look at reels. In the first ten seconds, no even five seconds, they're making a judgment about whether this is worth continuing. They may watch it to the end, but if they're not impressed in the first five or ten seconds, it's sad. It's over."

Presentation Slide Shows

These slide shows are more sophisticated, but they're still basically linear presentations. What they offer is the opportunity to add the sensation of motion and the element of passing time to the simple sequential format. Creating this kind of presentation should be simple for a designer with a good grounding in publication design and is within reach for almost every category of porfolio creator who has taken the time to work through the presentation concept.

Finding presentation software for such a portfolio is easy. Claris Works, Microsoft Works, Hypercard, PowerPoint, Persuasion…the list of commercial business slide presentation software is extensive. There are even full-featured shareware programs, especially on the Windows platform, that compete favorably with the better-known names on price and features. One of the problems with this software, however, (especially the commercial versions) is that sometimes the players created are simply too large for a basic diskette. The software itself is oriented toward business users and tends to show off for a portfolio presentation. The most useful options to work with are random access to images, adjustable effects and transitions, and good sound and text integration.

With more options comes the opportunity to develop a concept and polish the look and feel of your work. These options are also an opportunity to experience kitchen sink design—when you throw in "everything but the…" in an attempt to stretch out your material. In presentations, smaller and shorter is usually better. Go for quality, and use the additional transitions, movie, and sound options sparingly. If you've moved up

the food chain from the simple slide show just because you want to add a few transitions, that's fine. Stop there, and stick with your original agenda.

Bear in mind that the audience where this form of presentation will be most appreciated is in corporate communications or print-oriented design or advertising companies. For fine art or photographic material simplicity is usually better, and for media or small design firms, animation or interactive portfolios are a more impressive way to project who you are and what you can do.

Of course, all the guidelines for simple slide shows apply here also, but some additional issues need to be considered as well.

Titling and Type

The main thing that a more full-featured program can offer is typographic refinement, particularly if it is PostScript-based. If you are solid in typographic theory and practice, concentrate on an opening title and section dividers. Use type as a design framework around your individual portfolio elements.

If you are creating your titles and dividers as designed elements, consider using a vector drawing program (Adobe Illustrator or Macromedia FreeHand) for the artwork. You will want to have fine control over baseline leading, letterspacing and kerning. You might want to customize the type design, combine two letters or play with the alignment or overlap of individual characters. There are a host of typographic possibilities, most of which are either difficult or impossible to do in a paint or image editing program. Even things which seem relatively simple are easier to manipulate when you can click on complete objects. You can always save the file as an EPS and transfer it to Photoshop for additional embellishment later.

Keep your titles tight and to the point. Maintain visual negative space and avoid over-explaining. It's all too easy for a title slide to become too talky. If you need to explain a piece or its concept, continue on a separate slide.

Using Transitions

Your safest bet in adding transitions is to stick with the least obtrusive. A simple fade or dissolve from one frame to the next is often sufficient.

If you do want to experiment with transitions, analyze your material first. Are there strong diagonal elements in your image work? What about an underlying grid you can capitalize on? If necessary, make minor adjustments in the order of your presentation to highlight visual directions of motion that begin in one piece and continue in another. Then use transitions which make those links and play off them.

Don't just stop. The most important transition in an animated slide show is the transition out at the end. There is nothing more likely to ruin the mood of your presentation than a quick cut from your last image to the normal computer interface. Be nice to your viewer and transition them out. Add a black screen (black is the standard, but in fact any low intensity, relatively neutral value will work also) as the last frame of your piece, then fade from your work to black for about the count of three.

100

Figure 5.1
Example of a simple titling slide with minimal text and substantial negative space.

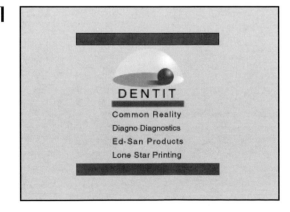

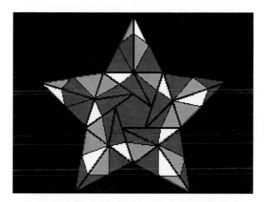

Figure 5.2
A transition based on the possibilities of the animated graphic. The glass star breaks into colored shards and spins into the center.

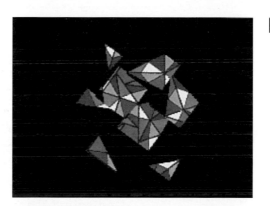

Figure 5.3

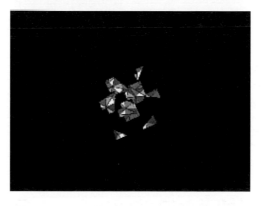

Figure 5.4

Interactive Presentations and Animation

An interactive portfolio piece may or may not contain prior art. In some cases, the previous illustrations or designs are used more as jumping off points for an excursion into animation. In others, the interface functions as a metaphor for packaging the existing material. Although some elements such as live navigation devices, random access to material, or non-linear action, are more or less common to interactive pieces, there is considerable stylistic and conceptual variety in this category.

Generally speaking, software for interactive presentations is both complicated and expensive. Macromedia Director is, rightly or wrongly, the most pervasive program for professional interactive designers on both platforms, as well as the growing medium of choice of displaying animations through the Web by virtue of its Netscape plug-in Shockwave. It's easier to deal with on an animation level, and many illustrators take advantage of this fact. A large percentage of portfolio players are really linear animations framed in a simple interface with options to begin, pause, back up, or leave.

At the truly interactive level, Director requires basic programming skills and high-level patience. It is a true multimedia program and is used to prototype and create a large percentage of the interactive and multimedia titles which find their way to

CD. As such, it allows you to incorporate graphics (usually PICT files), text, sound and music, animations created in the software, and QuickTime video. It is not for the faint of heart. On the other hand, once you get past the learning curve, Director is both versatile and powerful. *Director Demystified* is the best book available for leading you through the interface, explaining the somewhat arcane screen windows, and slowly building up your knowledge base.

There are a few simpler multimedia authoring tools that can be good bridges into the interactive world. For example, Digital Box Office is very affordable, can handle 24-bit files and is available for both the Mac OS and the major versions of Windows. If you are a Windows 95 user, Asymmetrix Toolbook is an elegant and undervalued medium for creating interactive work.

Controlled Chaos: Developing Your Ideas

The dos and don'ts of an interactive portfolio fall into two general categories: technological and conceptual. Both of them are important and should not be confused with each other. We'll start with the conceptual, because if you don't have a good handle on how to create and develop the mental space your work will inhabit, the technical structure will be of limited use to you.

If you decide to go interactive, realize that you are embarking on a challenging and time-consuming endeavor. Here is where the rubber meets the road. In Chapter 3, we talked about developing a portfolio "story."

For an interactive presentation, this need is multiplied by a factor of ten. Unlike other forms of portfolio presentation, an interactive design requires your viewers' active and willing participation. They must be persuaded to accept the mini-environment you create, which means that this environment must be internally consistent and offer symbols and rules that can be quickly understood.

Creating an interactive portfolio can be a wonderful experience because you are speaking to an audience that wants to see who you are through your work. By and large, commercial portfolios are comprised of artwork based on client problems, constraints, and solutions. They reflect the creative work of one individual, or of an individual directing the contributions of others. Media design, however, is truly a team process. A successful development usually means that all members have worked collectively to bring the piece to conclusion, often under pressure and long hours. Decision-makers in media firms are looking for potential collaborators, and a digital portfolio can act as a matchmaker in the process.

What are these media firms looking for? The list can sound like a personal ad: a strong sense of humor, a developed sense of self, enthusiasm, creativity, someone easy to get along with, and a unique problem solver. Your mission in an interactive portfolio is to frame your work and your ideas to clarify who you are, not just what you're capable of doing.

How can you do this? Obviously, there isn't and can't be a recipe. Good design is not the product of formulas. There is, however, a certain architecture that your personal solution can hang on. If you set up this architecture initially, you will at least have fewer false starts and can perhaps avoid some of the worst traps.

Begin by being playful. Don't say, "I'm going to do it this way" and rush through the process. Design is not neat, even if it's sometimes cool. Chances are your first idea is something that's been done before, and it comes up for you because the mental pathways are well-worn. Take the time to brainstorm your ideas, and take chances. Don't clamp down on a "stupid idea." Doing so will cramp your creative process and lead you back to business as usual. You're about to create something completely fresh in a medium that's new enough that it offers room for discovery.

After you've really given yourself the chance to break the rules, look at the ideas you came up with. Which ones appeal to you the most? Narrow down your list to the most compelling, and begin the process of elimination. First, ask yourself if you have the talent or can acquire the technical expertise to bring the idea to completion. Not everyone is equally good at everything, which is *why* full-fledged multimedia productions are handled by teams. If you're a terrific designer but a mediocre illustrator, you don't want to commit to a concept that will highlight this weakness. If you animate well but Lingo for Director makes your eyes

103

cross, don't plan an elaborate clickable interface. On the other hand, perhaps you have a side interest in music. This might be your opportunity to utilize your musical talent by replacing some visual cues with auditory ones.

The next eliminator is what I call the laugh-track syndrome. There is a difference between whimsy, outrageousness, and forced humor. Everyone thinks they have a sense of humor, but not everyone laughs at the same thing. If you keep trying to add bits of business to make your concept funny, you're probably forcing the issue. If your personal aesthetic runs toward the more formal and structured, don't work against that. Make it a virtue in your presentation by emphasizing an elegant interface and intelligently considered navigation.

Matching Existing and Created Work

This leads to the third issue: matching content to interface. You don't want to trivialize your existing material with the environment you use to negotiate through it. If the ideas you are considering will devalue your carefully scanned or transferred material, drop back and ask yourself again what your portfolio goals are. A good example of a mismatch would be a portfolio series of inner city sketches, or a group of sparse desert photographs. Pairing either of these with a playful flat-color interface or industrial typography could diminish both the original portfolio images and the work

that surrounds them. The dichotomy between the two will be too disturbing. Of course that irony might be your intent, but if so, you may have to choose the recipients of your finished portfolio very carefully indeed. On the other hand, if you have illustrations of athletic shoes, playing animation games with the original renderings could be very effective.

There is a possibility that, despite the mismatch between your existing art and your interface, you think the interface idea is simply too good to ignore. If so, consider the quality of the ideas you have brainstormed in comparison to your existing material. Is this the direction you would like to see your work evolve into, or is this a one-shot experiment? Despite all the scanning you may have done, if you strongly believe in the new direction you are pusuing, you always have the option of shifting gears. A new concept can be developed from scratch as a capabilities portfolio. As Mark D'Oliveira of Hatmaker said, "If I received a portfolio from someone that was created to show what they wanted to do, rather than what they had done, I'd react very positively, provided that the quality was up there. There could always be a followup discussion."

Last, avoid icon overload. Not everything you develop has to be represented by a picture. If any of your concept ideas are really about "I could make buttons that look like…", beware. I remember one technically stunning interactive portfolio where each category of project had been assigned a new graphical icon. I spent so much time trying to figure out what each picture was trying to say that I began to feel like I was participating in a game of Charades. ("Sounds like? Does it walk on two legs? Is it an annual report?") I would have been much more impressed with intelligently handled typography and a word like "Posters."

Moving from Concept to Development

One unbreakable rule is that the viewer's interaction with your work should be as seamless as possible. This should effect every possible situation, from the most mundane organizational issue to the most esoteric interface design consideration. This takes planning, some of which is easily related to design process, and some of which is more related to animation development.

Once you decide on your concept and its basic visual expression, it's time to develop your material into a complete presentation. To begin, leave your computer behind, sit down with a big pad of paper and some lined sheets. Write out in two or three sentences what your concept is. For example:

"My style is strongly geometric, and I've had years of experience in working with grids in publication design. I want to use the geometric theme to take elements of my work and collage them into a Kandinsky-like space. Viewers will explore this space, using it to access examples of my projects."

Keep this overview someplace visible while you move to the next step.

Create storyboards of your material, starting with your opening sequence. Make sure that your storyboards are in the correct aspect ratio. Space is really at a premium on-screen, and you want to make sure your work is designed to the correct proportions of the frame. 640×480 is a 4:3 ratio, so many people draw individual frames 3-up on an $8^1/_2 \times 11$ page, with space on the side for notes. Alternatively, you can get 6×4 index cards, flip them blank side up and work one frame to a card, and there are two advantages to this approach. First, it's easier to rearrange your work as you develop it. Second, you can spread your cards out and look at them all at once. There is less of a tendency to have problems with timing and transitions if you are not mentally dividing your presentation into thirds.

Note

Remember to number your frames in pencil so you can change them later.

As with more linear presentations, lead with something strong that will grab your viewer's attention. Try to avoid scenarios that begin in the center of the frame and never leave. Symmetry is boring. Elements dead center in the frame have less potential energy. To be effective, animation should do more than fill the frame. It should use the implied three dimensions, and all the conceptual space beyond the edges of the screen. Bring elements in from outside the image area. Keep them active.

Remember that you get to "set the scene" at the beginning, and the process of doing that can be used dynamically—experimenting with different key elements and trying variations of your original concept. Sketch this opening sequence out emphasizing the "key frames," those that will help you define the major visual actions. Imagine, for example, that you introduce lines, arcs, and geometric shapes from a variety of areas of the screen and then transform them together into typographic elements. You would want to show the entrance of each major element (or elements if many are entering at once), key places where they interact or change scale, and their final arrangement in space. The actual animation sequence will, of course, take up many more frames, but they will be transitional stages between your key screens.

When you've completed your key frames for the opening sequence, look at them sequentially. If you've never created an animation before, get a friend to look at them. If he or she can't understand what you intend to do, you are probably having problems with continuity, the logical way things flow from one key frame to the next. Add frames at the weak places to clarify your intention. Don't skimp on this process. Poor continuity is one of the most obvious problems in an animated sequence. You will want to repeat this process for any portions of your interactive piece that include animated elements.

If you are combining animation with interaction (elements that are clickable but do not stay in one position in space, or interactive elements that, when clicked, acknowledge that fact with an animated sequence), you'll want to annotate your sketch with explanations of what will take place and, if necessary, what link will be created between the interface and the next graphic displayed.

You should storyboard non-animated set-pieces also, but with the emphasis on function rather than motion. What's your portfolio's relationship to the viewer? Are you basically visualizing your viewer in a passive role, like a person sitting in front of a TV with a remote? In this case, design an interface where signposts are clearly marked and there is an identifiable sequence to your work. Let people know where they are and how many pieces of work you'll be showing them. If you see your audience as an active participant, you'll want to build in more options and random access. If you anticipate many alternatives and a strongly interactive presentation, consider creating a flowchart for viewing your interactive branches and making links between them. (This issue is covered in more depth in "The Web Flow Chart" section found in Chapter 6.)

Checking Your Design Decisions

Once you storyboard your entire presentation, look at some of the implications of your design decisions. Make sure that your viewer knows how to leave your portfolio presentation, or return to a specific image. There is nothing more frustrating than having to search madly through screens you've seen several times to find the one that lets you out. Interactivity also involves respecting the wishes of your audience. Otherwise, you run the risk of setting up an adversarial relationship that no one will appreciate.

Have you marked out an area for text to explain your projects? Make sure there is enough space to say what you need to. In print design, you can count on more freedom of point size and typeface than onscreen. If something doesn't work in 12 point, you can always move it down to 11. That's a limited option here. No creative director will read more than one line of ten point screen type. Although it's better to use scrolling text than to downsize or move to a thinner typeface, it's even better to cut your text to the essentials. That way you don't have to compromise your negative space or legibility.

In some cases, particularly in academic environments, you may have to supply more text with your imagery. If so, don't plan your presentation so that video or animation takes place at the same time that text is provided. Give people time to read before you start your video or animation, or run the animation first and show the text later. Since it's next to impossible to ignore a moving image, it will overwhelm simultaneously presented text, forcing the viewer to read it several times…to read it several times…to read it several times…

If you incorporate analog video clips into your portfolio, ask yourself if they translate well into the new medium. Analog video, because it has so much information, will probably have to run in a fairly small window. Details will disappear, as will the benefit of SMPTE coding. Your work will be at the mercy of a wide variety of computer processors and CD-ROM player speeds. If the work is a few years old, it may seem dated compared to earlier work which was created for the computer environment. Make sure you really need to show this work before you commit the time and energy to digitizing. If you decide to go forward, choose the portions you plan to show carefully. Don't cut a sequence in the middle because of space constraints. Such a decision will look as arbitrary as it is. It's better to show fewer individual works than to have a serious case of video interruptus.

Check the timing of your animated material. Are you rushing the viewer out of the frame or keeping them there too long? Generally, it's better to err on the side of too much going on than too little because people like to be kept involved. However, if you are presenting an animation sequence, you don't want it to move so fast that no one can figure out what's going on. Particularly at the beginning when you are setting up your environment, make sure that the viewer will have enough time to comprehend the space and shift their perceptions to deal with it.

107

Technical Details

Transferring your ideas to an interactive software program involves a steep learning curve if you've never done it before. Even worse, there is no commonality of interface in video, animation, or interactive software the way there is in other categories of programs. In illustration or paint programs, there are some things you can take for granted. There is a canvas space, some common icons that represent familiar functions (like the paint bucket for the fill function, the letter A for type, a looping line for freehand drawing), and a set of dialog windows which offer more detailed choices that can be accessed from a common file bar or tool space. Not so for animation or interaction. It seems as if every interface was designed from scratch. Although there are some growing standards for transferring animated clips across programs and platforms, the container files themselves are usually strictly proprietary to the software that created it.

Even given this wide variety of software, technical issues crop up again in interactive or animation portfolios. These little details can make a tremendous difference in how well your work will be received, and most of them are relatively easy to handle.

- Always enclose a ReadMe file with instructions and system requirements! Make sure your ReadMe clearly states that the viewer should turn off virtual memory. Otherwise, your viewer could become trapped in your application, unable to quit without shutting down their system. They should know better, but they'll blame you.

- Make a custom icon for your presentation. Creating a custom icon not only identifies your disk when it's in someone's drive, but acts as a memory reminder of who you are for the busy creative director who needs to find a supplier quickly.

- Create a compressed file of your presentation as a self-extracting archive to fit more material on the diskette. Stuffit Installer Maker SEA 2.0 will also allow you to create a customized splash screen for your archive. Generally speaking, the more completely you can customize your presentation, the better.

- Watch the names for your player or projector files. In Director, for example, when you make a projector file, "Projector" is the default name. Don't accept this default. Give your projector a custom name. Many art directors copy portfolio players onto a common disk for viewing and evaluation. If your file is copied last, it will replace the Projector before you. If it's copied first, the art director will never see your work, because it will be replaced by the next file of that name.

- If you are working with QuickTime movies and transferring them to

108

CD-ROM, CinePak your video files. CinePak is a lossy format but given the usual onscreen size of a video clip, the lost visual information is almost never noticed. Other forms of video compression (like standard Apple Video) retain more information in each frame, but this is actually a negative feature. Access times are considerably slower from a CD than on a hard disk. The larger (and less compressed) your movie file is, the more likely it is that frames will be dropped when your movie is played.

Note

CinePak and QuickTime Versions

Apple's QuickTime is an evolving video standard. Each time Apple changes or improves it, these changes are reflected in the QuickTime file format. Just as with other file formats, if you take a movie which was created on a new version of QuickTime and try to play it on a machine running an older version, you may have unexpected problems. For example, color palette implementation has changed over time. A CinePaked movie created with QuickTime 2.1 can look positively awful if run on a system using QuickTime 1.6.1. Make sure to specify your version of QuickTime as part of the system requirements to view your work. Be careful! If you are providing your work on CD, you can't simply add a copy of QuickTime 2.0 or better to it. You need to contact Apple to obtain a license to distribute QuickTime versions above 1.6.1.

 Never provide an editable copy of your animation or interactive piece. There is no way to prevent a diskette or CD-ROM from being copied, but as long as you have created player versions of your work, it is protected from being "reverse engineered" to duplicate your imagery or your code. If your software doesn't create a player, make sure it has some form of script hider or remover. When working in Director, it is possible to bring a movie file from one platform to the other, although it is not possible for a single projector file to be read on both platforms. This might make it necessary to violate the "only projector" rule to be able to present a single-platform piece. If you Update a copy of your movie to protect it, it will become a play-only version.

109

Testing Your Work

Both before and after you create your player application, you'll want to test your work under a variety of conditions to make sure that it will always be seen the way you designed it.

 Try your animations on computers of different speeds, especially if you have moving icons you want viewers to click on. We're so used to creating commercial applications for the lowest common denominator that we can make life a video game exercise for the creative director. You can really challenge their hand-eye coordination if you optimize your work on a Quadra 650 and they view it on a 604 Power Mac.

 Particularly if you plan on moving your work to CD, test it again and again. Launch it and stop it at different places. See what happens if you reboot the system and try to run it again. Check every link and follow it all the way through.

110

 Have someone else test the application and watch them. Do they click in places that you never intended? If they do, does anything unexpected happen in the application? Do you have links that lead nowhere or which abandon the viewer without a way to move on? If your guinea pig seems confused by your interface or slow to understand your environment, don't ignore the problem. Either provide some form of online help, or rework the difficult sections.

 Have you been developing your work to be viewed on more than one platform? If this is the first time you've every tackled such a thing, be aware that almost nothing moves from Mac to PC (or vice versa) without some problems, ranging from shifted colors to typographic changes to files

that "should" be readable by both platforms refusing to run on one or the other. Unless you are sticking to cross-platform file formats (like JPEG or EPS) without any slide show software, take nothing for granted. Develop a separate presentation on the other platform so you can test your work for embarrassing errors. Ask for help from more knowledgeable users and find every multimedia developer's information site on the Web.

Diskette or CD— Choosing Your Delivery Medium

Once you've completed your portfolio, whether it be an interactive piece, an animation, a slide show, or some combination of files, it's time to decide what physical medium you plan to deliver it on. This may seem obvious, but think again. Just because you have more material than will fit on a diskette doesn't mean that you need to write a CD. First, if your work is made up of several different elements—an interactive piece, some 3-D artwork, excerpts from video—you might consider targeting components of this work on different diskettes rather than going for the complexity of a CD. Everyone can load a diskette and play it. Not every computer has a CD-ROM attached to it. Additionally, some viewers can actually be put off by a CD-ROM presentation because of the time commitment involved.

Unless you are a multimedia developer by profession, you should guard against the tendency to decide in advance that you need a CD-ROM. This can lead you to gather more—older work, work of dubious quality, unnecessary versions of existing work—to "fill" the CD. After all, there's up to 650MB of space on these things, and just providing 10MB seems somehow wasteful. Don't give in to this temptation. You should never show anything in your portfolio, on CD, or in any other medium just to fill space and air time.

Check that your presentation size is not the result of technical issues you can control. Besides using files with too many colors or too high a resolution, you might have incorporated sound, but at too good a quality. Just like imagery, sound can be downsampled to take up less space and still be recognizable. Most good studio sound runs at 22 KHz, but you can take many clips down to 11 KHz and still be able to use them. If you are not using sound at all, check your software to see if you can create your player without a sound track included. This will automatically shrink the size of an animation. Once you slim everything down, you may discover that you have a tighter presentation than you thought.

If your material is too large to fit on a diskette, you can compress it, although that does add another layer of action between your prospective viewer and your presentation. If compression doesn't solve the problem, don't despair. You could create a diskette "package" instead, two to four related sample disks that you can link with

label and package design. You can either ship them out as a completed set, or send them as a series. The series can be a terrific marketing ploy, because it keeps your name current and ensures that new reviewers see your work.

Note

Although it involves specialized technical issues outside the limits of this book, integrating broadcast-quality video into a digital portfolio is worth discussing briefly.

Analog video can be successfully edited on digital systems and can bear extensive compression without the average person perceiving any major image degradation. Work created or composited digitally can be output to standard videotape or to CD-ROM equally effectively. Just the fact that things are moving keeps the eye engaged. However, the fact that you can get away with a surprisingly low level of resolution in moving images should not blind you to the fact that you will require professional quality equipment and a powerful computer to make the transition. Moving from interlaced video at 30 fps to non-interlaced digital display can result in dropped frames and unsatisfactory matches of sound and action. At this moment in time, most design and production houses involved in broadcast work still expect to see broadcast-quality material. This makes video a nice tool when integrated as a small element in a larger presentation, but less than ideal for a video artist looking to replace the videotape with a CD.

There is also no rule that states you can't do work with both a CD and a diskette. You could create a CD with an extensive, high-quality assortment of your work, then

excerpt teaser pieces of it to create a diskette portfolio. Your CD will always be a more static piece since it takes more time, energy, and money to create it, but your diskette can be more flexible. If you work back and forth between the two, you'll occasionally create a new diskette presentation, update or add to an older one, and hold the new version for the next time you are ready to compile a CD. In the meantime, if a prospective client or employer shows an interest in your work, you have a more comprehensive medium to present to someone willing to spend the time with it.

Burning a CD

Few people actually take their CDs from concept all the way to completion. Until recently, cost has been prohibitive. CD recorders no longer cost as much as a complete computer. Some recorders are under $1,000 and media has dropped from $15 to $50 a disc to $6 to $12. These prices are still high for portfolio pressing, and even many companies who could afford the hardware tend to send the work out.

There are many good reasons to limit yourself to preparation only. To record with your own equipment, you'll need an enormous amount of dedicated disc space— enough to hold your CD information twice over. This dedicated space must be reformattable (not just erasable) before every session. And it must be fast enough to keep up with the transfer needs of the recorder. During the period of time that the recording is in process, your system cannot be doing anything else and I mean *anything*. No incoming faxes, email, or network traffic. No screen savers or other memory-resident utilities. No automatic backups. No power brownouts or interruptions. If any of these things take place, the recording session will automatically abort. And once that's happened, the CD media you've been using is worthless, because it's been partially written.

Preparing Your Files

Even if you plan on using a service bureau to master and duplicate your CD, you'll still have plenty of technical preparation issues to deal with.

 Resize and organize all of your windows. Open what will be your main folder/directory and arrange all the icons in it. Shrink the window size down to the optimum size for displaying the icons. Open and do the same for every folder that your users will search through. Whatever you set up in this stage will be the default view everytime the CD is loaded. You don't want your viewers to have to hunt for their icons, or be distracted by files that you include to run your animations but are not the movies themselves. If you have a folder with a substantial number of small files, consider having them viewable by name rather than by icon to conserve space.

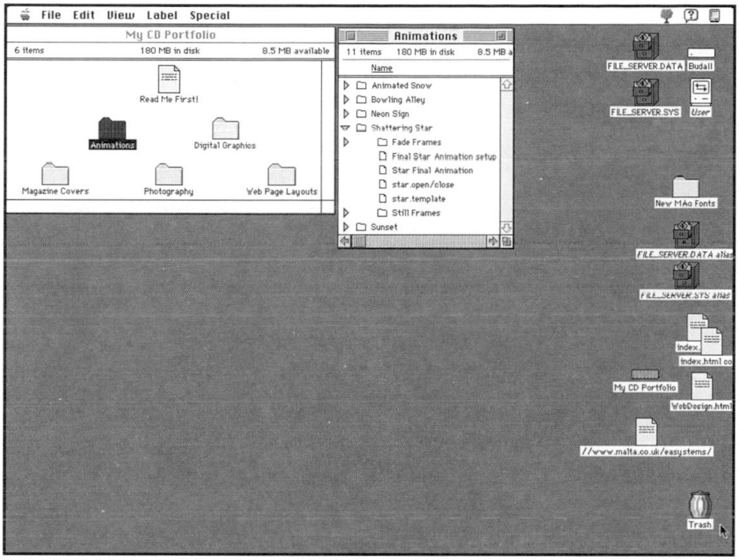

Figure 5.5
Examples of two windows properly organized for CD mastering.

113

 Know how to name files for different operating systems. Creating a digital portfolio is work enough without being forced to go through 90 files at midnight, renaming them to fit the ISO 9660 standard for Wintel CD creation. Despite the fact that DOS allows some characters other than alphanumerics (letters and numbers), ISO 9660 allows only the underscore (_) as an additional character.

 If you have a choice between creating many small files or compiling them into one large file (like whether to maintain separate QuickTime movies or to nest them together in one larger movie), always go with the larger file. Lots of small files mean lots of disc seek time during the recording process. If the operating system has to slow down to find many small files, it might not keep up with the recorder. This could result in the whole process crashing to a halt.

It's also a good idea to minimize the folder directory depth and the overall amount of individual files in a folder or directory. This is particularly critical on the Mac side. Try to limit the number of files in any folder to below 50, and the level of folders nested inside other folders to 8 or 10.

Preparing Your Drive for the Recorder

Whether you've decided to try the process yourself or simply want to prepare your work for the service bureau, you shouldn't simply drag your files to a disc from wherever they've been stored and send it off. The disc should be properly prepared to maximize the possibility of a successful recording session.

Begin by making sure that your material is completely organized. Delete any extra files that you may have nestled among your CD files. It's all too easy to have a folder full of duplicate or transitional files somewhere in your CD hierarchy.

The ideal situation is to have a virgin disk or hard drive the right size with no extraneous software, disk utilities, or other files on it. Since you can almost never count on such a situation, you'll need to start by reformatting your target drive. Don't cut corners here and assume you can just delete everything on the disk. Deleting only trashes the directory; the files are all still there. When you copy over new files, fragments of the old material can remain in untouched segments, ready to come back and haunt you on your CD.

Once your disk is reformatted, you need to find out exactly how much of that disk is actually usable. Disks are mass-produced and almost all of them have a few bad sectors—physically unwritable segments. During the normal course of using a disk, the drive finds these sectors and works around them. Unless the sector problems are particularly awful, the average person will never notice them. The CD recorder, on the other hand, can grind to halt unless the sector has been located and tagged as

useless. To do this, run a disk utility that checks for bad sectors on your target medium. On both the Mac and DOS/ Windows, Norton Disk Doctor will do the trick.

Your next step is to copy the files you'll want on the CD-ROM onto your disc. Before you begin this procedure, run all your original files through an up-to-date anti-virus program. Don't make any assumptions. It is generally considered a marketing no-no to infect the discs of potential employers and clients.

When you begin to copy, don't just drag the files or folders over. CDs are written from the inside out. Material that takes a lot of processing (3-D animation or video) should be copied over first. Other "first" material should be files that are accessed on a regular basis. If, for example, you have a movie that frequently calls up a screen with interactive buttons, copy over the screen and all its linked elements together. Keeping files that are used together physically near each other will improve your CD's performance later.

If you've been copying your files in a different order than they were in their original folders, bring your newly created disk to a different computer and try to run your files. It's very easy to get confused and miss something. If you don't check the disk or drive on a different computer, your software could just go looking for the missing file and find it on the original source disk. You'll never know it's AWOL until the finished CD comes back with missing elements. (One cautionary note: remember to check the second computer for viruses, too!)

If you test the new disk and everything seems to be there but something doesn't work as you expected, run your disk utility software again. It's possible that there was some minor glitch while the copying process was taking place and one of your files was corrupted in transit. If so, you'll find it through this process and can replace it on the disk.

Run a disk optimizer to defragment your files (yes, that disk utility is getting quite a workout) and you should be ready to either start the recording process, or hand over your files to your service bureau.

Blank CDs

If you're handling the master disc recording yourself, you'll need to buy some blank CD-R media. There are several types to choose from. Different brands use various forms of chemicals on their recording surfaces, the most popular being referred to as "green" and "gold" based on their dye color. A heated discussion in the young CD-ROM industry exists on the relative merits of the different methods. "Green" discs were the first type developed, and they tend to be more universally readable on CD-players than most of the "gold" discs. "Gold" discs are generally considered to perform better at 4x speed and above and are rated to last longer. (Of course longevity may not be

much of an issue for portfolio discs, since you'll want to revise long before the master disks give out.) Manufacturers of CD recorders sometimes recommend brands that they think work best in their devices, but the only way you can be absolutely sure you're buying the right brand is to test them. Begin by buying only one or two discs, making a master pressing and then testing the result in several CD-ROM players. Surprising as it seems, you can run across discs which seem to record without a hitch but won't play in some standard players. Whatever you do, don't run out and buy in bulk until you've recorded and tested on the exact media you expect to use.

The Actual Transfer

You've planned for the worst, tested your material extensively and provided your CD recording service with the right material, so the transfer itself should go smoothly. A surprising amount of minor details specific to your software, or to the service's recorder, can cause problems. Talk to the people who will be recording your master disc and ask them for a premastering checklist. Make sure they understand what kind of disc you'll be bringing them for the transfer, and verify that they can accommodate the method. Leave plenty of time between when you hand over your material and when you really need to have it finished. As with any service bureau, if they run into problems with your file, they'll have to call you and work out the issues. If they are also going to

115

create copies for you to distribute, make sure
that you get to check the master before the
copies are made. When the process is
finished, you can breathe a sigh of relief and
pat yourself on the back for having completed a major undertaking. If Murphy's law
hasn't plagued your steps, you're now ready
to take your material, design a package for
it, and distribute it as you please.

CHAPTER SIX

Work on the Web

I like a state of continual becoming, with a goal in front and not behind.
— *George Bernard Shaw*

There must be dozens of books on creating a Web site and surfing the Internet. There are Web books for newbies, Web books for the masses, Web books with cool techniques, and Web books for the serious programmer. They'll lead you through the basics of HTML, or CGI scripting, or beautiful buttons. Please see Appendix D for an extensive listing of reference titles.

This chapter's goals are very specific. I assume that you have browsed the Internet and are familiar with the basic concepts of URLs and links. I am not offering an exhaustive compendium on how to create every form of Web site, or how to implement plug-ins, tags, or browser-specific technology. Nor will I attempt to provide a universal style sheet for "correct" Web design. These things are worthy of books unto themselves, some of which are mentioned in Appendix D. This chapter deals with only the issues, both conceptual and technical, that are most critical if your primary goal for a Web site is to display your portfolio. I'll discuss what you might want to have on your Web pages and how to get the material into a usable form. I'll also take a look at the major technical constraints that will affect your design, and suggest how to work around them or with them.

Pros and Cons of the World Wide Web

For those who want to take advantage of the Internet, it is one of the best marketing and promotional venues available. For others, it can be a black hole, sucking up energy and free time and giving nothing back. Why do artists or designers put up portfolio Web pages?

 Target audience—A properly designed Web site can bring visibility, recognition, and unsolicited business.

A recent survey by Nielsen Media Research indicated that 17 percent of the US population alone had Internet Access in 1995, and that well-educated professionals constituted the bulk of those users. The chances that your target audience is online are fairly good already and increasing daily.

Immediate gratification—Unlike the digital portfolio on CD or diskette, the Web portfolio need never be out of date. As Diane Fenster (see CD) once said, "If I had another life, I would learn Macromedia Director. I had wanted to do an interactive CD, but it was too much work and too expensive to create. But on the Web, I could take my planned hyperlinks, translate them to HTML, and put them up on a site. Now, when I have a mind to make a change, I can do it instantly!"

Web design advertising—Maybe no one has hired you to design Web graphics yet, but that's unlikely to change if you don't have a site as an example to prove you're up to the task. The best way to show that you can handle online design is the fait accompli.

Demonstrate technical capabilities—You're hoping to move to interface design. Maybe you've been working on Director scripts and you want to post your résumé and some samples in the virtual world.

The Web as a visual medium—The Internet has its own set of possibilities. It's a wonderful place to explore a personal vision and to reach a much larger group of people than you ever could traditionally. As Robert Odegard of The Ark noted, "We're realizing that the Web site can be more personal, and that we are a personal company. We can take that a little further. It can be more playful and narrative based."

Everyone seems to have one—You're probably not surprised that this is the most frequent reason firms as well as individuals decide to create a Web page.

Shotgun Web Design

In some circles the need for a URL on the business card is becoming as important as an email address a mere two years ago. Pushed by the image more than the real need, some design firms or corporate communications departments take the low road. They farm the project out to their most junior artist, or to the person on staff they view as the "techie." He or she scans in photos of printed pieces, converts the logo, and tries to build a site around these static pieces and some existing promotional copy. Depending on the quality and imagination of the Web-designing guinea pig, and whether any design and organization direction comes from above, it can be a stellar effort or a cosmic waste of time.

Individuals or small partnerships feel the pressure too but don't have a convenient soul to stick with the project. Their sites fairly scream "Just do it!" With no time to actually become knowledgeable, they settle for basic HTML or blindly use a Web page layout tool, with mixed, and frequently mediocre, results.

Never let pressure for time make you forget that a Web site is a publication, and as much a statement of corporate identity as any other self-promotional piece. For a designer or artist, it should be done right or not at all. It is better in the short term to confidently say, "I'm working on my Web page, but my client work comes first", than to publish something that reflects badly on you. Of course, once you've said you're working on the site, you have committed yourself to actually doing so!

Time to Do It Right, or ...

About this time you're asking, "So how long will this take?" There is no right answer to this question, but good Web sites aren't an overnight charette, especially if you're doing them alone. Like any other artistic project, creative time is unpredictable. It's easier to talk in terms of production. Assuming you already have all your graphic elements created, your artwork scanned, and you're reasonably good at picking up new software skills, the actual composition, with a Web layout program, might take as little as two hours. A sophisticated Web site, however,

will demand considerably more preparation, knowledge, and time, and it can take weeks to go from original concept to completion. Most Web sites fall somewhere in between. It is possible to start very simply and grow your site in stages, allowing you to manage the time-crunch issue according to your schedule.

As with most projects, you can't do it right if you don't know what you're trying to do. If your online time has been limited, remedy that first. There is no substitute to actually surfing through the Web and becoming familiar with its delights and frustrations. Go to Yahoo (http://www.yahoo.com) and search under your own category—photography, art galleries, graphic design, architecture, multimedia—for examples of how other people have dealt with the task. You'll find the good, the bad, and the mediocre. Pay attention to what you like and create bookmarks so you can return there later. Make sure you go through a few sites in their entirety to see how they've handled organizing their links. If you get lost, go back and figure out why. There's nothing more efficient than learning from someone else's mistakes.

Be Realistic About Your Goals

After you've decided to forge ahead, be specific about why you are embarking on a Web portfolio, and have realistic expectations. Too many people think that once they have a Web site with images and a résumé the job offers will pour in. Like the myth of movie stars being discovered in drug stores, it's nice to be able to fantasize.

Don't mistake exposure and visibility for cash flow. Although a Web portfolio can lead indirectly to income, no one yet has gotten rich on their home page. Your Web portfolio will be used in conjunction with all your usual activities—making phone calls, answering or placing ads, and networking. It's a billboard on the fabled Information Highway. If it gets one person in a hundred to send you email, or one in a thousand visitors to make a serious inquiry, you have accomplished your goal.

120

The Maintenance Plan: Long Term Commitment

In one respect creating your Web portfolio is like buying a car. If you don't allow for maintenance when you make the commitment, eventually it will stop performing. Expect to spend additional time to update the site after you've created it. Although portfolio Web sites are comparatively easy to maintain because you're not expected to change material as quickly as other destinations, they do take a certain amount of periodic vigilance. Especially for design professionals and photographers, a static, unchanged site quickly gathers conceptual dust. Layout ideas that looked fresh in January can look pedestrian in March and be trite in June.

Preventive maintenance is even better. If you set yourself achievable goals rather than

trying to get everything in place all at once, you will learn from your mistakes and be able to upgrade your site in small increments. This is particularly important if you'll be starting your site using WYSIWYG layout tools and learning code later.

Designing for Your Audience

If your portfolio has a self-promotional purpose—and whose does not?— you have to consider your audience. You should either be intimately familiar with your target's interests and biases, or you should be back at Chapter 1 re-examining research references. Know who might be interested in your work and why they should visit your portfolio site. Their expectations and their technology must be factored into your design. As Robert Odegard, speaking for The Ark said, "Lots of people used to call us from places, like India, and say they were really interested in our work, and could we ship them some samples? We invested a lot of time and energy for what was essentially spec work. Now we can just say, 'take a look at our Web site.' Since everything we do is digital for the screen, it doesn't suffer in translation. We know that people seriously interested in our work should have access to that technology."

Cause and Effect

Many popular sites were initially designed for a specific audience, while some "big tent" sites remain quiet backwaters. By and large, it's easier to design a good site when you have a vivid picture in your mind of who you want to visit it and how they'll use the site once they get there.

Everytime you consider solutions that will effect the way someone relates to your site, you should try to envision the result. I once spoke with a non-designer who had a very successful site in terms of hit rates. He was disappointed, however, because no one visited the more creative areas, despite the fact that he was an excellent amateur photographer. Everyone went to his hot list, which was simply a gateway to other sites. He had never noticed how the logical design of his home page discouraged the recreational surfer he really wanted to reach, and encouraged a more task-oriented user.

An in-demand hotlist can be a useful way to bring traffic, but never lose sight of your portfolio material as your primary purpose. It's ideal to have the maximum amount of visitors to your Web site, but if they aren't interested in your work, you've spoken to the wrong audience. If you have tangential interests and want to "curate" a list of other sites, make sure that your own work dominates. Don't make it too easy to jump away. Plan to put images on the home page and hotlist, rather than "saving" them for a portfolio section. If people are intrigued by the initial images, they may be persuaded to linger. Set up a competing attraction like a quiz, puzzle, or narrative to add to the richness of your site. Use humor or visual

teasers, and break up the strict linear grid of the site as much as possible.

Focus on Your Real Goal

It's more straightforward to design for yourself than for potential clients. If your goal is primarily artistic rather than commercial, you can hardly do it any other way. On the other hand, the fun of Web design—and it can be a great deal of fun—can easily blind you to your original purpose, overwhelming your existing art and design. A painter's Web portfolio, for example, should emphasize existing artwork, just as it would in a traditional presentation. Anything that makes your work an afterthought is unlikely to serve your purposes.

The Technical Threshold

If you want to be accessible to the broadest range of Web surfers, you face major limitations in color, layout, and image which you must build into your site architecture. In addition, your portfolio work itself may have to be altered to fit display constraints.

There are millions of computer users in the world, and not all of them are using a Pentium Pro or the latest, greatest Power Mac. If you design for fast connections and 24-bit color, only the most technically blessed will view your work. It is possible to make a Web portfolio accessible to those with lesser capabilities while still catering to the digital elite, but you must plan for it as you develop the work. If, on the other hand, you are a cutting edge multimedia producer, perhaps you can get away with warning viewers on your home page and concentrating on the high end.

As for your own technical expertise, a respectable site concentrating on existing content can be developed by using a Web page layout program. This means that you can get some version of your personal portfolio online relatively quickly. If you are trumpeting your ability to design sites for others, on the other hand, you must display technical expertise. This means actual HTML coding. The special language used by page layout programs can identify their pages quickly to experienced designers, and the products are still too primitive to serve as high-end tools.

Planning Your Site: Web Flow Chart

For your Web site to stand out from the crowd, your material must be easy to access and attractively packaged. Your presentation should encourage people to view your work, not just your home page. Above all, your site must be intelligently organized for navigation. Before you can consider the visual interface, you should create a skeleton of your site based on your content. This flow chart will be your bible and will enable you to recognize links which belong within your pages, or out to other sites. It will also help you to organize your ideas logically, so visitors to your site won't feel lost as they

wander through it. An organically grown Web site might be fun for you but will send the message that you are disorganized and undisciplined.

As long as all the elements you need are accounted for, there is no standard form this chart must take. Post-its on a large sheet of paper are a great low-tech way of visualizing your site. A small site can start as a clean sketch on paper or as a FreeHand or Illustrator file. On the other hand, flow charting software can make the process easier, particularly if you anticipate a very complex site. It will make additions and deletions possible, as well as reorganization without redrawing.

No matter what physical form it takes, make sure that it's easy to add items both horizontally and vertically to your chart. Hypertext, by its very nature, is information- and user-driven, rather than provider-controlled, and you want to be able to reflow your site architecture when the content demands it. If you can't remember what page links to which topic, or where to find a graphic, neither will your viewer. A disorganized Web space discourages people from staying and exploring your work in more depth.

What will your chart contain? Initially, you'll start with broad categories of material, based on the portfolio "story" you've developed. Maybe you'll have a separate section for types of design work, like collateral material or books. You might have both an illustration and fine art portfolio area. Reflect such categories as branches from your home page.

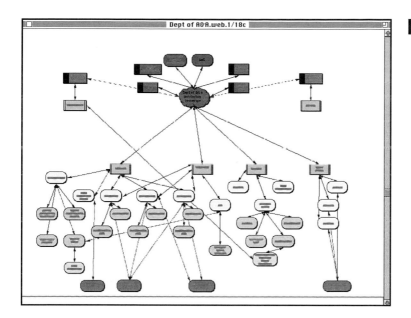

Figure 6.1
Example of a Web site flow chart.

123

Next, identify and name your individual pages. Let's say you have 15 illustrations in one category. If they have natural groupings, reflect that by planning for them on the same page. If they don't, or you're unsure about how you want to lay them out, list each one. As long as you decide how you want to display them before you create your file links, you can always delete the extras.

It may seem strange to be naming your files before you've even created them, but doing so will help you think of them as containers for changing material. You'll be updating your portfolio before long, and it's easier to do that modularly. The Web administrator where your files will reside should know if your pages must be named in a specific way.

Although you may be creating your files on a Mac or PC, chances are good that the files will be living on a Unix operating system and will have to conform to its specifications. Remember to refer to Appendix C for characters to avoid in naming your files.

Once you have your files named and represented in your chart, reflect their major elements on information thumbnails. Not only will this make it easier to find everything you need, but it gives you a visual reminder of what elements you'll need to incorporate in your designs. An information thumbnail should not be an attempt at designing the page. It should simply account for the elements that you'll be working with.

Figure 6.2

Example of an information thumbnail sized to fit a standard Post-it format.

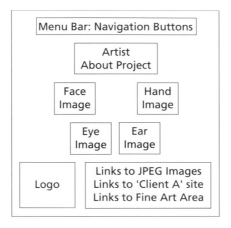

Every page thumbnail will list content, including all text and portfolio images, and navigational elements—buttons, menu bars, imagemaps. You should also document your planned links. All pages should have a "home" navigation option, but there may be other sub-connections to consider. If you have images that you want seen as a sequence, you'll need to link their pages together. If you have a scanned, finished piece that you'd like to link to your client's site, document that. Don't set up your site so people have to constantly hit their browser's Back button to return to the beginning of a section. Make it easy for visitors by planning links between branches.

Last but not least, plan for some form of logo and/or branding information, such as a verbal or visual key to identify a site. It's too easy to forget that search engines can jump people literally anywhere in your site. You can't control which of your pages they'll see first. Especially for portfolio sites, your name, email address, and some clear identifier should be visible on every page.

Be sure to hang your chart on the wall near your computer, so you'll be able to name your actual files and directories to match your documentation. Avoid renaming your files, or moving them from their original positions in your local Web site directory. If you do, you will break any links you have made to them and have to reestablish them. Troubleshooting broken links is one of the most frustrating aspects of the Web creation process.

Speaking of files as containers, remember your on-disk portfolio file management and mirror it here. If you are going to have a separate section to display a new project, you will probably want to put all the pages that relate to that project in a common folder, which will make it considerably easier to upload to your provider. Images should live in an Image folder, which should be documented in your chart. You will need

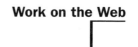

this information when it comes time to transfer your Web pages to their server. Some Web page layout programs, such as PageMill, have default preferences that allow you to specify where such information should be placed.

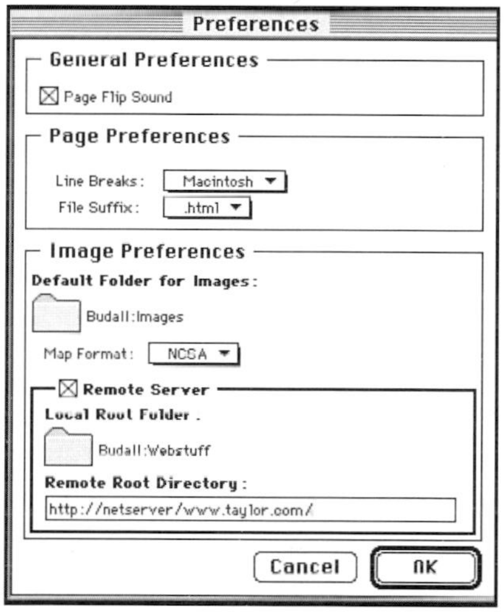

Figure 6.3
The Preferences dialog box in PageMill 1.0.

Preparing Artwork for Web Use

The major agony of Web site portfolio creation is transferring visual work to this new medium without sacrificing its essence. It is a craft, and sometimes an art, in and of itself. Doing it without sufficient knowledge can negate the point of having created a personal Web portfolio. In fact, transferring artwork is so critical that we can't really address design issues until we've worked with imagery.

To adequately move your work to the Web, you will need an image/photo editing program, plug-ins or stand alone software for creating GIFs, transparent GIFs, interlaced JPEG images, and software that enables you to optimize your image's color palette. Other options are available for this purpose, but I work primarily with two commercial cross-platform products, Adobe Photoshop and Equilibrium's DeBabelizer. In doing so, I am breaking the general rule in this book of avoiding non-Photoshop software specifics. DeBabelizer is a Macintosh OS program that I consider absolutely indispensable for Web and interactive portfolio design. It simply has no duplicate on any platform. On the Windows side of the house, a commercial software package which offers some palette editing and file format conversion is Hijaak Suite. It is quite comprehensive in format conversion, but nowhere near as effective or elegant at palette editing and batch processes. There are also some good shareware products which handle file format conversion and palette editing. On the Mac, I recommend GIF converter. For Windows users, try LView Pro. See Appendix A for download information.

Moving Existing Material to the Web

If you have not created a portfolio on disk or CD-ROM, this is probably your first foray into scanning material for electronic viewing. For the most part, this topic is covered in the scanning and resolution section in Chapter 4.

125

Even if you've already converted your work for a digital diskette or CD portfolio, it may not mean that you can use these images as is. It is possible that some of your indexed color images will need no additional work other than a change in file format. On the other hand, a file that seems lean and mean in the context of an interactive program running off a computer CPU may be positively bloated on a Web site. You may need to return to the image to re-optimize your color palette, separating images that had been batch converted. In addition, you may want to radically change the image size, as interpolating or downsampling can

introduce artifacts that would be easier to deal with from a new scan, or a file which had not yet gone through any editing. Don't make assumptions that will prevent you from staying on target with your portfolio. The sizes of your image files are so important that they can drive your design decisions.

Bandwidth, and Why You Should Care About It

Why does it matter so much how big your image files are? For that matter, what constitutes a big file on the Web? The answers to these questions go to the heart of why a digital portfolio online is different from other purposed Web sites. Your imagery is what you have to offer, so certain compromises for bandwidth are more difficult for you than they would be to the average person.

If you're like most people, you access the Web through a dial-up modem connection and an ISP or online service like CompuServe or AOL. The ISP routes your URL request to whatever Web server is responsible for the pages you are interested in. If there is an open line to this server the connection is made. The pages are routed back to your line through the gateway of the ISP, where your browser interprets the stream of bytes into text, graphics, and sound.

How fast will this take place? This depends somewhat on the remote server's line, a little on your ISP's connections, but mostly on your line and modem, which is where the information bottleneck is created. Table 6.1 illustrates the situation.

The T-1 speed sounds very tasty, and it is. But few individuals or design firms have deep enough pockets to own their own T-1 line, which can cost about $1000 to $2000 per month. Educational institutions and large corporations (as well as ISP providers themselves) probably do, but limiting yourself to them really narrows down the number of people you can reach.

The same image that might take a mere second to download on a T-1 line will take almost a minute (53 seconds) on a 28.8 "fast" modem connection. A Web surfer on a 14.4 modem might as well send out for coffee. Even worse, these figures assume a best-case scenario for each download. If the phone line is bad or the service provider is overtaxed, that 53 seconds could easily

Table 6:1

Maximum Throughput Speed on Various Types of Connections

Connection Type	bps Speed	Maximum in 1 Second
14.4 modem	14,400 bps	10-line email message with header
28.8 modem	28,800 bps	One simple Web page, with basic coding, light text, no graphics
ISDN line	56,000 bps	One 256 color GIF image, approx. 100×80 pixels (lg. button, sm. thumbnail)
T-1 line	1,544,000 bps	One 72ppi, 24-bit color JPEG image, approx. 500×350 pixels in size (about 153K image), with caption text

stretch to 75 seconds or more. If the Web server your image is sitting on is itself only connected to the Internet through another 28.8 modem, even viewers on a T-1 line will suffer, since they can't receive information any faster than the server line can send it out.

This math can be a real shock to those of us who are used to thinking of a 153K image file as small potatoes. Ask yourself "Would I wait a long time to download an unknown image?" Probably not, particularly if several minutes had already passed and the image was still creeping down the page. But what if you had a sense that it might be worth it, and could estimate how long you were actually committing yourself before being rewarded by the finished picture?

Small Is Better

Unlike the typical corporate site, you can't really design your portfolio artwork with small color palettes and broad flat colors, although you can take this strategy for the Web graphics you create specifically for your site. You'll need to develop strategies to minimize the download times for your existing imagery without sacrificing so much of the image that the effort isn't worth the game.

Various studies and surveys have surfaced, trying to quantify exactly how long a viewer will wait for a site to download before they give up and go away. The number of seconds seems to hover somewhere between 10 and 30. In my own experience, this number can stretch in either direction, depending on how motivated someone is to see the information, and whether the site is giving them anything to occupy their time while the download is taking place. Since a 28.8 modem's throughput is approximately 3.6K per second, this means that any page that is much bigger than 30 to 35K in total size could scare people away.

Speed Maximizing Strategies

The vast majority of speed issues revolve around image editing and color palettes. However, you can incorporate some relatively simple strategies in your Web site design to help you meet this goal.

Coming Attractions

One of the simplest ways of lengthening the amount of time and patience people will give your site is to let them know in advance what they're waiting for. This can be accomplished by offering thumbnails images on your first image index page. A thumbnail image shouldn't be larger than 5 or 6K, and you should avoid showing more than four of them on a page at that size. Don't treat this thumbnail as a throw-away, however. If you experiment with optimizing, you can make it a close enough approximation of your actual piece for the viewer to be able to determine what they'll be seeing next. Otherwise the whole thumbnail strategy can boomerang on you because the image looks too grainy to be identified.

Figure 6.4
Diane Fenster's Illustration home page with thumbnail images as icons.

Some images are too large or visually complex to be recognizable at such a small size. In this case, you may be able to use the art book trick of showing a representative detail of a section of your image instead. If you decide to go this route make sure that you have kept an original scan copy to crop your thumbnail section. Unless your cropped piece will be on the same scale as the larger version you'll be showing, don't try to make it from an image you have already converted and resized.

If you're using thumbnails, clearly state on your Web page that you have done so, and that a higher resolution image can be viewed by clicking on the preview. There are enough sites out there that show tiny images at various levels of quality that you shouldn't take for granted that people will notice yours are linked images. Additionally, make sure your thumbnail caption tells the viewer how large your good-quality image is. People are much more patient if they know in advance how long downloading will take.

Arsenic and Interlace

Interlacing is the function that allows an image to load progressively. The entire image comes up at once in very low resolution, then adds information in additional passes until finished. This doesn't objectively load the image any faster, but it does provide immediate gratification for itchy surfers.

Until recently, the GIF format was the only one to support this venetian-blind kind of loading, forcing artists to choose between color depth and image loading speed. With the recent release of the PJPEG (progressive JPEG) format, you have the option of interlacing without necessarily having to

minimize your color palette. Adobe offers the GIF89a Export plug-in as part of Photoshop for writing interlaced files. Note that it is not part of the normal Save or Save As dialog box, but must be accessed through the Export menu.

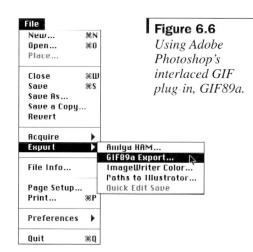

Figure 6.6
Using Adobe Photoshop's interlaced GIF plug-in, GIF89a.

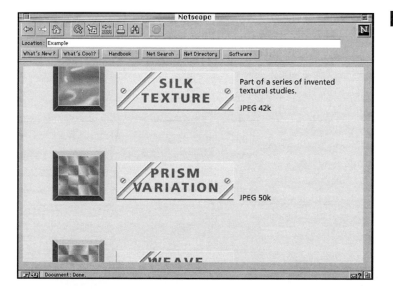

Figure 6.5
Example of thumbnails used as previews for specific images.

Two commercial plug-ins, Transmogrifier and ProJPEG, do the same for the new PJPEG format. DeBabelizer 1.65 handles both functions and is the better place to handle the file format changes if you have the option.

Editing Imagery for Color Issues

One of the least-favorite surprises to a visual artist or designer is how bandwidth and platform independence affect image color on the Web. Even if he or she has been working with animation or interactive media and is familiar with indexing, the new and unexpected twists of Web display can be irritating. For those of us who have primarily worked in print or on slide, the 8-bit limitations of the Web world can be positively painful. Though general adaptation of JPEG has made 24-bit color attainable, not all imagery looks good in this format. It's the wrong decision for navigation elements, banners, and many imagemaps. As with any visual problem, however, you can find workarounds to minimize the image degradation that most artwork suffers. These workarounds involve compression and palette manipulation. In general, anything you can do to simplify your imagery will result in smaller files and shorter download times. Image editing should always be done before you shrink your image or attempt to convert it to one of the compressed formats you need for Web viewing.

One of the problems of the palette minimizing process is how colors are chosen for deletion. Using DeBabelizer, you can watch the results of this process by going into the Palette menu and sorting a palette by popularity. Colors that are simply artifacts of the scanning process can represent a large percentage of the color palette. This is particularly true if you are working in Photoshop or other image editing programs rather than DeBabelizer, which is more astute about recognizing rogue colors in its indexing process. When you then go to minimize the palette, these colors represent such a large percentage of the options that they are remapped to the exclusion of more critical shades. This can cause two problems: overemphasizing unnecessary background colors and eliminating critical but sparsely used ones.

De-emphasizing Background Pixels

In a scanned image, seemingly monochromatic areas are full of multicolored pixels which fool a compression or palette conversion program into wasting color depth accounting for them. If they represent neutral space and are not critical to the feel of the image—like the white painted wall of a gallery—there's no reason not to replace them with a simple blend based on two or three existing shades in the area. Since JPEG looks for similarities in areas, it will simply add value changes to its information for this section, usually allowing you to compress the entire file more than you could otherwise.

For images that will become GIF files, a useful trick is to replace such background areas with one flat color. The color should either be one that currently exists in the rest of the image, or one chosen from the non-dithering palette discussed below. See the files StudentWorking and StudentEdited to see an image which had had its background material removed.

Emphasizing Spot Color

The flip side of this process is when an image has a critical spot color. Representing a small fraction of the pixel count, it's one of the first to be compressed out of existence. This usually forces artists to keep their image files artificially large to accommodate it.

The trick here is forcing the program to recognize how important this color is to you. Try these steps.

1. Enlarge the canvas area on one side.

2. Using the Eyedropper, select the critical color.

3. Fill the blank canvas area with your spot color.

4. Index the image. Your color will be part of the new palette.

5. Crop the image back down to its original dimensions and resave.

You can see the results of this tip on the accompanying CD. In the folder Portfolio Helpers, open Xmp61.GIF and Xmp62.GIF. The first is an indexed image created without applying the spot color tip. The second is the same image with the spot color tip used.

If instead of one isolated color, you have a photograph or an image with a small blend, a variation on this trick can be used:

1. Enlarge the canvas area.

2. Grab a chunk of the original image that holds your blend or color area.

3. Copy it to another file. Scale it up in size.

4. Select the empty canvas area on the original picture.

5. Copy the scaled image area into the selected canvas section.

6. Index the image.

7. Crop the image back down to its original dimensions and resave.

Once you've edited out anything that might distract you or your palette indexing program, you're ready to save your image and a copy of it. We'll work with copies only from here on in, because you'll probably need to return to the original as you go through several stages in testing the conversion process.

131

Conversion Experience

Palette conversion is a necessary art. It will define how fast your images load, how closely they will resemble the original art, and how large your images can be. But why is it necessary?

Let's start by thinking about the cross-platform nature of the Web, using the Mac OS and Windows as examples, but not forgetting that Unix systems are important elements in the Web mix. You've probably noticed that color can shift a little if you view an image on one machine, then look at it on another one with a different type of monitor. If the two machines have different operating systems the color shift can be striking. Add in a difference in color depth—an 8-bit display on one, a 24-bit display on the other—and you can think that you're viewing different versions. We've talked about this shift in the context of creating hybrid CD-ROMs and interactive pieces. But in those cases, we either decided to show 24-bit imagery, or we were able to deal with the differences by telling each platform exactly what group of colors to use to best view the image.

As anyone who creates hybrid CDs for a living can tell you, translating palettes between platforms is a complicated and frustrating issue. 8-bit on a Mac or Unix system is not the same as 8-bit on a Windows OS. While Macs have a full 256 fixed colors, most Unix-based machines have no fixed system palette; they make their colors on the fly depending on what's available at the time. 8-bit Windows computers, although they have 256 colors in theory, have only 236 in fact. Twenty colors in the palette are reserved for the operating system.

The 256 Non-Dithering Colors— Not!

When Netscape created browsers for the different platforms, they decided that more people were likely to be Windows and Mac users than Unix ones, and that the Unix method of assigning colors was too difficult to use as a standard. That left them with 236 colors that could potentially be displayed equally well and dependably on both systems. Out of these, they reserved 13 to display their logo. Then, for mathematical reasons of even division, they decided on 216 as the magic number (6 * 6 * 6).

This decision created the 216-color palette that we live with today. Colors in this palette will display on screen as true, flat colors. Any that are not present in this palette are approximated by dithering. Dithering is somewhat like pointillist painting. The computer comes across a color that doesn't exist in its palette and hunts in its paint box for two other colors it can combine to give the appearance of the missing one. When it finds them, it replaces the missing color with a tightly woven pattern of the two colors it has used.

You can see the result of this by viewing a 24-bit color image in 8-bit mode. Grids, cross-hatching, or multi-colored dots all indicate that dithering is taking place. This is actually less of a problem in photographic images than it is in flat color, unless the computer is really hard pressed to find the right shades in its system palette. Dithering is much more distracting in illustrations, cartoons, or logos. That's why most knowledgeable Web designers have been using the undithering Netscape palette colors for most graphics designed specifically for the Web.

What does this tiny palette have to do with 24-bit images? Well, they aren't 24-bit on a system which can't display millions of colors. They'll dither using the 216-color palette. But if your target audience has 24-bit capability, the only real issue is image size, not the number of colors. A 24 bit image will still look like a 24-bit image, even if viewed on a different platform as long as the receiving computer can process that many colors.

Finding the actual 216 colors can be quite a treasure hunt. On the CD, you'll find a Mac-based Photoshop palette which you can load into your palette swatches window to make life easier. In Appendix E is a chart keyed to the swatches, with the numbered squares translated into Hex code for use in creating backgrounds and specifying text colors. If you load the swatches into Photoshop as we walk through the process of image conversion, you'll see how the colors are expressed in GIF indexing.

Choosing Your File Formats

Most image file formats that artists and designers work with are meant to capture a

significant amount of information, usually for some form of print application. On the Internet, our options are essentially limited to GIF and JPEG. Both of these are formats developed to compress information to conserve bandwidth for online viewing. Neither GIF nor JPEG files are usable in print applications, nor are they interchangeable with each other. Which one you use should be determined by the kind of image you are trying to show, and what you are planning to use it for.

Just Enough About Compression

A section on compression algorithms practically has "skip this" written all over it. Most explanations do tend to get technical. But understanding just a little about how GIFs and JPEGs work to minimize your image file sizes will help you determine which one you'll need to use to get the best possible quality for your portfolio pieces.

Compression works because visual information is, to some degree, redundant. If we paint a simple line on a white background, we see the whole image as an entire piece, with the line defining our position in the space. Yet you could look at the image in another way, as white and not-white. Anything that was white would be redundant and could be ignored, with one small bit of information holding all the white areas. Anything that was not-white would simply have to be positioned in relationship to the entire image area with specifics on its not-whiteness archived as information. Strategically, you might do that by creating a grid

133

and scanning from the top left of the image to the bottom right, keeping track of the horizontal color changes and linking them together as you went down row by row.

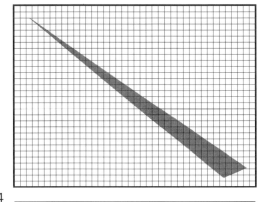

134

Figure 6.7
A visual interpretation of how a compressed file might be seen by the compression algorithm.

It might have occurred to you while reading this explanation that not all images lend themselves to this kind of method. Think of a continuous tone photograph. Instead of large, solid areas of one color, there are hundreds of levels of color and tone. How do you find the redundancy here? Well, you could begin by looking for areas of similarity. If you have a photograph with a sky, for example, you'd notice that some areas are somewhat uniform in color, blending toward other areas that are lighter or darker. You could lump all the blueness into one category and keep track of how much an adjoining section changes from your originally examined area. Then you only keep track of the change. When your eye

finds a cloud, it might become another defining area and be treated much the same way.

In a nutshell, these two ways of finding redundancy describe the different ways that GIF and JPEG compression do their work, and the kinds of images that they are optimized for. GIF uses the first method, looking for large, identical areas in an image. This makes it excellent for flat color work, line art, and high-contrast images. The downside of GIFs is their tendency to posterize continuous tones, since GIFs only have an 8-bit color space. This means 256 is the maximum number of individual colors that a GIF file can recognize.

JPEG uses the second method and does a very effective job at compressing photographic images or graphics with multiple blends. JPEG's downside is its tendency to add incorrect information to flat areas and sharply defined color changes. Unless the banding from blends is extensive, don't save flat art in JPEG format. JPEG can dither previously solid-color areas or add grain or anti-aliasing to clean lines. For an example of this problem, look at the FButton folder/directory on the CD for Xmp63.JPG (saved as a high-quality JPEG), Xmp64.JPG (saved as a good/default JPEG image), and Xmp65.JPG (saved as a medium JPEG image) series. Only the 10K high-quality JPEG version is acceptable. All other versions add progressively more artifacts to the background flat color. Anything below medium level would not even be worth trying. As a comparison, look at

Xmp66.GIF, the same graphic with an optimized indexed palette. It not only looks better, it's smaller.

On the other hand, there are some occasions when you have to save a photographic image as a GIF. Older or non-standard browsers do not all support JPEG images and require helper applications like JPEGview to see them offline. Although you might not want to sacrifice your large version of the image, GIF thumbnails could make sense. You might also want a portion of the file to be transparent, a necessity if the image shape you want is not rectangular or has rough frame edges and you want to drop out the surrounding background color. JPEGs do not yet support transparency.

There is one other characteristic of these two compression formats that can have an effect on your image quality. GIFs do not throw out image information. If you save a 256-color image as a TIFF, then resave it as a GIF, the two images will still be identical. You can compress and decompress infinitely. JPEG, on the other hand, throws out information that it thinks is unnecessary as part of its compression process. This lossy method, so called because you lose some information permanently, does give you a number of different levels of compression to choose from. A high-quality compression throws out very little information but does not result in a tremendous amount of savings in file size. A low-quality compression can create a miniscule image barely 5% the size of the original but is correspondingly less

detailed and more likely to have ugly artifacts.

Converting an Image: Step by Step

Now that you know the ground rules, we'll take a test drive. This will be very detailed, but hopefully worth the effort. Your images are the most important element in your portfolio, and cutting corners on this process will come back to haunt you later.

Pull out an image you've already edited. As I go through the process with my photograph (Xmp67.cps) on the CD, you can see what happens to your own artwork. Make a habit of saving your work after every step until the process is complete. You may find yourself having to go back to step one or two in your quest to optimize sizes and color.

Your first task is easy. If you have not already done so, downsize your image in your editing program so its maximum horizontal width fits within your monitor target. Although ideally your vertical measure should also fit in one screen's worth of space, width is more critical for a landscape image. The experience of viewing an image at 600×400 and 480×320 is different, but probably not different enough to sacrifice download time. For a portrait image, on the other hand, asking your viewer to scroll is preferable to showing an image that would otherwise be pointlessly tiny.

135

Step two is to change your resolution to 72 ppi if it is not there already. (See Xmp68.eps.) You are never going to print this image out, so there is no advantage to holding on to more information than the screen can display. Save without a preview from this point on. You'll have a better sense of the real size of your file without the extra PICT Resource image the icon uses. Make sure to keep a backup copy of this stage, because this is where preparation for JPEG and GIF formats diverge.

Step three is to create an alternate file with an Indexed palette. (See Xmp69.eps) Although as far as file sizes are concerned, DeBabelizer's algorithm for determining colors is considerably better than Photoshop's, and Photoshop's standard conversion mode is functionally identical to DeBabelizer's Fastest scheme with duplicate colors removed. DeBabelizer's algorithm is less likely to be fooled by color artifacts and isolated pixels added by scanning. In addition, its best quality indexing decreases the size very little, but allows you more room to play if you want to do manual work on your palette. Either way, you'll want to be using an adaptive palette with diffusion dithering. (For more on these options, see Chapter 4.)

Making the JPEG Files

Let's start with the JPEG files, by far the simpler and more straightforward file format. Photoshop allows you to save your files in JPEG mode, but it has fewer com-

pression levels and can't save them as progressive without plug-ins, so I'll be discussing DeBabelizer.

We'll create four files with different levels of compression to compare their sizes and image quality. Let's open Xmp68.eps (or your own 72 ppi file) in DeBabelizer. Note that DeBabelizer will not display more than one open image at a time, although it can apply batched commands to several images in succession.

Figure 6.8
DeBabelizer Open dialog box.

All JPEG conversion is done through Save as under the File menu. When we choose Save As, we see the following dialog box:

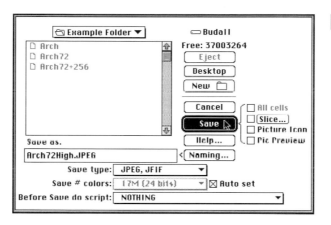

Figure 6.9
*DeBabelizer Save
as dialog box.*

1. Choose JPEG/JFIF from the Save type: option. Note that DeBabelizer defaults will automatically add an extension corresponding to your file type to whatever you name your file.

2. Choose 17M (24 bits) as the Save # colors option, then check the Auto set box. This will lock 24-bit color in as a default until you change your file type. Don't choose the 256-color option for a JPEG unless you want to automatically turn your pictures into greyscale images.

3. Click on the Save button, and you'll have one more dialog box.

4. For our first image, we'll drag the slider bar all the way to the right for the High option, which gives us a Quality of 100%.

5. We'll also check the Progressive box (so readers can open the image in

stages). Note that the sample pictures on the CD have been saved in non-progressive mode, since any image editing program which does not support progressive JPEG will have problems parsing a PJPEG file.

6. Click OK, and you're done. The result on the CD is Xmp610.JPG.

137

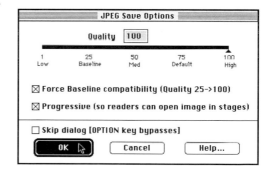

Figure 6.10
*DeBabelizer JPEG Save Options dialog box
with Quality set to 100%.*

From here, we simply repeat the process, using the original saved image, not the JPEG one, for each of the lower quality images: Default (75%)—Xmp611.JPG, Medium (50%)—Xmp612.JPG and Baseline (25%)—Xmp613.JPG. It is possible to create a lower quality image by unchecking the Force Baseline Compatibility box, but the results for portfolio imagery are probably below what most people would consider acceptable.

Now let's compare our file sizes. Note the massive jump in size between High Quality and Default, without a correspondingly large change in image acceptability. Open these images in Photoshop so you can see them all on-screen at the same time. Now zoom your images up and make the same comparison. You'll begin to see changes in details, especially in subtle shadow areas. These changes become more obvious as you go up in compression and down in quality, but even the Medium image quality might be usable on your Web page.

If you don't like the quality of any of the images that are 30K or below in size, you'll have to return to the original image and do some tweaking there. Change the size, recrop the image if possible, and edit non-essential detail if you can. Don't try to bring a JPEG image back into Photoshop for editing. Lossy really does mean lossy, even if the human eye can't see the difference on-screen. JPEG works so well because it gets rid of information it knows you can't see.

The extra data in your scans that you used to adjust levels of brightness and contrast no longer exists.

Making the GIF Version

We'll take the same original image and save it as a GIF for comparison. You'll find this file as Xmp69.gif on the CD. Note that some of these steps are the same or similar to the process we discussed for preparing your work for an interactive presentation. Your goal is still to have the smallest possible palette, but batching functions to create a super palette are worth little on the Web, unless the entire Web page is made with exactly the same palette. On 8-bit displays, you are locked into the 216-color palette for good or ill, and all indexed images will dither from this color space. So why bother to use the adaptive palette and work so hard at optimizing? On a 24-bit system, the browser will use the adaptive colors instead, providing far better quality.

DeBabelizer has multiple ways of dealing with a minimized palette. It can make the palette changes based on its own automatic algorithms, which remap the colors it sees as being similar to a smaller group of shades. Alternatively, you can minimize the palette yourself color by color or specify colors you definitely want to merge. The automatic function is infinitely easier, so we'll concentrate on that. We'll need 72 ppi original that you used to create your JPEGs (backed up, of course!). In our case, this is Xmp68.EPS.

We know from our guidelines that our photographic images won't look as good as GIFs as they are as JPEGS. But how bad will they be? Let's look at the size of the file we indexed, Xmp69.gif, for a cluc. It's larger than the recommended maximum size of 30K, which will make it too big for downloading and there is already some evidence of posterization. Go back to Indexed Mode in Photoshop, and change the resolution to 7-bits/pixel. Notice how much the example on the CD (Xmp614.GIF) has changed. We have substantial banding of the background behind the rock arch and our GIF file is still larger than any of our JPEGs.

Reducing Size by Editing

Obviously for a photographic image, JPEG is the way to go. But what if we have no choice? Let's look at another file. It's original is Xmp615.EPS. In an effort to maintain the important information in the picture, we've edited out the background and replaced it with a flat color. You can see the result of this strategy in Xmp616.EPS. Let's save this image as an 8-bit Indexed file with an adaptive palette and open it in DeBabelizer to see what our options are.

1. If your image has a flat background color like this one, you'll want to block this background from dithering. The first step is to go to Palette > Options > Dithering in the menu bar. Remember that the 216-color palette will not work as effectively on a Unix system. This option increases the

likelihood that a flat color will be substituted for our background even if there is no exact color match.

Figure 6.11
The Palette pull-down menu bar with the Dithering & Background Color... option highlighted.

2. We can specify the value we want recognized as the background color in many ways. In this example, I placed my pointer over the background color to find out its RGB value, then copied these RGB numbers into the dialog box.

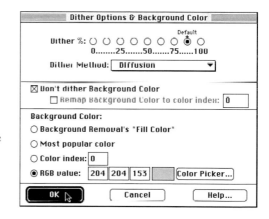

Figure 6.12
The Dither Options & Background Color dialog box, with DeBabelizer's default Diffusion dither setting chosen and the Background Color fixed as non-dithered.

3. Now we'll try a reduction in colors to 128, or 7-bit color. Under the Palette menu bar, choose Reduce Colors.

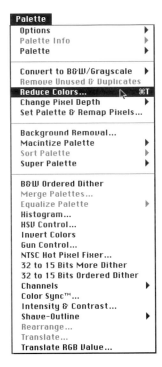

Figure 6.13
DeBabelizer Palette menu with Reduce Colors... chosen.

4. This brings up a new dialog box. Choose the Slow option. Although the Fast radio button is usually recommended, especially for large images, I have usually found that Slow often creates slightly smaller files and in this exercise, size counts.

5. Our target number of colors is 128, so choose the radio button next to it.

Notice that, unlike Photoshop, we have the option of choosing numbers in-between the standard size reductions. This can be very useful when working with graphics created for the Web with a small color gamut and when saving 500 bytes can make a cumulative difference in the load time of our page.

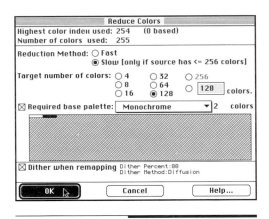

Figure 6.14
The Reduce Colors dialog box.

6. Although doing so can take up two slots for colors we don't seem to use, I recommend specifying the Monochrome base palette as required colors. Having black and white to dither with can be very useful, as well as improving image contrast.

7. Last, we'll check the Dither when remapping box, so the settings we've requested earlier in the Dither dialogue will be implemented.

8. Click on OK, and we're ready to see our results in Xmp617.gif.

Reducing by Eliminating Color

Besides going back and editing the file
again, we can try to eliminate colors that add
nothing to the image, but take up a dispro-
portionate amount of the palette. Scanning
and anti-aliasing can add color artifacts. In
this edited indexed image, Xmp618.gif,
these artifacts in the purple and magenta
range take up a disproportionately large
percentage of the 256-color palette. This
leads to extensive mottling in the fleshtones,
which are the most important colors to
maintain, and will certainly make things
worse when we reduce our colors.

Luckily, DeBabelizer has a method for
isolating these colors and eliminating them.
Let's step through this process.

1. Under the Palette menu, choose
   Palette > Save....

2. The Add Palette to List dialog box
   comes up. We will add the current
   image's palette to DeBabelizer's
   palette database, and name it
   'testreduce.' Click the Add button and
   the palette has been saved.

3. Under the Palette menu, choose Set
   Palette & Remap Pixels... This will
   bring up a dialog box with the last
   palette. DeBabelizer will usually come
   up with the local system palette as a
   default the first time you do this.

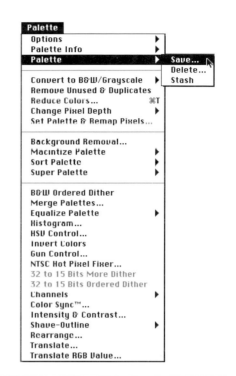

Figure 6.15
DeBabelizer Palette Save... pull-down bar.

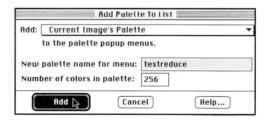

Figure 6.16
DeBabelizer Add Palette To List dialog box.

141

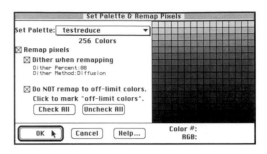

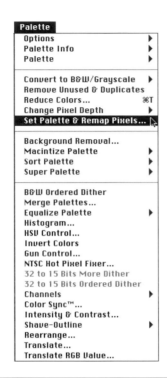

Figure 6.18
The Set Palette & Remap Pixels box, with all settings checked.

7. When you've chosen all your colors, click OK.

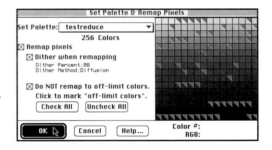

Figure 6.17
DeBabelizer Palette > Set Palette & Remap Pixels… pull-down bar.

4. Pull down the Set Palette menu in this dialog box and scroll until you find your newly added palette name. Set this as your working palette.

5. Check all three available boxes in the menu.

6. Look for the colors you want to eliminate. Each time you find one, click inside the color box. The box will be greyed out on the diagonal to indicate that this color should not be considered when you remap your image palette. If you make a mistake, just click inside the box again.

Figure 6.19
The Set Palette & Remap Pixels box, with colors checked as off-limit.

8. DeBabelizer will remap your image without those colors as part of the palette. If you like the results, your next step is return to the Palette menu and choose Remove Unused and Duplicates. The offending colors will disappear from your palette window. Return through these steps as often as you like until you have eliminated any colors your image does not need.

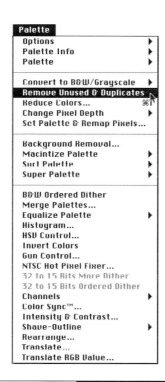

Figure 6.20
The Palette pull-down menu, with Remove Unused & Duplicates chosen.

9. Now you can return to the Reduce Colors option. (Refer to Figure 6.14.)

To compare the same image at 128 colors before and after the Remap process, open Xmp619.GIF and Xmp620.GIF on the CD. Both files are the same size, but the Xmp619 is much closer to the original 256-color file than Xmp20, which was not manually remapped. You can repeat the process to reduce the image palette and its bit depth even further, particularly if your objective is to create a thumbnail. As a final comparison,

look at Xmp621.GIF for the same 64-color image with all indexing and palette conversion handled in DeBabelizer. Using the palette remap strategy and scaling the image down to thumbnail size gives us the final Xmp622.GIF, a 6K file which holds the most important color information of the file.

Working Within HTML Constraints

We've made it through the hardest and most complex issue in preparing a Web portfolio. Now you can move to actually designing your site. This requires some basic understanding of the environment you're designing for, and *that* means HTML (HyperText Markup Language). This is the underlying coding language that defines what you can do graphically.

HTML was developed to make text and visual information universally available, no matter what platform, system version, or monitor the user might be working on. The individual, rather than the source, could determine how they wanted or needed to view information, based on their system's capabilities and their personal viewing preferences. In keeping with this philosophy, Mosaic, the first browser software, was very simple, straightforward, and tiny, which is why it could be written by a graduate student working on a personal project. At first, users accepted its limitations just for the novelty of being able to see information

143

and navigate through it, rather than having to work through Unix line editing and code-based FTP. But the eventual frustration with the HTML standards committee's slow progress towards releasing new capabilities made Netscape inevitable. Netscape broke with the commitment to universality by developing unauthorized tags and de facto new standards. Its existence led directly to the evolution of the Web as a full-employment act for computer-savvy designers, as text-based sites have given way to the image-rich pages we see today.

Unfortunately, the fact that we have many more tools and options today does not change the root assumptions of HTML. Many of these continue to shape the kinds of pages we can create. To design an effective Web site, you must recognize that it is *not* a printed page, or even an interactive screen. Your design constraints are freer in some areas and mind-bogglingly tight in others, but they are definitely different.

Some of those differences may be minimized as the browser war-to-the-death between Microsoft and Netscape accelerates in a blinding whirl of new tags, plug-ins, Java applets, and typographic solutions. But even so, the ability for most viewers to take advantage of these solutions constantly lags behind their release. Recognition of basic ground rules of Web page layout will be necessary for some time to come.

Rule #1: You Have No Control Over Page Dimensions

Differences in platform and browser insure that your page can appear somewhat wider or narrower even on a system equivalent to your own. But that's only the beginning. The same page must look acceptable on a 14-inch, 8-bit screen as well as on 21-inch, 24-bit one. What does that mean in design terms?

Unless you are quite certain of your audience, it is generally a mistake to design based on your own personal high-resolution desktop. There is an enormous variation in viewing resolution and screen sizes, and the higher the resolution you design on, the fewer people will be able to comfortably view your work. For example, on a standard Mac OS 640×480 (13–14") monitor running at 72 dpi, 622 pixels is the largest horizontal dimension for an image in Netscape, once you've subtracted scroll bars and the image area's eight pixel left border.

But even this limitation changes. A designer raised on a Macintosh is practically hard-wired to believe that all on-screen resolution is 72 dpi. In fact, pixels are not like inches, or centimeters. They are not a one-size-fits-all phenomenon. Their size is dependent on the monitor resolution, as well as a factor called dot pitch. The higher the resolution, the more pixels there are displayed on-screen, and the smaller those pixels are. For many years, monitors for Macs were made to Apple specifications, so they were standardized at the same pixel resolution for each size screen. PC/Windows monitors had no standard, so they could vary widely, mostly to the worse, because it was so much cheaper to produce them that way. Now, multisynch resolution has been introduced on the Macintosh side, but old habits die hard. Actual screen resolution can easy go to 90–100 ppi, or down to 65ppi on a 640×480 screen with a low-grade video card and a large dot pitch. On such a system, an image optimized to 622×360 will fall off the edge of the screen. Conversely, a design created on a Windows video system set to 1024×768 will not be seen as designed on a Macintosh with a 16"–17" monitor running at its default resolution. Viewers can scroll right

to see something larger but will not see all of a page which violates this constraint.

Picture tubes for PCs have a quoted pixel pitch in the range 0.25mm to 0.28mm. A pitch of 0.254mm would be exactly 100 pixels per inch. Here is a further breakdown:

 .25mm = 101.6 ppi

 .26mm = 97.9 ppi

 .27mm = 94.9 ppi

 .28mm = 90.7 ppi

If a picture is sent at 72 pixels per inch either its size will be shrunk or pixels will be repeated (or interpolated) to maintain the picture size.

Certain monitor sizes are optimized for specific resolutions. For any specific

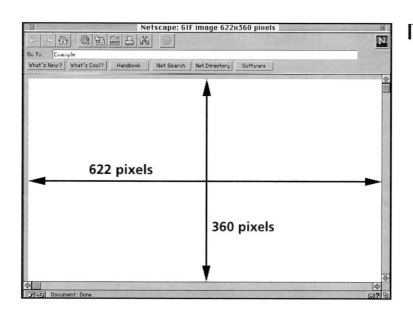

Figure 6.21
A Macintosh 640×480 screen, with an active image area inside the Netscape window of 622×360 pixels.

monitor size a lower resolution means less information on the screen but bigger text that's easy to read. A resolution too high for a specific monitor size means lots of information but text that is too small. A high-quality monitor with great focus and small dot pitch will make the smaller text more readable. The optimal monitor size for a specific resolution is different for Windows versus Macintosh computers.

Note

What is Dot Pitch Anyway?

The first time I heard the phrase "dot pitch," I fuzzed out. Later I found this was an appropriate response, since dot pitch is the major factor determining how sharp and crisp, or fuzzy and grainy, a screen appears. Monitors work by sending electrical light through a grillwork of tiny RGB dots to the screen phosphors. The size of a monitor's pixels, the individual picture elements used to form the display, is gauged by the dot pitch. The smaller the dot pitch, the crisper and clearer the picture. Apple monitors are generally around .26mm dot pitch. Other multisynch monitors for today's Macs and PCs can run between .25mm and .39mm. This means that two monitors which have the exact same physical size may not display a picture the same way.

Knowing your target viewing audience is critical for deciding what to make your maximum dimension. The surfing public, as well as most corporate sites, use Wintel computers. Only in the worlds of graphic and interactive design and desktop video is this ratio reversed. Whatever you choose, be consistent in applying this maximum and design with your window set to your chosen size.

In addition, the browser default window is always more narrow than the maximum viewable area of a screen. Many people like to be able to access other portions of their desktop and avoid resizing their browser window. To be on the safe side, avoid putting critical navigation information in the area between 472 and 622 pixels. It could easily be missed.

Variations in text column widths are one of the traditional tools in page grids and are normally a factor of page dimensions. However, only the frame tag actually gives you full control over column widths, and it is implemented somewhat differently on the various browsers that recognize it. Tables work best in situations where you want to take advantage of the elasticity of the Web screen width to keep columns evenly spaced relative to each other, or to control text running around graphics.

Screen Depth Variation

As goes the width, so goes the depth. Since almost all computer screens are in landscape configuration, the screen depth available without scrolling is even smaller. This figure varies according to browser and the user set-up preferences, but a depth of about 360 will probably be the maximum on a 14-inch screen. This dimension is less critical for text information than it is for imagery. For design purposes, it means that

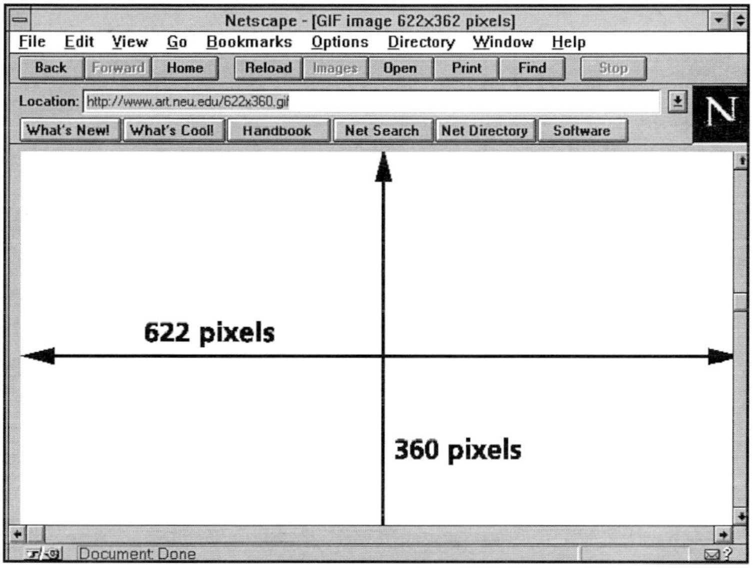

Figure 6.22
A Windows 640×480 screen, browsing the same image as the previous Macintosh 640×480 screen.

portrait-shaped imagery will suffer more from design constraints than landscape-based work.

"But they can scroll!" you say. Yes, they can and they will, particularly if they are very interested in what you have to show. But presentation of your work may suffer. It's better to design small pictures which can be linked to larger versions for those who have larger screens than to force your audience to see your work in pieces.

Rule #2: You Have Little Control Over Text Specifications

This rule is on the verge of being over-turned. As this book goes to press, Adobe and Microsoft have inked a deal to create a superset of their two competing font

standards, Type 1 PostScript fonts and TrueType, to be usable for consistent downloading from Internet pages. If accepted by the World Wide Web committee, supported by other browsers, and dependably implemented, it would mean that a Web site could download a screen representation of the font you specify to the viewer's computer. This would finally offer the control Web designers have been hoping for.

However, licenses to the newly formatted fonts will not be free. To function as Web-downloadable on-screen faces, these new versions will probably need to be purchased afresh by the company or designer who wants to display them on their pages, even if they are already owned in an earlier format for traditional usage. For many of us, this may continue to limit typographic design possibilities. Other considerations also intervene. First, recoding fonts, even by such large companies as Adobe and Microsoft, will take time and the entire library of options will not be available overnight. Second, many other foundries with popular fonts will need to retool to adapt to the new font technology. Third, Microsoft has announced Internet Explorer's support of the new downloadable fonts, but the timetable for Netscape Navigator may well be different, since they are not primary partners in the deal.

One of the ways that people tend to get around inherent HTML typographic restrictions is to create headlines, small blocks of text, and logos as graphics instead. (Books like *PhotoShop Type Magic* have many creative ways of spicing up words on the Web.) Any type you see on a Web page that has textures, effects, dimensionality, or

even just good letterspacing has probably been made this way. But every time you replace a standard piece of HTML text with a .GIF, you increase the amount of time it takes your page to load. This is simply not practical for running blocks of text, especially text you might have to edit later.

Until typographic technology is freely available and widely supported, you will still have to design your pages with the possibility that they will display with different typefaces and default sizes than you would wish. To test your designs under these conditions, change your browser's definitions from the font you've been using during your Web design to one as radically different in width and character as you can find. You may discover that you need to alter some of your page geometry or create hard returns in flowing text or headlines to allow for these variations.

Figure 6.23
Netscape window with text displayed using a condensed typeface.

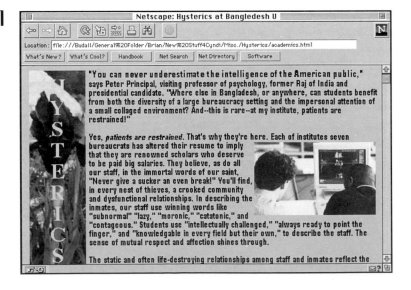

It's also important to recognize that a choice in typefaces still won't mean control of sizes, which are determined by header levels and HTML rules, not by the typefaces themselves. Each individual can set their default size browser preferences to anything that suits their fancy. Although you may still see a header which is larger than the body text around it, the entire text material will be scaled up or down within your layout. Pages designed without this in mind can have stray lines that wrap into areas that should be blank, headers which break strangely, and weird leading around images.

Figure 6.24
Netscape window with the same browser text displayed using an expanded type-face.

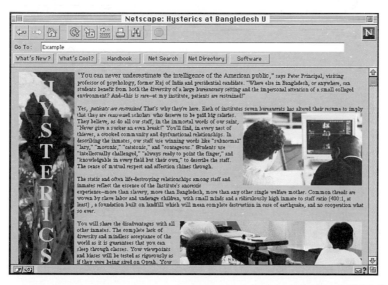

Figure 6.25
Netscape window with preferences set to 10 point as default.

Figure 6.26
*Netscape window
with the same text
set to 14 point as
default.*

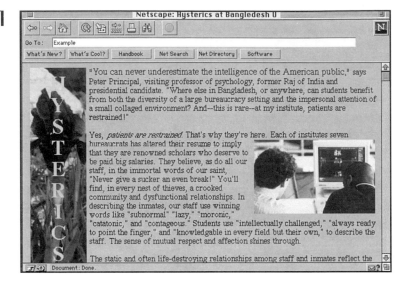

Rule #3: White Space Can Be Negative Space

In print, it's hard to have too much white space. On the Web, white space can occasionally be a negative factor in design, unless the page is so small and self-contained that the user can see it all at once. Given the clogged wires and heavy traffic, even a site sitting on a zippy server with a T1 line can seem to take forever to provide a page. Big chunks of white space on a scrolling page will frustrate viewers who are waiting not-so-patiently for your page to finish downloading. They need every second of additional load time to be filled with new viewing material.

Laying Out Your Web Pages

No matter what tool or method you plan to use for your foray into a Web-based portfolio, you will work more efficiently if you limit repetition. Obviously, you need a home page, the place where most people will enter your site and navigate to the meat of it. You'll want a résumé page (or, if a design firm, a corporate statement and client list), and a link to your email address on every page. Of course, you'll need specific portfolio pages. Add links on pages within your Web site (simple text links and buttons are the easiest to implement), and your basic ingredients are in place. Backgrounds, if they support your work well, can be a simple way to make your site distinctive without adding a tremendous amount of additional work. As for the rest—clickable imagemaps, tables, frames, forms, chat rooms, bookmark pages, small animations, Acrobat PDF files, personal interest pages—they're all very nice but tangential to your initial goal.

Figure 6.27
Attractive Web home page with white space problems that takes 50 seconds to load on a shared T1 line, but gives you nothing to do during that time.

An uninviting home page almost guarantees that your image pages will wither unseen. Your home page is like the cover of a book, or the first view of a building space. It can be a full-featured gateway to the rest of your site, or simply a visual title before the actual navigation area. Either way, it must be carefully laid out and executed.

A home page should always be unique to the individual site, although stylistically linked to other pages. Nothing is more disconcerting than leaving a black and red home page with navigation tools on the left and having a textured background with buttons on the bottom take its place. Establish a position and style for buttons or menu bars on your home page, then remain consistent throughout.

The text template will be used for any pages that are solely or primarily informational,

like your résumé. This doesn't mean that you can't have graphics on this type of page, but you do want to keep them simple, non-distracting, and secondary to the page's delivery of information. A text page should not be difficult to read and understand if the graphics on it do not load.

The image page can take one of two forms: a table of contents for your pieces, or as a portfolio page with captions and/or commentary. Approach your image page decision and its organization in the same way, and with the same criteria, you have been applying to all your other portfolio decisions. If you want to show both fine art and design work, or different categories like illustration and animation, lay out the page so that you can separate these portfolios subjects into different sections.

Figure 6.28
Example of a portfolio home page in the process of construction. Note the visual teaser and the playful tone.

Figure 6.29
Example of a text page layout. Navigation buttons remain in a predictable position; graphics are separate from basic text information for easy text download.

Figure 6.30
Simple solution to the visual table of contents issue.

153

Don't plan on cramming so much on this preview page that it takes forever to load all the pictures, or forces you to show thumbnails that are too small to give an adequate sense of the larger work. It is better to show fewer pieces on a page than to show them all badly. If you really need to display a significant amount of work, plan on dividing it into categories by theme or style, and offering versions of the thumbnail image page as gateways to each one. Then give descriptive names to each different path, not generic labels like Portfolio 1 or Portfolio 2. Remember that even people who are interested in your site will not spend more than a few minutes exploring it. You want to make sure they have the right impression of

who you are and what you can do before they move on.

Enhancing Your Work

It is generally a good idea to provide some text to accompany your work. At the very least, you'll need labeling captions. Remember that your images online, even if they were always on-screen art, are unlikely to be as rich an experience for the viewer as the originals. You can't control how each individual monitor or operating system will display your images, and you will probably have had to make some alterations in the original to optimize it for the Internet's structural limitations. Your Web site must fill in the gaps that you would during a real presentation. An artist's statement, a discussion of a client's problem and your design solution, or a photojournalist's commentary on story photos can go a long way toward providing a context in which to view your work.

On the other hand, don't add text and commentary unnecessarily, or add information that isn't relevant to your work. The online environment is not optimal for heavy text, and most people will react to content-free material by moving on. No caption or design discussion should extend longer than one paragraph. If you have material that absolutely must be delivered in long text form, like a résumé or curriculum vitae, keep it simple and easy to save as one file. Don't put critical information, like your name and contact addresses, in a graphic without creating an <ALT> version in simple text. Some people will only skim your résumé to get a sense of your experience, then save the page as text for future reference.

Optimize Critical Pages

As people move through your links, they will come across some *nexus pages*, main pages that your other pages link back to. One of these, obviously, is your home page. The other may be the image index page where you keep thumbnail versions of your images. Others may become obvious to you as you build your chart with its links. If you are pressed for time, you should concentrate your efforts on these pages. This effort

should extend beyond their layout and design. They should also be as quick to load as possible. Even though browsers only download most page elements once in a session, loading from the cache can still take time. People get impatient with slow loading pages that they see frequently and that irritation is cumulative. If the nexus pages are speedy, your viewers will be more inclined to wait for a larger image page to download.

Pitfalls You Can Control

People tell you that rules in art and design are constantly being broken as times and processes change. Most of the time, what really changes is the stylistic response to those rules, not the basics themselves. Good Web design still rests on adapting basic tenets of visual space and design principles to a new set of limitations and possibilities. If you want to create a professional-looking portfolio, you'll want to avoid the easy mistakes that will hurt your site.

Stupid Word Processing Tricks

Artists and designers who are very articulate in person can come off rather badly in written material. Although text is not what you are promoting, simple errors can distract people from your visual issues and send the message that you are sloppy on details. Even if you are only writing a brief introduction to your site and very short headings and paragraphs to accompany your work, don't write them as you compose your Web pages unless you are working with a layout program with word processing tools. You'll miss typing errors while concentrating on the layout. Use a program with a spell-checking function, then import or copy and paste the text into your template layout.

Make sure to check acronyms and proper names that the spellchecker won't catch. I was once asked to comment on a former student's new corporate Web page and had to mention that the company name had been misspelled! Last, ask a friend or coworker to read what you've written out loud. If something doesn't make sense, the two of you will be more likely to hear it in spoken words. This may also help you catch the kind of errors no spellchecking program can, like two "the"s in a row.

Legibility

Even if your text content is clean and clear, how you deliver it visually can have a big effect on your viewing audience. Many things that are elegant in print, or useful emphasis in a slide presentation or interactive piece, are inappropriate on the Web.

Micro-type

Small type can be very difficult to read. This is a particularly critical issue given the variety of default typographic specs your target audience could be using. You may be working in a wide, legible serif face, but someone else may be viewing it in a version of Times Roman, a typical default on a Windows machine but not a terribly good on-screen font. If the information you are

155

Figure 6.31
A typical typing error published unnoticed.

offering is important to your work, you should make sure that no one you want to reach will avoid it. If you really want to use a small point size, at least keep the column width small and the text terse.

Loud Type

No one likes to have someone shout at them. Long headers in all caps, header type sizes specified where normal text belongs, and big, bold, italic words hammer at the reader online. One quick shout can get attention. A continued dose of it just makes people tune

out and drop away from your site before they see your work.

Wallpaper Type

Column widths and text type sizes should be somewhat proportional to each other for maximum legibility. However, with Web layout programs to help organize your page, there is no reason you should have large chunks of text running the full width of the screen. The longer the line length, the easier it is for people to lose track of where they are and the less likely they are to continue reading.

Figure 6.32
Web page with font specification too small.

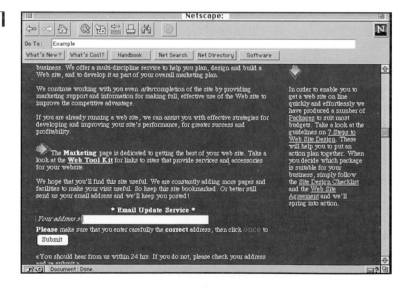

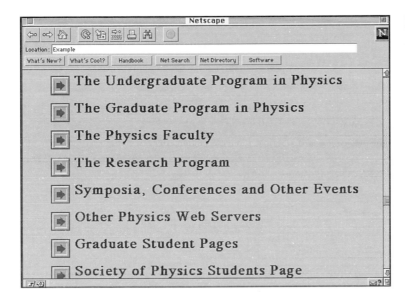

Figure 6.33
Web page with font specification too large.

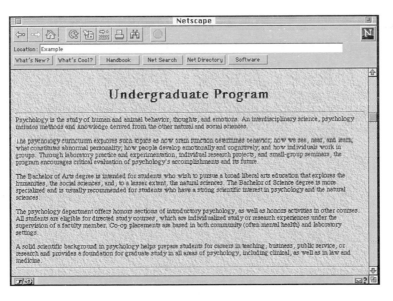

Figure 6.34
Web page with type too small for column width.

Technology for Technology's Sake

Just because you can do something doesn't mean you should. Anything that distracts from your online portfolio is a mistake. If you are an interface designer or programmer, your Web page itself will be a portfolio piece to highlight your expertise in these areas. Concentrate on simplicity, clean organization of information, and design to highlight your content not its container. Make your page visually distinctive and use technology sparingly, especially if you are new to it.

158

Busy, Busy, Busy

Most people by now know that the blinking text tag is the mark of a net newbie. It's irritating and ugly. However, with the advent of animated GIFs, flashing text has made a return in other forms. Type can cycle endlessly between two colors in a screen-width banner. Buttons blink. Animated GIFs are simple enough to create that such distracting uses of them seldom serve the purposes they were created for. Unless you have an excellent reason for doing so that integrates seemlessly into the design of your site (unlikely, but possible), avoid them.

Invasion of the Marching Ants

The same argument applies to marquee banners marching through the bottom of a window frame. The marching marquee is particularly irritating when its Times Square message is merely a duplication of material posted elsewhere on the Web page. There may be good justification for using a

Figure 6.35
Marching ants at the bottom of a page advertising Web design. Note that the marquee text is a reiteration of the existing Web page material.

marquee in informational sites where it can be used to highlight new material or draw attention to late-breaking news, but there is little use for it in most portfolios.

Keeping Backgrounds in the Background

Backgrounds are a wonderful way to give texture and richness to an otherwise flat medium. However, they can be overused or poorly chosen. Before you commit yourself to a decorative background, consider the effect it can have on other elements that may be more important. How will your images look on the background? Sometimes people design a portfolio site, then plug in their scanned images, and discover that the effect is similar to hanging a painting on patterned wallpaper. As with most rules, this one can be broken very effectively if it's done with

great deliberation and for a planned effect. However, there are good reasons why galleries show art on solid-colored walls. Look at your artwork first and choose background elements which work with your material, not against it.

Just to be on the safe side, you should also take a look at what happens to your site if you load your page without the background. All too frequently, whether through individual access lines, browser memory issues, ISP problems, or server overloads, portions of Web pages do not all load up on a page. When this happens with a background, the entire page can become completely illegible and the unwary viewer may make incorrect assumptions about it. Always set a default background color in your body tag which is close to the background tile's dominant color to guarantee legibility if loading problems arise.

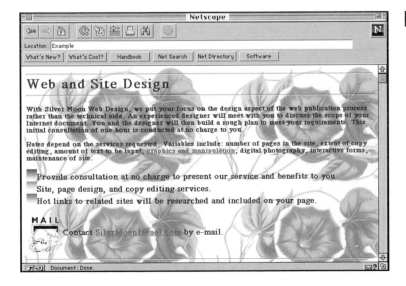

Figure 6.36
Background/type combination with insufficient contrast. Note in particular the lack of contrast in the anchor type for email.

Doing this is easy, even for the HTML impaired. Below is the HTML coding for a tiled background with a white, powdery chalk texture (chalk.gif). The portion of the tag that follows it changes the default background to white from the usual neutral gray, using the Hex code for white. (See Appendix E for Hex codes translated to RGBs.) This is a useful thing to do for your viewers even if the background loads as it should. Hex background colors, since they involve no searching and interpreting files by the browser, load much faster than tiled backgrounds. Your viewer will be able to appreciate your site more quickly as they wait for the background picture to finish painting.

160

Pitfalls You Can't Control

Since few companies and even fewer individuals are likely to own the hardware and Internet addresses needed for their portfolio, they must, like Blanche, "depend on the kindness of strangers." These strangers can be very efficient, knowledge-able, and inexpensive. However, the growing number of providers guarantees that not all will be equally successful on all three counts.

Figure 6.38 shows something you've probably experienced in Web surfing, the server maxed out screen. If you really need

Figure 6.37
Web page with unloaded back-ground image and insufficient type contrast with default background color.

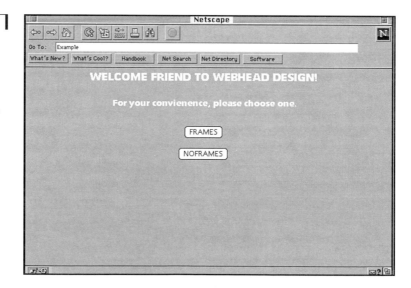

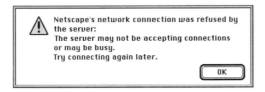

Figure 6.38
The dreaded server maxed out screen.

to reach a site, you try again and again until it either seems hopeless or you finally get through. If you're merely following a Web search or checking out a URL someone mentioned might be worth viewing, you'll probably just go somewhere else and never make another try. There's simply too much else available out there. Obviously, you don't want your Web site to be the one that people bypass because they can't get through.

Every Web server, even the most technically well-supported, will occasionally have too many requests for connections to field at one time. If this happens too frequently, however, the provider has probably done a better job of advertising their services than supporting their site with appropriate hardware and technical staff. Changing providers when you are just browsing and reading email is one thing. Changing your URL, notifying your business contacts, and moving your site is something else. You can minimize the chance of having to do this through several strategies.

First, ask around. Check out what your potential ISP's domain address is and search in Deja News for postings by people in design, photography, or artist's Usenet groups with this domain in their address. Chances are some of them have Web pages and are experiencing the things you will later. Send them email asking them if they'd recommend their provider. Most people are happy to praise their ISP if they're happy with their connection, or talk about where they might be moving instead if they're not.

Second, sleuth some sites with your ISP's address at different times of the day. There are many exact and technical ways of doing this, which can include separating your own phone line's deficiencies from that of the provider, but they're really overkill unless you anticipate a highly complex and heavily traveled site. Simply hit the same sites early in the morning when things are quiet, again in mid-afternoon as traffic heats up, and finally during the 6 p.m. to midnight prime time. Then choose another ISP and visit equivalent sites at the same times. Even if some of the slowdowns are at your end, you'll still be able to tell whether your ISP is performing well in comparison.

Third, make sure that your ISP is prepared to give you the service you'll need. At the beginning, your Web site may be very simple and low-tech. If you ever want to create clickable imagemaps (those wonderful graphics with live areas on them) you will need access to something called a CGI-BIN. Without it, you can make single button links only. Some ISPs are very security-conscious and make you jump through hoops if they let you add code at all. Check out your options before you sign on.

Whatever you do, don't settle. Unless you live in an isolated area where ISP choices are very limited, new ones are probably cropping up all the time. Monitor your own site from time to time. See if you have problems connecting to it and whether the time it takes to bring up your pages has degraded. Don't take performance for granted because it was good when you started. You may have begun as one of the earliest users of a new ISP, and additional traffic can make all the difference.

Do You Need to Know HTML Coding?

In the past, implementing your designs required learning HTML. Although irritating and tedious for most artists or designers, HTML is very misunderstood and unnecessarily feared. Excepting CGI or Java scripting, anyone who can type and follow simple instructions can be an HTML programmer in one week, and write a simple site's code in a day.

I can make this statement because HTML is not a programming language, with complex grammar and command sequences. It is a shorthand means of describing visual attributes and file locations using simple ASCII text. As such, HTML coding needs no special software to use. Any word

processor, including DOS's EDIT and the MacOS's SimpleText, works just fine. A plethora of word processor tools, most of them either shareware, freeware, or very inexpensive commercial products, can make the process easier by calling out the codes with color, or using keyboard shortcuts to insert the tags. A list of the codes can be found in Appendix E.

Web Page Layout Alternatives

Despite HTML's basic simplicity, most of us have viewed it as a step backward from the WYSIWYG world we've know since the Macintosh arrived in 1984, followed quickly by Ready, Set, Go! and its more sophisticated descendants.

The first alternatives to coding were offered by existing print-based page layout programs. As mentioned in Chapter 4, Adobe Acrobat PDF files are quick ways of transferring text-heavy documents to the Web. Users of other Adobe programs like PageMaker, as well as QuarkXPress users, can purchase plug-ins, extensions, or sophisticated stand-alone programs to convert their pages direct to HTML.

Although these approaches certainly save the user the trouble of learning a new layout program or the dreaded HTML coding, they perpetuate the incorrect assumption that Web pages are like print pages. Many converted documents show their roots with text-heavy material, pages that are too long or too wide, color choices that are terrific in print but disastrous online, or type being way too small or in a bad face. They also require purchase of an expensive full-featured program when Web requirements alone are considerably simpler and less expensive to support. Few non-graphic designers, for example, own page layout programs, even though they may have several types of image-creation software.

PDF files, so useful in other contexts, are really inefficient for Web portfolio use. First, they're simply too big and can take a long time to download. Second, having been created originally for text (mostly standard paper size), they are frustrating to look at on-screen. If you're interested in the actual content, you have to scroll madly around the page through columns. If you just want to see what the page looks like, you'll need it small enough to fit on a standard monitor, and at that zoom factor, you could probably manage just as well with greeking.

Given these options, it's not surprising that the first attempts at WYSIWYG Web design programs were snapped up quickly, despite the limited tags they supported and their extensive problems. It would be dangerous to try to review the current crop of these tools here, because six months from now half of them will be radically different and the other half will be gone. If you've decided to buy one to help you with your initial layout tasks, look for specific features that you need rather than the brand name. Unlike layout programs, the files created by

Web design software are all cross-platform, recognizable code, so there's no need to worry about creating a file that no one else can read. Ideally, your program should be truly WYSIWIG, unlike the text editor and browser combinations that require you to reload to see your changes. Another good feature to look for is a program which will transfer your pages to your ISP's Web server for you, without having to use a separate FTP tool. Make sure it has its own spell-checker and that it won't write over tags it doesn't recognize. An ideal feature would be a program that lets you preview your site's look with different browsers.

163

Making the Decision

Whether you choose to create your pages with a WYSIWYG program, directly with HTML, or a combination, your decision will have a lot to do with your general comfort level with getting under the hood. Layout programs are a tremendously more efficient use of a beginner's time. You can concentrate on the design aspects of your site without being sucked into the tedium of tags. Unfortunately, the current crop of editors can set up false assumptions and limit your design options. It is important to realize that we are dealing with first generation tools, not the highly refined, feature-rich publishing programs they resemble. As browser development races ahead, layout tools won't always support the wide range of tags, nor do they show you how your page may look on all browsers. Although they convert graphics to the correct file formats, they do not optimize them. Many use coding language specific to their program. If you want to add unsupported tags, you may no longer be able to work in the layout program with the edited files.

Despite these problems, I recommend the use of Web layout programs for basic page architecture, as long as the one you choose supports the functions your design requires. A layout program which doesn't support tables or frames, for example, could make it impossible for you to position your elements as you had originally sketched them on your template grid. Short of an attack of coding macho or a true desire to master HTML, there is little justification for a beginner to create basic page geometry any other way. Even an intermediate user of HTML will probably find these tools at least as useful as they are frustrating. Get your pages as close

as you can to what you had envisioned with the layout program tool. Do all image manipulation except the actual placing of the picture on the page in dedicated image processing software. Then, move to text editing software to add to or amend your program-generated code, and test the amended pages through browsers.

Steal This Code!

Whether or not you decide to begin with Web layout software, at some point you may discover that you really need a tag that neither you nor your program recognizes. That's when its time to view and copy source code. Just by viewing a source through your Web browser, you can match the straightforward HTML coding with the finished piece. Seeing how tables and frames are implemented can help enormously in helping you improve your first efforts. Some

Figure 6.39
Adobe's home page with its source code revealed.

beginners have actually used existing pages as a template, replacing other pictures, colors, and backgrounds with their own. As long as you don't stop there, it's an excellent way to see how an unfamiliar tag works.

Some functions will be beyond your grasp because they require CGI scripting. This is real programming—well within the capabilities of anyone who can handle Lingo but not something to tackle in your maiden Web voyage. Don't get in over your head. Your ISP may not even allow you access to their CGI-BIN folder.

Testing Your Work: The Web Version

Never assume that your work is done until you've tested your pages under different conditions than those you made them in. If you have used JPEG, view all your pictures in 8-bit to see what happens when they dither, particularly on a different type of operating system. If you've created GIF files without using the non-dithering palette, or have converted other artwork into GIF form, you could be in for a real surprise.

Try to test your work on more than one browser. Netscape Navigator is currently the standard for Web browsing, so chances are that you will have designed your page using it. Microsoft's Internet Explorer is gaining ground though and online services still offer their proprietary browsers as well as browsers like Apple's Cyberdog or the

former standard, Mosaic. If you have designed your work to be seen by a specific browser, or you are using HTML tags that not all browsers support, be sure to say so on your home page.

If you've designed on a Mac, try to bring up your pages in Windows, and vice versa. See Xmp623 through Xmp625c on the CD for comparative views of the same Web page on different systems, each set to 256 colors. Xmp620 is a 17" Windows screen set at 640×480, Xmp621 a 17" Macintosh set at 832×624, and Xmp622 a 17" Sun Microsystems Unix-based system running at 1280×900. Note the wide variety of image quality and amount of material displayed on-screen.

Besides discovering image display problems, you may see strange color shifts, even if you've limited yourself to the non-dithering Netscape palette. You may be the victim of gamma correction or the lack of it. Gamma determines image brightness and effects the visual proportion of RGB on-screen. The Macintosh OS handles gamma differently from Windows or other operating systems. Because of this, artwork created with the Macintosh OS will tend to look darker in Windows and variations in the intensity of the red, green, and blue voltage can change your color percentages. It is not possible to compensate for this problem completely; there is just too much variety in systems and monitors. You can, however, use the Gamma control panel which comes with Photoshop to approximate how your work will look on other systems. Mac users can set this control panel to 2.2 to approximate what their work will look like on other systems. Windows users can do the same, using the Macintosh setting of 1.8. Catching these problems before you advertise your site is very important.

A Little HTML Goes a Long Way

One simple coding strategy can make all the difference in the world to how people react to the waiting game. Even if you want to stay as far away from HTML coding as you can, you should make sure that you learn this one by heart, or that your Web layout program supports it automatically.

Figure 6.40
HTML tag with IMG WIDTH and HEIGHT definitions specified.

In Figure 6.40, the HTML <IMG> tag calls the name of the image file you'll be showing, gives a phrase that will print if your image does not load, positions it relative to the text around it, and defines its horizontal and vertical dimensions in pixels. These WIDTH and HEIGHT definitions are incredibly useful. If they're not used, a browser reading your file tries to compose

the page from scratch, referencing the browser window dimension and the actual image file or files you have placed on the page. If you have several images, even if they're just thumbnails, this means your viewer may wait several seconds with a completely blank browser screen while the entire HTML code for the page is interpreted. With WIDTH and HEIGHT included, the browser simply "saves" the space for the image like an FPO in print, gets your other elements on-screen, and loads the pictures as it finds them. If you have text with your pictures, viewers can read it first and orient themselves to your page, making the effective wait time seem much shorter than it really is.

Broken Links, Coding Errors

It's very easy to create a wonderful Web site, put it up on a server, and have nothing work properly. To avoid this, make sure that all your link references to other pages in your site are relative, not fixed, links. A fixed link is one in which you reference the entire URL. A relative link only references from the top of your hierarchy. For example, look at this line of HTML code:

```
<AHREF="http://home.netscape.com/
comprod/mirror/client_download.html">
```

This is a fixed link. It specifies that the browser will look for a hypertext document called client_download.html and that it is

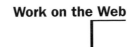

found on the specific host server called home.netscape.com , in a directory comprod and a subdirectory inside that called mirror.

Now look at this version of the same thing:

```
<A HREF="/comprod/mirror/
client_download.html">
```

The second version is not just a short-cut. It eliminates information about the specific host so the browser will look for addresses relative to your root page, not your local hard drive. If you use fixed links in preparing your Web site and don't change them to your server address, browsers will follow those links into oblivion. No images will load; no links except your outside links will work.

HTML Testers

The hardest part about HTML is finding the inevitable typos that can prevent your page from loading or linking. If the error is buried deep in your site, you may miss it. You'll want to test every text and picture link twice—once when you've finished your site on your local hard drive, and again once you've transferred it to the ISP.

If you've been using your own HTML code or have altered code generated by a page layout program, it's a good idea to the online HTML testers, who'll check submitted pages for HTML syntax errors. They'll generate a report to make it easier for you to figure out what might be wrong so that you fix it before anyone notices it. The two

leading sites for this service are WebLint (http://www.unipress.com/cgi-bin/wwweblint) which costs $9.95 for six months of unlimited checking, and WebTechs HTML validation service (http://www.webtechs.com/html-val-svc/index.html), which is currently still free. Imagiware at http://imagiware.com has recently developed a software tool called RxHTML, which checks everything from URL links to spelling errors. For those pesky spelling errors alone, I recommend WebSter spellchecker (http://www.eece.ksu.edu/~spectre/WebSter/spell.html).

167

Keeping the Site Current

Once you have your site up and running, you'll have to deal with updating it. Modularity and simplicity are very important to a portfolio Web site. As you develop experience, you might want to add images, document an exhibit or project, or advertise an interactive CD you've just finished. This is considerably easier if you don't have to rename and relink everything in your site as you add complexity. The last item on our list involves strategies to make that easier, or at least less pressing.

Don't Date Your Pages

Avoid putting "last updated" tags on your pages. All it does is create a sense of guilt every time you visit your own pages, and draw attention to the fact that your site hasn't changed lately to everyone else. Last updated lines are only useful if you are displaying time-sensitive information, and most portfolio work doesn't change like this week's top 40.

Don't Date Yourself

Unless you have one very specific page that you expect to update for current information, try not to put any references to future events in your pages. If you feel that you must provide teasers, give a sense of what you'll be doing but nothing to indicate when to expect them. As long as you have the basic look and feel of your site in place and are satisfied with it in its initial form, resist the temptation to mention that your site is under construction.

Exchangeable Folders/ Names

This is not a tip to try if you have any qualms about how frequently you backup and how good your overall file management has been. Although it's tricky, it can be very effective if your site is modular and you have a limited amount of server space available. It requires that you have kept your Web chart current and have access to removable media.

If all you want to do is replace one set of Web pages with another set of the same number (like a rotating gallery with the

168

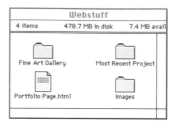

Figure 6.41
Two folders on two different disks. They have identically named files and links, but the files themselves contain updated text and different graphics.

same number of elements shown on each page), clone the exact names for the new version. Name everything the same as the first group, test them for accuracy, and simply exchange one folder for the other. Remember that exact cloning of naming and general layout similarity is critical to this trick.

Next...

Overwhelmed but still standing, you've made it through the worst portions of visualizing your portfolio, researching the best ways to showcase it, and the right people to show it to. You've decided on your physical format and learned what it will take to create a disk, CD, or Web site portfolio. Now you're done! So why isn't this the last chapter in the book? Unfortunately, we must next discuss the pressing need to safeguard your massive investment in time and energy.

CHAPTER SEVEN

Intellectual Property

...being invited to hear a man who admirably imitated a nightingale, he declined, saying he had heard the nightingale.
—Plutarch

We're very close to having a fully-functioning portfolio. In fact, you have good reason to believe that you're ready for the presentation phase. Unfortunately, digital portfolios are more subject to legal scrutiny, and more affected by the changes we've experienced in technology, than the traditional portfolio. What follows is an overview of how law affects the making, showing, and ownership of creative work.

Current Trends and Portfolios

It would be a mistake to think that intellectual property issues are new to the art and design community. Copyright protection has long been an important and evolving issue. It is true, however, that its visibility has recently been written in bright red flashing capital letters, when it used to be gray and lower case. There are so many new and wonderful ways that works of art can be borrowed, sampled, copied, altered, and out-and-out stolen that a chapter could be filled just with horror show anecdotes.

But what does this have to do with portfolios? More's the pity, a great deal. Both as creators and users of material, we must be aware of the legality of where we find our inspirations and raw materials, who might have helped to create them, and who might be tempted to misappropriate them.

Until the digital age, it was much easier to control intellectual property and much harder to break the law by mistake. Frankly, there was also less temptation. Appropriating creative work often took as much time and energy as creating it from scratch would have—or simply calling the artist and asking permission. Today, even the simple act of asking for the rights to use something can involve special expertise. The artist who created the work might have no copyright to it. The stock photos you think you have the right to collage because you paid for the royalty-free CD may in fact have reverted to the copyright of their original creator.

Note

The Government and Intellectual Property

The government, in its own endearing way, is attempting to wrestle with the issue of electronic copying. Unfortunately, being the government, it does not speak with one clear voice, nor does any statement ever rest uncontradicted or unmodified. At this point, those of us involved in art and design stand to both profit and lose from the current state of affairs.

The NII (National Information Infrastructure) Intellectual Property Preliminary Report, for example, has recommended that, among other things, "browsing" an electronic work could be a copyright infringement, because to do so you must download it to your system, thereby making a copy of it. The implications of this are potentially staggering.

On one hand, it would certainly cut down on the myriad little copyright violations that plague the Web—people's artwork appearing on unauthorized sites, for example. On the other hand, it could kill or at least hamper such things as the burgeoning digital gallery movement. (In the real world, you can just walk into a gallery and browse around. You can't walk out with a copy of the work unless you've paid for it.) If the NII recommendations become law, only people willing to pay to see screen-resolution art would visit a site, or only artists willing to weaken their copyright protection would make it available.

You want to be able to assure that you only show work that is yours to claim, and that the work you show digitally on Web or disk

172

won't turn up in someone else's project. These laudable goals are often impossible to meet in practice. All we can do is be aware of our rights and responsibilities, and try to avoid making assumptions that could get us into trouble later.

Do Unto Others... The Golden Rule of Avoiding Violations

Artists and designers are vocal about retaining intellectual property, and with good reason. In the good old days BC (before computers), there was a very thick line drawn between looking at other work for inspiration and appropriating it. Only unethical clients would use an artist's ideas without hiring him or her, not our peers. In addition, no reputable art director would consider the possibility of taking an illustrator's work and altering it for a new project. But today these things happen with increasing frequency, although sometimes in complete innocence.

How easy is it to step over the line? A small design firm in a major city experienced a massive upheaval in personnel as a creative director, junior art director, and salesperson left to begin their own firm. Projects, in various conditions, were left unfinished, many of them only existing on the departing workers' Macs. New creative people were hired and oriented almost instantly to make deadlines. The new junior art director was delegated to complete one project. She came up with one version of her own but found some artwork on her predecessor's disk that she really liked. She used it in the mock-up, changing colors, altering some aspects of it to fit the layout. The client loved it and the design firm produced it.

It was quite a shock to the entire new crew when they received a phone call from a lawyer informing them that the work had been stolen. It turns out that the drawing had been part of an illustrator's digital portfolio. The portfolio had been copied, moved from disk to disk, and all memory of its beginnings lost. The case was settled by paying the illustrator for the artwork, plus her lawyer's basic fee. From the illustrator's point of view, it could have been much worse. The design firm could have been less ethical, or the illustrator might not have had the resources to engage a lawyer. What are the lessons of this story?

Copyright Your Work— Visibly and Actually

Before you put your work into a digital portfolio format that could be reproduced and re-used, spend $20 for a copyright registry. Call the Copyright Office in Washington, DC at 202-707-9100 and have them send you a copy of the form. (No, they don't yet have online ordering!) Make sure to ask for the right form: Form VA (Visual Arts) for all forms of artistic or graphic work.

Current law states that copyright is implied without the actual need for the symbol ©, and that you have five years after the creation of the work to register it. You can't, however, actually sue for copyright infringement unless you have taken the time to register the work.

In addition, using the copyright symbol with your name will stop innocent appropriation. The proper form for doing this is:

Copyright © 1996 Your Name. All rights reserved.

Follow Up Your Leave-Behinds

173

If you have been distributing digital media around town, make a practice of checking in with the person with whom you left it. Not only is this good marketing practice to make sure you're remembered, it helps you to keep track of your work. "Oh, you're the new art director? Congratulations! Can I send you a copy of my most recent digital portfolio?" You might have to present again, but at least you have an even chance of preventing an on-disk image from taking on a life of its own.

Do Look a Gift Horse in the Mouth

You will be held responsible for the consequences of using an image, even if you were acting in good faith. If you did not personally purchase material from a reputable

source, don't use it. Like mother used to say, you never know where it's been.

Treat the Artistic Output of Others with Respect

This might seem an unnecessary admonishment, but it is surprising how many creative souls who would never use the work of another in their profession develop a blind spot when it comes to supporting material. How many illustrators, designers, or artists actually have paid for the typefaces they use? Many legally own only the fonts that shipped with their computer, although their drives are stuffed full of fonts. All too many times I've heard, "But I'm just a poor (student, artist, freelancer—choose one). I can't afford it and I'm not hurting anyone." Yet these typefaces are the product of the intellectual and creative work of other artists and designers. When fonts, photographs, and illustrations can all be dragged and dropped to your disk, everything looks like a tool. Under pressure, it's too easy to grab the nearest thing at hand and justify it later. If you're willing to do it to others, don't be surprised if someone is willing to do it to you.

What Is (and Isn't) Fair Use?

What about work that you're using just a few frames, words, or pixels of? Isn't there such a thing as "fair use"?

Fair use was intended as a vehicle for "purposes such as criticism, comment, news reporting, teaching (including multiple copies for classroom use), scholarship, or research." In other words, it is an educational and free speech vehicle. You'll notice that the listed purposes hardly cover the typical reasons for visual appropriation. In practice, however, the list of purposes is not a closed book. Satire and parody, for example, are not listed explicitly, but in practical terms have been the basis for successful fair use challenges. Even in circumstances that clearly meet the "fair use" purposes, you can step over the line, depending on whether or not your use will result in commercial gain, particularly for you the user at the expense of the original creator. Violating copyright of a commercial item for educational, non-profit purposes is generally seen as less serious than if the violator profited handsomely (or at least hoped to profit handsomely!) from the act.

In addition, the law takes into account how much of the piece you're using, and how critical that piece is to the original artwork. If you liberate a bank of clouds from the background of a photograph, chances are your theft won't be noticed or result in devaluing the original, although the practice certainly is still illegal. On the other hand, if you adopt a distinctive visual element, it doesn't matter how small a percentage of the artwork it was, or how much you've reworked it, you are still accountable. Its centrality to the concept of the piece will be a clear violation of copyright.

What about those "gray area" situations, where you think you've altered the piece to such a major degree that it qualifies as a new piece of art? The law tends to take a common sense approach to these actions. If you plucked a typical person off the sidewalk and showed her both images, would she recognize their similarity as substantial? If so, even if you have changed color, flipped, flopped, scaled, duplicated, or collaged, you have also violated the law. It's so much safer not to do it at all.

Note

There is a big difference between copying an actual artistic creation and using the idea behind it. Neither ideas nor facts can be copyrighted, only the specific means of expressing them. For example, one of the best known graphic posters from the '70s is Milton Glaser's "Dylan." If you come across this image and it inspires you to create a totally new graphic combining a solid color form and strips of curved, stylized lines, a savvy viewer will recognize that you are working in Glaser's style, but you have not violated any of his copyrights. If, on the other hand, you scan a copy of his poster, change the colors in the hair design, and straighten Dylan's nose (or replace him with a profile of Alanis Morrisette), you have done more than use an idea. You have created a derivative work and violated his copyright to the original.

Fair Use versus Derivative Work

Many people who use the phrase "fair use" are actually trying to apply it to derivative work: work that is based on the creative output of others, not the fair use of copyrighted material. The difference is a matter of type and intent. The kind of sleight of scan we're discussing here would be very hard to construe as a "fair use" situation. It is clearly the creation of a derivative work, which is defined in the Copyright Act as:

...a work based upon one or more preexisting works, such as a[n] ...art reproduction, abridgment, condensation, or any other form in which a work may be recast, transformed, or adapted. A work consisting of editorial revisions, annotations, elaborations, or other modifications which, as a whole, represent an original work of authorship, is a 'derivative work'.

The Copyright Act is very clear that only the copyright owner of the original work has the right to create a derivative work from it without first asking for and receiving written permission to do so.

Students transitioning from school to the working world are particularly likely to misunderstand this issue. They've been raised on music sampling, as well as Picasso and Braque (two artists who collaged found material like newspapers with objects and drawn forms), and often make the transition from art project to design project to commercial project without ever having been told the potential legal consequences of their actions. When the fine artist Robert Rauschenberg can be sued successfully for copyright violation in his collage work, where does a work for purely commercial purposes stand?

175

Ready for one more horror story? This one involves a student on the brink of graduating from an art school. He had been exposed to several collage projects where he was encouraged to find material in magazines. His instructor neglected to mention—or perhaps was unaware of—the difference between this time-honored process of exploring craft and material, and scanning artwork into the computer. The student went on to create illustrations for other projects by scanning and compositing from commercial magazines and design annuals. Finally, he went out to present his portfolio at an advertising agency. When the interviewer went ballistic, he had his first life lesson on copyright law. She had created one of his key images.

Copyright Retention: Who Owns Creative Work?

It must be obvious by this time that the copyright owner, and only the copyright owner, has the right to copy, duplicate, reprint, alter, or adapt their work. It is not, however, a given that because you were the creator of the original material, that you own the copyright. In a surprisingly large number of cases, the artist has no claim to the work. This can have profound implications for the creation of a digital portfolio, which by its very nature will involve copying and adaptation. Under what circumstances can an artist lose his or her rights to creative work?

"Circumstantial" Evidence of Ownership

The circumstances under which a work was created determines who owns rights to its reproduction. If you have created an image on your own time, for your own purposes, it remains yours to duplicate or alter. Even if you sell the original artwork itself, you retain the right to show copies of it in your portfolio, no matter what form that portfolio might take. If you choose to make a series of unique images in the same style, on the same theme, or with elements from the original piece, you are still free to do so.

On the other hand, work created under any other circumstance might conceivably belong instead to your employer, your client, yourself in combination with one of the above, or a third party entirely. The key to this distinction is your working relationship to the other parties.

Work for Hire and Your Portfolio

Were you an employee at the time you created the work? Did you do the work as part of your job, at the company site, while having taxes and social security deducted from your check? Did you have a supervisor who told you what the terms of your assignment were and directed your work? If so, the work you did belongs, and will continue to belong, to your employer. You can certainly claim that you did the work on your résumé, and probably carry a single copy of the work around to show others, assuming that trade or non-disclosure contracts are not in effect, but you can't copy it, sell it to someone else, or adapt it for a freelance job. If you want to use the work as part of a digital portfolio, you will need to get permission in writing from your employer to do so, because the work will be duplicated and "published" on creative director's machines.

You (or your employer or client) can't have it both ways. If you want to retain rights to the work, you can't also get the benefits of employment—sick days, health insurance, overtime, and so on. Conversely, your employer can't deny you these benefits on the grounds that you are an independent contractor unless they also treat you as such in the copyright arena.

What if you are a freelance artist or designer, not an employee? If so, you must be an independent contractor. Under those terms, you use your own materials and computer, work at home (or at least not usually at the client's office), set your own hours, and get paid for the project not by the hour. A freelance designer creating a corporate identity for a start-up firm might be a good, clear-cut example of this situation. Unless there is a contract stating otherwise, the designer retains copyright on the artwork, and the client simply has rights to use it. The nature of that use (how extensive and broad) should be negotiated at the beginning of the project. The designer has every right to reproduce this work in portfolio form.

Unfortunately, a tremendous amount of visual work changes hands in a no-man's land between where "work for hire" stretches the employer-employee relationship and is applied to a variety of other freelance situations. This is a growing problem for artists and designers, some of whom can end up in a situation where large chunks of their creative output belong to someone else. Although the work for hire law hasn't changed for decades, the problem has increased dramatically in recent years. An old-fashioned portfolio situation, where one copy of a finished work was carried around, shown, and returned to its case seldom resulted in a legal action. As long as the artist or artists made no attempt to copy or distribute the work themselves, did not claim to have done more work than they actually did, and didn't try to reuse any original art, most copyright owners looked the other way. The existence of digital artwork—infinitely and immediately duplicable—has changed all that and made the work-for-hire provision in a contract an increasingly ugly by-product of doing business.

What allows a commissioned freelance project to be termed a work-for-hire? A surprisingly broad category of work fits.

 A contribution to a "collective work" such as a large corporate Web site, a newspaper or magazine, an encyclopedia

- Something that's part of a motion picture or other audio/visual work—contributions to an interactive CD or storyboards

- A translation, a test, or answer material for a test

- Instructional text—a textbook or training package

- As a "supplementary work"—everything from maps and tables to indexes and bibliographies

- As a compilation—a database or bookmark list

If you've been looking for a common thread, you've probably noticed that the law assumes that the work would not have been made without the larger project, and that the work would not necessarily stand on its own without the larger work. On the other hand, both parties ostensibly have to agree in writing that the project should be considered a "work made for hire." This means that any item that both parties put their names to that calls it such could be considered a binding contract. The phrase has, therefore, been known to be tucked into a work contract and printed on the back of payment checks.

Assignment of Rights

As a freelancer, try to avoid being pushed into work for hire situations. This is, of course, easier said than done. But if you bear in mind that you are being asked to give up

more than the time you spend creating the work, without any of the benefits and protections an employee would receive for the same favor, you might be able to at least negotiate for some residual rights to display the work in your portfolio. This can frequently be accomplished when the freelancer and the client draw up and sign a contract at the beginning of the project, stating the artist's intent to assign the rights to the client after the work has been completed and paid for in full. This differs from a work for hire because the two of you can write the specific provisions necessary to give your client the rights they need to market or use their material without denying you the right to claim your contribution.

Team Work and Individual Rights

It is a sad commentary on human nature that people will always give in to the temptation to claim ownership of work created by others. Student team projects are a particularly obvious example of this, although the tendency for this to happen does not, alas, disappear with age.

Of course, the value of the team creation concept is that the whole should be greater than the sum of its parts. The most successful collective design projects are those in which a focus on a common goal is paramount. However, every such project is the result of individual creativity and effort, with specific elements assigned (or chosen) by individuals precisely because they have the skills, abilities, and time necessary to create, develop, and complete.

With the growing need for groups of people with different roles to work collectively on design projects, it becomes more important for the artist or designer to document such involvement. From the beginning, your contract should delineate the scope of your involvement in the project. If you will be responsible for a section of a project, or a specific group of illustrations, photos, or layouts, make sure you keep copies of your process work. If, as it sometimes happens, you are called upon to handle more material than was originally planned, make sure that the change is documented, not just to make sure that you are appropriately paid, but so you can ask for rights to show the material you created.

How to Protect Your Rights

On the CD accompanying this book, most of the participants elected to provide work that would look fine onscreen— much of it is material from their Web sites—but could not be output and appropriated. This is partially because intellectual property considerations weigh on more than one mind. Anytime an artist provides an image for mass consumption at a resolution or in a format that would allow the work to be edited or printed, he or she runs the risk of piracy without any guarantee of reparations. Besides threatening to sue, and then backing up the threat—

as one contributor is currently in the process of doing—what preventive measures exist? Can you do anything if you must provide reproduction-quality work in an intrinsically unsafe setting?

Watermarking and Digital Signatures

Until recently, the only way you could claim copyright to a digital image file was to actually overlay the copyright symbol and information directly onto the file. Although more than adequate warning for the innocent, this was not much protection against anyone with a good eye and a cloning tool, especially since you couldn't put the notice any place that was critical to viewing the work. The other method has been to provide low-resolution representations of work perfectly fine onscreen, but ugly and bitmapped when output. However, with so many images being shown on the Internet, there is nothing to prevent a determined violator from simply copying your image to their computer and placing it on their equally low-resolution Web site.

Responding to the obvious need, companies are beginning to develop invisible digital watermarks that are impossible to erase and follow the file through most forms of alteration. One company that has recently made the process elegant and simple on the Mac OS is FBI (Fingerprinting Digital Images). Their Photoshop plug-in Writer and Detector enable you to digitally imprint your images with an electronic "fingerprint." This fingerprint can be detected by a free Detector plug-in, which could eventually become a method for prospective publishers or licensees to contact you for reproduction rights. A more professional version of the software would allow someone with a large backlog of images to run the fingerprinter in batch mode. A limited version is available for downloading and experimentation (see Appendix A for software contact information). Other alternative technologies have been announced, but they have not yet been implemented in existing software. In the foreseeable future, artists will have multiple options for protecting their digital work and proving its ownership.

What To Do If the Worst Happens

There are few things more awful than the feeling of personal violation. Anyone who has ever found their work being passed off as someone else's creative output, or felt the shock of recognition when they see a portion of their art looking back at them from an unknown source, knows that feeling. Everyone's first reaction, after the shock passes, is to *do* something about it. But what?

Reacting Effectively to a Violation

Your first reaction should be to make sure that you have applied for copyright of the material. Neither you nor your lawyer can take any form of legal action without a registered piece of art. It is possible to rush through a copyright registration, but it costs more than the nominal $20-$200 to be exact. A high price to pay for procrastination.

Don't run to call a lawyer unless you happen to have one hanging around the house. Copyright law is very specific as to what you can recover from a violation and you may discover that the legal fees will hurt you more than the thief. Instead, calm down and look into the nature of the violation. If your artwork was appropriated and used in a major national publication, the time and energy you are about to expend is more likely to result in a payback than if you've seen it used on some teenager's Web page or a non-profit circular. A non-profit use doesn't mean you should give up and do nothing. It should, however, make you ask realistically what you are willing and able to do to recover your honor. If there is little or no financial impact, and no damage to your reputation, particularly if it turns out that the violator clearly thought they were operating under fair use provisions, your time might better be spent educating them.

It's also important that you be able to assign a realistic dollar value to your artwork and the effect of its loss. Legal fees don't come cheaply, and if you want to force someone to stop using and profiting from your material, you might have to have a lawyer file an injunction against them. Immediately, you've committed to more than a thousand dollars of out-of-pocket expenses. You will not be able to recoup this by simply assigning an inflated value to the work. If you have been getting a few hundred dollars an image, suddenly claiming $10,000 for this one may not be believable.

Instead of a lawyer, send a certified, business-like letter (not a hot-tempered set of empty threats) to the infringer. Let them know that you've discovered that they are using your copyrighted artwork without your permission. State clearly the nature of the work appropriated and the date or dates the violation was discovered. Then send them a realistic invoice for the use of the artwork, with a deadline for payment before you take action. If the violation took place on a Web site, make it clear that they must stop displaying your work immediately. You may receive a shocked and contrite phone call, a request to work something out, or an apologetic note with a check attached.

In the meantime, conduct a search for a lawyer versed in intellectual property issues and take a cold-eyed assessment of your risk and return. Copyright law states that you are always "entitled to recover the actual damages." This means that you can recover the money you should have been paid for legal use of the artwork, including any profits that the infringer made because they used your art, minus their own deductible expenses. However, if your art accounts for only a small portion of their profits (one design element used in one screen of a multi-megabyte CD, for example), the profits will be pro-rated accordingly. Even so, if the vehicle for the infringement was a

major publication, your actual damages could be substantial. Contrast this with the actual damages from a non-profit, personal Web site with no commercial content. Your honor could be satisfied, but not before a legal battle costing far more than your lost profits. It is also possible that you could be awarded legal fees if you prevail in court, but these are given at the discretion of the courts, which are overcrowded with tort actions and are possibly unsympathetic to an action they feel should have been settled out of court.

This less than encouraging assessment changes somewhat if you had the foresight to register your work before the copyright infringement took place—particularly if you did so within the first three months of the work's creation. Besides demonstrating that the work was, in your opinion, a valuable expression worthy of copyright protection, you may be rewarded for your diligence. Statutory damages have the potential of punishing an infringer more seriously than actual damages can. Let's say that the use was an obvious and deliberate infringement. Statutory damages in lieu of actual damages can run as high as $100,000—not trivial at all.

If your infringer stonewalls, or you receive a corporate "up yours" letter, it's time to consider legal action. If your financial assessment says that the process could be worth it, call the lawyer you've researched and provide all the documentation you can. Make sure your lawyer makes every effort to settle the case out of court before taking that

final step. Even if you get less money than you think you deserve, anyone who has ever spent serious time in the court system will tell you going to trial is worse. The wheels of justice turn slowly and expensively when they turn at all.

You may decide that you can't afford to go to court. If the infringer is a professional and they choose to stonewall you rather than apologize or negotiate, this is the time to call in your network of friends and associates. Speak to relevant professional guilds and associations. Some of them have funds set aside for copyright actions. If the work has been used to create a commercial printed product for a company, consider contacting the client directly. Send a cover letter with a clipping of your stolen artwork and ask them to compare it to the non-original art and judge for themselves. If your work has appeared on a Web site, contact the Internet service provider. They may find it in their best interests to exert pressure on the violator. Sometimes public shame will do what good conscience will not.

Next...

With luck, common sense, and some proactive work, you may never have to be the recipient or the initiator of a copyright lawsuit. Being aware of the potential for problems is not, alas, a guarantee against them. However, minimizing your exposure can allow you to move toward presenting your portfolio with more peace of mind.

CHAPTER EIGHT

Finishing Touches

It usually takes me more than three weeks to prepare a good impromptu speech.
—Mark Twain

Well, we've made it to the final stretch. You've created, digitized, altered, and designed your way to a new expression of your work, but we're not finished yet. We need to integrate your digital portfolio into the real world, and then invite that world to view it. How effectively you do this will have a tremendous effect on whether you'll end up feeling that the result was worth the effort.

God Is in the Details: Putting the Package Together

Just because you've done the byte thing doesn't mean you're ready for the next presentation. If you still have non-electronic materials, you'll need to make sure they are organized, sequenced, and in good traveling condition. Then, you'll need to pull the disparate elements into one presentable package.

Mounting

Chances are you have some treasured pieces that are worth presenting in person. Some might be oversize or three-dimensional pieces (like a CD jewel case, a small package design, or an annual report) that you might carry separately in a case. Flat art, however, should always be mounted on a stiff, solid color board. Mounting board or foam core board is available in black and white only. Mat board comes in a wide variety of colors, but there is a de facto assumption that everything for a portfolio should be mounted on black. Black shows the effects of wear and tear more slowly and tends to be a neutral element.

If you have material of different sizes that is not too radically different in dimensions, consider standardizing on one consistent board size and finding a portfolio case that holds them with little or no room for the material to shift. Not only will this keep your materials' wear and tear to a minimum, but it is also a satisfying presentation solution. This is a particularly useful suggestion for architects, whose original work is usually too large and unwieldy to present as is. Because almost everything will need to be resized anyway, you can "build" your presentation to an optimal size (see Figure 8.1).

184

Add-Ons

If you have slides or transparencies, bring a loupe or a small light box (see Figure 8.2). You simply can't count on your contact

having one on hand, and the amount of time it might take to locate one will reflect badly on you. Unless your contact tells you that a slide carousel will be available for you, don't request or expect one. If it's actually there when you arrive, almost inevitably you will find it placed in an awkward position or will be difficult to focus. Having to fuss with low-grade technology will make both you and your audience impatient.

Non-Electronic Leave-Behinds

Despite having a digital portfolio, it's always a nice touch to have another form of portfolio leave-behind to accompany it. Sometimes clients or potential employers appreciate tear-sheets or digitally printed reprints. If your work involves printed art or photography, this can be a good way of showing your work in tangible form.

Figure 8.1
Elegant graphic design portfolio with material optimized to fit within a carrying case.

Figure 8.2
Versions of the photographic loupe, a magnifying lens of varying quality for viewing details in photographic images.

Incorporating the Résumé

Obviously, your résumé should be as carefully thought out as the rest of your presentation package. Despite the fact that your portfolio will be your single most important element, your résumé will be used as a filter. Most design directors won't even look at a prospective artist or designer until they've seen his or her résumé, because they know how time-consuming a full-fledged presentation can be. Therefore, it should act as an extension of your portfolio, both in concept and in presentation. If you treat it as a lesser element, you run the risk of it ending up face down in the circular file.

This is not just good advice for the neophyte. If you've been sending your résumé around for years, it might be time to reevaluate it. Does it convey the same impression you've worked to develop in your portfolio? If not, it's time to redesign. From design firm to corporate environment, a creative person's résumé is expected to stand out. The plain word processed résumé is not for you. Such a non-presentation makes it so much easier to toss the excess paper. Even in the more predictable environments of corporate communications or desktop publishing, your résumé should be distinctive, albeit tamer.

Distinctive doesn't mean overwhelming. It is possible to make a résumé that is so "creative" that no one would want to hire you. Your résumé must still legibly inform. I once received a piece that liberally used tinted spot varnish as a second color and flowed text into amorphous containers. The whole exercise seemed like overkill, particularly when I realized that the artist had neglected to include a telephone number.

Be Concise

Unless you are in academia or an artist listing exhibits, try to avoid creating a two-page résumé. Be concise. If you've had an extensive professional history, eliminate those lines about personal interests, software skills, and your earliest job positions unless they were particularly unusual or important. If you put your personality and expertise into your design, you won't need to state that you are fascinated by good typography—it will be obvious. As for your software skills, young professionals are usually told to list them because their résumés are thin and they need the extra edge for those early jobs when production abilities are critical. For an established professional, a phrase like "expertise in a variety of graphic software on the *X* platform, specifics on request," might be sufficient, unless you happen to be unusually knowledgeable in one package.

Choose Type with Care

A graphic designer should be typographically literate, but many artists or people in other design disciplines know little about typographic conventions. If you don't know much about typography, don't pretend that you do. Stick to one typeface with a bold and italic weight for headings, avoid all caps, and use indents and extra line spaces between sections to keep the résumé open and easy to read. For further reading on typography, I recommend *Digital Type Design Guide* (Hayden Books) and *Branding with Type* (Adobe Press).

Text Is Craft, Too

One of the most consistent résumé problems is sloppy text and bad grammar. Such errors couldn't happen in a worse package than your résumé. I've seen QuarkXPress spelled with an E and Photoshop with an initial F. Maybe you're a terrific artist but a lousy speller. That's okay, but this is your résumé, not email to a friend. Acknowledge the problem and use a spellchecker. Proof proper names carefully, and look up things if you're not sure. Even if no one will ever ask you to spell anything again, errors in a résumé say that you're careless. And if you could be careless about something so personal, what type of work will you do in the job?

Packaging the Digital Portfolio

Designing a disk or CD portfolio is only part of the task, albeit a very critical part. Now you have to get people to view it. Almost anywhere you send a résumé and diskette probably gets dozens of them in a month. Why should a design director pay more attention to your offering than the one that comes tomorrow? Remember that diskettes in the raw are non-communicative and omnipresent. You probably have a few in boxes, lying around on your computer table, or stacked somewhere. So does the typical contact. If your material looks generic, it could easily be relabeled and reused without ever being looked at, or tossed in the trash in a fit of house cleaning. This is a particular problem with CDs, which don't even have the cache of reusability that might make someone keep them around for future reference.

Completing the Image

To raise the odds that your work will be given a hearing, your digital portfolio should be attractively packaged. Ideally, this means a label on the media itself, a mailer, or case that is designed consistently with the media label, and, possibly, a contents insert.

Diskette

Never use an off-the-shelf label on your portfolio diskette. At the very least, you can buy laser-safe Avery labels 9-up on a sheet. Design a diskette label and output on a decent 600 dpi printer with good black coverage. If the coverage in solid black areas is insufficient, touch it up with a black permanent marker. Some inexpensive ink jet printers can also print on these labels, and it might be a good alternative to introduce spot color into the design. Color laser prints have come down in price and more service bureaus now offer them as options. Using these for short-run color printing can be very cost-effective and enables you to create labels that incorporate portions of your diskette artwork as an easy stylistic reminder for the busy art director. Nothing says you can't use normal paper stock and printing

processes for your labels. Have them trimmed to size and glue them carefully to the label area. This may take a little longer, but the range of paper choices it offers can make the extra work worthwhile.

Note

Although many people create templates from scratch in publishing software, dedicated labeling packages make the process considerably easier and are worth considering if you might have additional uses for them.

On the PC side, there's Soft Keys Key Label Designer CD-ROM for Windows (http://www.softkey.com or 1-800-227-5809). It comes with over 350 preexisting formats and imports artwork from all standard graphics formats.

For the Mac OS, Synex has a commercial product called Label Press. With a list price of $299, this is not a product to buy on a whim, but it offers text and drawing tools, a multiplicity of template formats for many more labels than just diskettes, and is very customizable. Contact Synex at http://www.snx.com.

Ideally, you should continue this process to its logical conclusion by creating a mailer or disk holder to protect the media and providing information about system requirements or installation instructions (see Figure 8.3). This level of detail not only makes your material more memorable, it keeps your diskette separate from the pile of other diskettes on your contact's desk.

Figure 8.3
Sample diskette package. The mailer format protects the diskette and identifies the material.

CD-ROM Disc

CDs look naked without some type of label. Many people try the do-it-yourself approach. Unfortunately, this is a very bad idea with recordable CDs. Rolling ball, pencils, or standard ball-point pens can damage the delicate media. Most standard issue pre-stick labels, including many laser-safe brands, are made with an adhesive that eats away at the disk's coating. This is also true of most tapes and glues. The most professional way to label your work is have it directly printed on the CD, but that generally is too expensive for the individual or small firm. Alternatively (and more cheaply), you can get a 100-label kit with labels and an applicator for under $50. One company that manufactures this product is Pro-Source, which can be reached at `http://www.inter-look.com/prosource` or at 1-800-903-1234.

There are many creative ways to deal with a CD-ROM's external packaging besides the standard jewel box that are cheap to mail and environmentally friendly. Most of them require professional printing and die cutting. For very short runs of demo CD portfolios, it is probably easier to create the front cover as a single fold insert and design an inlay card for the back of the jewel case.

Getting Professional Feedback or Hands-On Advice

Once you've completed your work, whatever its form, you might want some feedback from fellow professionals who will look at your work with a fresh eye. Trusted, knowledgeable, and discriminating friends are a valuable source. When you have created something in a format that is new to you, objectivity is very valuable.

If you're a student, people are often generous in providing feedback. Some schools are beginning to post student work online for critiques, but the old-fashioned method of presenting to faculty is worthwhile. Take advantage of any opportunity that arises. The tried and true route of informational interviews can be applied to the portfolio package itself. You'll get feedback on your work and your presentation of it.

The online community is a particularly good resource for feedback, although there are several important caveats to consider. It's very import when soliciting help from strangers that you have some sense of who and how qualified they are. This isn't always easy to do online. A little common sense, however, goes a long way. Before you ask for a critique, follow the comments of the newsgroup, list, or chat participants first. This is called lurking and it will help you separate the knowledgeable posters from the impostors. If one exists, read the FAQ (Frequently Asked Questions) file for the group. You may discover that posting "Please critique my Web portfolio" is frowned upon there.

It is better to post requests for feedback in online lists dedicated to discussing your area than to send out a multi-newsgroup Usenet request. (See Appendix A for subscription lists in relevant areas.) Serious professionals are more likely to subscribe to such lists because they want to avoid off-topic flame wars and spamming, as well as complete newbies and amateurs in their fields.

Don't ask for help, however, if you aren't prepared to take the heat. People are often more honest in their opinions if they don't have to watch your face when giving them.

Advertising Your Portfolio

The most terrific portfolio in the civilized world may be lurking in the hands of a humble, shy artist waiting patiently to be recognized for his or her evident genius. If so, we can only hope that the artist has another form of income. A sufficient number of good artists and designers practice the art of self-promotion such that our brilliant hypothetical will have to be very lucky indeed to be noticed.

Promotion is not a dirty word. True, there are people whose tireless and egotistical pursuit of attention has given the practice a bad name. Yet if you believe in your work, if it gives you pleasure, and if you'd rather be creating for a living than anything else, you should be prepared to be your own advocate.

Being Visible

The world will not come to you. Unless you are an established artist or illustrator with an agent representative who takes your book around, you are condemned to getting out there and getting noticed. This involves developing a protective shell, because with self-promotion occasionally comes rejection. If you are an artist and you land a show, you should create your own promotional material and send it to media outlets and reviewers. If your work has a tie-in to a local issue or neighborhood, contact an advocacy group working on the subject for help disseminating the material.

Never leave the house without carrying a few business cards. This may seem extreme, but a few cards in your wallet could prevent a missed opportunity. I know of one young designer who landed a CD cover for an alternative record label by being at the right club at the right time.

Go to art and design events, and talk with people there. Remember that contacts in the community can lead to recommendations and referrals later. You'll also have the pleasure of talking with other people who care about some of the same things that you do, which is a wonderful spark to creative ideas and new directions.

Web Site

Publicizing your Web site is the other side of researching your audience. All the connections you made in lists, Usenet groups, and chat areas are places to let people know what you're up to. Once your site is up, add its address to your email signature, along with one or two lines about its content. Be descriptive, short, and subtle. If you're good with words, try to include a teaser to draw people in.

Don't neglect all those search engines and directories either. You want your site to pop up when someone does a search looking for your specialty. Every one of these sites

encourages you to add your URL because you're helping them do their work. Some sites let you bundle your efforts into one simple form. Visit `http://www.submit-it.com` and register with several of your targets at once.

Make connections to the new interest-related sites that are organized as online source books for people in your profession. Most of them have no fees (at least not yet!) and usually take the form of searchable listings as a resource for buyers. The Digital Directory, for example, covers everything from illustration to multimedia at `http://www.DigitalDirectory.com`. Virtual Résumé at `http://www.virtualresume.com/vitae` maintains a résumé and portfolio database, as well as job search information. There are more and more of these source book sites coming online everyday.

Note

Although it might be excessive, it's possible to skew searches to guarantee that your site is one of the first to match a query for design, architecture, video, or any other area. If you use the keyword frequently on your home page, the engine will consider it to be a better match than a similar page that mentions the keyword only once. Don't go overboard with this, or what you're trying to do may be all too obvious to the viewer.

If you haven't made a Web site yet, don't try to get around the issue by buying a listing online on a general site. You may think that you're adhering to the self-promotion principle, but in fact you're throwing your money away. When most people hit those sites, they tend to do what any right-thinking person would with cheap advertising stuck in the middle of a book—they ignore it.

Presenting Your Portfolio

Your portfolio will speak for you, but only to a degree. Unlike many corporate settings where Human Resources sets the hiring specs and people are plugged like Legos into existing work groups, most design jobs or art contracts are awarded on intangibles. With many good artists and designers out there, why should a contact give the job to you?

Getting in the Door

A surprising number of positions and assignments are filled through word of mouth. People rely on their network of sources to find the right person for a job. Use your network to help you here. If you're a student or recent graduate, try to find a faculty sponsor who is willing to make supporting phone calls or write letters in your behalf. Maybe you graduated from the same art school as your interviewer. Many people are strong partisans of the programs at their colleges or grad schools. If an appropriate occasion arises for you to mention it, do so.

Don't just mass mail your portfolio; it's a waste of time and materials. Start by looking for agencies or studios where you think your work and interests will fit. Read *Ad Week*, visit Web sites, and look through design publications to learn more about your target firms' work. Use the strategies mentioned in Chapter 1, and check Appendixes A and B for specific information. Once you've narrowed down your field, call ahead and find the right person to direct your inquiries. Be straightforward about what you want, don't make them guess why you're calling, and above all, be polite. Ask if you can send your résumé and a diskette sample of your portfolio. Describe succinctly and clearly the kind of work you do and why you would fit in at her firm. Don't run on, and don't make the person at the other end say those nasty words, "I'm sorry, I have a meeting to attend." End the phone call without being prompted.

Even if your contact tells you no positions are available, or that he's happy with his current suppliers, send a short follow-up note thanking him for giving you his time, and enclose your résumé for him to keep on file. Situations can change quickly and your résumé could land on his desk just as another employee unexpectedly leaves.

Targeting the Individual

If your initial contact results in an appointment to show your work or to send your digital portfolio, begin to plan your presentation. Under some situations, a portfolio can be customized to fit individual situations. It's worthwhile to do so if you know or can find out anything about the individual or group you'll be presenting to. This kind of information used to be difficult to track down. Not anymore.

People leave a trail. If they design in a well-known firm, you should search *Communication Arts*, *ID Magazine,* or *Architectural Digest* for mention of them and their work. If you are presenting in a corporate setting, check out trade magazines for that industry. Look for a personal Web page, a résumé, or any biographical material. Check Deja News for postings. This is not dirty pool; this is research. Remember that anything posted on the Net is not a private communication. You will be presenting to people who will have your résumé in hand, have references to check, and will expect to know a fair amount about you and your work. It's only fair for you to even the odds a little.

Even if you don't know much more about your contact than his or her name, you can tailor your digital presentation to him or her. If you are planning to bring a diskette with your digital portfolio as a leave-behind, go back to the original software. Create a new title slide with his or her name on it and a short letter, and remake your player or projector application with this new frame at the beginning or end. If you are a freelancer and expect to do these presentations on a regular basis, make this frame when you make the original work, then merge it in with a new name for future situations. If you created a portfolio animation, ask what specific computer model your contact will

be viewing your work on. If it's significantly faster or slower than what you originally optimized for, adjust your timing.

The Presentation Itself

Whether you are presenting digital material, a video tape on-screen, or showing printed work or slides, you should be prepared to put your material in context for others. This is inextricably linked with how you present yourself and your work.

Looking the Part

Even if you have very strong opinions about working in a loose, casual environment, you don't improve your chances of finding it by showing up for an interview in torn jeans and a T-shirt. (This even holds true for artists visiting gallery owners, unless the gallery's work and general appearance indicates that such an approach might actually be useful.) In almost anyone's book, extreme clothing telegraphs a lack of respect for the interviewing company, or an ego so all-consuming that the person is unaware of the impact on others. It also, paradoxically, implies that you are inflexible and might be difficult to work with, as well as being someone who would have to be kept insulated from clients.

This doesn't mean that you must show up for an interview clad in a corporate uniform. Precisely what you wear should be dictated by your common sense assessment of the kind of place at which you're interviewing and the image you want to portray. For example, an interview at an established, large company's in-house design department demands a more conservative presentation than the local, two-person animation studio. In fact, the animation studio partners might be put off by a white shirt, power tie look. As a rule, it's a good idea not to use your personal wardrobe to make a statement. Your creative work is supposed to do that. The best all-around interview attire is a happy medium—clean, tasteful, and professional.

The guidelines for presentations are slightly different if you are working directly with clients. You need to give the impression that you are enough of a solid citizen to get the work done, but a total button-down look can sometimes be the wrong image. It is strange but true; many clients expect a creative person to "look" creative. This still doesn't mean bizarre, in-your-face clothing, but sharp, good quality clothes that telegraph a personal style are very acceptable for professionals in the arts.

Talking About Your Process

Once you are contacted to come in and present, go through your portfolio and rehearse what you are going to say about each piece and your work in general. You'll want to clarify your role in creating the work, especially if you have done more than the design. Did you also create the illustrations or write the copy? Was the work completed in a tight time-frame?

Don't just do this in your head—speak out loud. Be aware of time-stalling mannerisms and work to minimize them. "Like" is a word for comparing two things, not an alternative to "um." Go through the actual physical act of presentation to make sure that it's easy to pull out mounted boards from a case, and that you can access each individual element without rummaging around for it.

Rehearsal doesn't mean memorization, which leaves no room for personality or spontaneity. Nor does it mean developing a sales pitch. That tends to turn off other creative people, especially in smaller firms. It does mean feeling prepared for the process, which should make you feel more confident. Expect questions about your experience and your goals. These are eminently predictable questions, but it's surprising how many people seem unprepared to address them in interviews. Above all, know why you made the design decisions evident in your work. "It just came to me," will sound as weak as it is. How can you be hired as a client problem-solver if you can't describe the problem?

Above all, never apologize for your work. You can discuss design constraints, your client's specific requirements, or problems and solutions, but never point out what's wrong with a piece, or with your skills. That isn't perfectionism, it's suicide. By this time, you should have eliminated from your portfolio anything that doesn't reflect well on you.

On the opposite side, don't sling the bull. If you are presenting to other knowledgeable professionals in your field, they will be able to tell if you don't really know what you're talking about. Telling your audience, "The process of developing this identity helped the client redefine their product mix," might be reasonable. Telling them, "My logo design resulted in a 20% increase in employee productivity" is absurd. If you are asked a reasonable question that is based in knowledge that you don't have, it's better to admit it than be caught trying to cover up your ignorance of the subject.

Talking about your work can also involve listening. I once attended a presentation by a highly respected design professional who turned every query about how he might approach a specific client problem into a lecture about how good he was at addressing client problems. Despite his star reputation, this introduced doubts in his audience about whether they could work with him. He too clearly projected his own agenda.

Don't be thrown by questions geared toward finding out who you are and what you might be like on a design team. Your personal chemistry with the interviewers is something you can't control. Either it's there or it isn't, but if you're prepared for the questions, it will be easier for you to loosen up and let your personality come through.

Tips on Presenting Your Material

Once you're in the process of presenting, there are some general guidelines to help you make your presentation more fluid.

Present your work facing the client. You should know your material well enough to be able to glance at it briefly and point to relevant places on-screen or off without having to turn your back for more than a brief set-up period.

Speak up. If people keep asking you to repeat what you've said, you are talking too softly or quickly. People who are naturally quiet or shy tend to go monotone when they present, because they are afraid of being embarrassed. Even though it may go against the grain, try to keep a normal conversational tone, and pitch your volume to that of the other people in the room. Think of the audience as if they were your colleagues.

Make eye contact. Don't get obsessive about this or it will come across as a Dale Carnegie ploy. And certainly don't play Svengali, holding eye contact so long that you make people uncomfortable and draw attention away from your portfolio. Eyes are the windows to the soul, and if you want to know how you're doing, or whether you can work with people, try to catch their eye occasionally as you speak.

Don't be afraid to show interest and enthusiasm. If you were excited about a project you worked on and proud of the result, talk about that. Energy and good humor can be infectious,

194

particularly if you are looking for a position as part of a development team.

 Be aware of your audience. If they are fidgeting, you're probably moving too slow or going into too much detail. In most presentations, you'll have about 30 minutes from the moment you walk in the door and shake hands to the moment you close the book and leave your business card, résumé, and samples. If they want to prolong the interview, they'll ask questions, offer you coffee, or invite someone else in to look at your work.

Following Up

The presentation isn't finished when you walk out the door. If you are interested in the position, you should make that clear by making your interest tangible. The form that takes will depend on the nature of the interaction and the position. For job interviews, a thank-you note, particularly on your own letterhead, or a nicely designed card can make a big difference.

Some presentations are made because a specific project is on the horizon. If the interview itself seems to have gone well and you've been asked to develop a proposal, act quickly and responsibly. How you follow up will color your presentation and crystallize your contact's impression of you. If you promise to call the next day, do it. It's an indication of whether you can be trusted to treat a deadline seriously. If you're excited

by the project, make your enthusiasm clear. As Mark D'Oliveira says, "Some people call back after a weekend with, 'I really like this thing and here's what we can do in these 10 areas.' A company that just says, 'Yeah, we can do it—just tell us what you want us to do' doesn't sound as if they'll contribute as much." No one wants to baby-sit a supplier through a project. The whole point of hiring someone from outside is the hope that he'll bring a special creativity and expertise to the project.

Note

The text for a thank-you note should be professional, short, and warm but not effusive. It should be addressed to the person who conducted the interview. Make sure you spell his or her name right, and don't refer to other people in the interview by name unless you are certain of who they are. Such a note could go something like this:

Dear Scott,

Thank you for the opportunity to present my portfolio to your group yesterday. I really appreciated the give and take, and hope we'll have the chance to continue the process in the future.

Hope to hear from you soon,

Linda Jones

Some presentations are made because a specific project is on the horizon. If the interview itself seems to have gone well and you've been asked to develop a proposal, act quickly and responsibly. How you follow up will color your presentatio and crystallize your contact's impression of you. If you promise to call the next day, do it. It's an indication of whether you can be trusted to treat a deadline seriously. If you're excited by the project, make your entusiasm clear. As Mark D'Oliveria says, "Some people call back after a weekend with, 'I really like this thing and herc's what wc can do in these areas.' A company that just says 'Yeah, we can do it—just tell us what you want us to do' doesn't sound as if they'll contribute as much." No one wants to baby-sit a supplier through a project. The whole point of hiring someone from outside is the hope that he'll bring a special creativity and expertise to the project.

Finally, don't get discouraged if the presentation doesn't result in a job or assignment initially. Your style may not fit their current concept for a project, or they may have found someone with more of the experience they need. Stay in touch. If you have a new collection of work in a few months, send it to your contacts with a cover letter reminding them of who you are. Make phone calls on a regular cycle (once every six weeks is reasonable) to see if there's something new available, or if they'd like to see more work. Keep the conversations short and upbeat. If you add a Web site to your portfolio, make sure you send a note announcing the URL and inviting your contacts to visit it. If your work is good, persistence will usually be rewarded.

Conclusion

If you've stuck with this program to the end, congratulations! You have entered the world of digital portfolios and you'll probably never leave it again. Most of the hardest work in any new endeavor is found at the bottom of the learning curve and you've finally crested the top. From this point on, your focus should be on refining your presentation and updating as you work on new projects. A digital portfolio isn't really finished unless you decide to stop creating and learning. There are always new possibilities, better solutions, and stronger concepts to be developed. Never before could an artist or designer expect her portfolio to truly reflect the immediacy of her creative process. Now it's possible. Approach each new iteration of your portfolio with the knowledge that if you truly love what you do, each process of portfolio creation is another chance to convey that continued commitment to the world.

APPENDIX A

Internet Resources

Stepping Through a Profile Search on the Web

This search is based on the hypothetical situation outlined in Chapter 1.

You know that the client is a large Asian telecommunications firm trying for a broader international presence. What does this tell you about where to go next? First, you'll need to search telecommunications as an industry. How many large international firms are there based in Asian countries? How many already have Web sites?

Your first stop is Yahoo (http://www.yahoo.com), the best-known and most comprehensive subject index of information on the Web, and a search of Trade & Industry. This has many sub-categories, one of which happens to be Telecommunications. One of its subcategories is Organizations.

Scrolling down this list, we find something promising: a link to the Pacific Telecommunications Council home page.

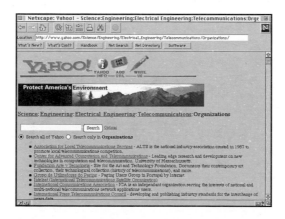

Figure A.1
Result of Yahoo Telecommunications: Organizations search.

Figure A.2
Pacific Telecommunications Council (PTC) home page.

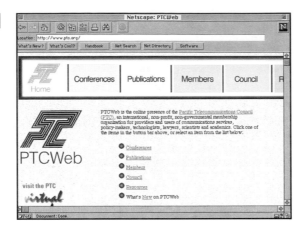

Here on the PTC home page, we have several buttons. All of them have research possibilities, but one button will actually give us a list of members.

Knowing who the competing players are can be very useful. The members page gives an alphabetical list with countries of origin, enabling us to narrow our search. By the member names, we'll be able to eliminate any companies that are consultants or PR firms, and concentrate on Asian-based companies.

Stage two is to find out more about these telecommunications firms. Let's move to the search engines. One of my favorite sites is the Internet Sleuth (`http://www.isleuth.com`). It submits queries to a large number of individual databases, allowing you to choose those most likely to result in appropriate information. It's also relatively easy to reach, even during Web prime time.

Let's try a broad search on the word "telecommunications."

Figure A.3
PTC member list.

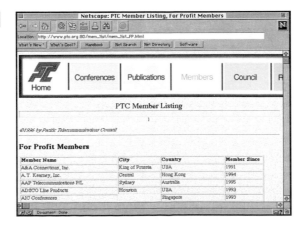

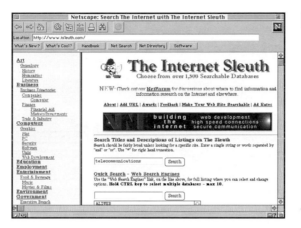

Figure A.4
*Internet Sleuth
home page.*

The result of our search gives us a list of searchable databases. The first one on the list is Singapore Web Sites. Since Singapore is right in our target area, we choose this link as the first one to explore, and once again search on "telecommunications."

Only one company comes up, the Singapore Telecommunications Ltd. It links to the corporate Web site.

Hmm. The home page takes over a minute to load on a T1 line. When it finally does, it's just one collaged graphic and a corporate heading. If this is the potential client, could we be looking at part of the company's dissatisfaction?

From here, we can explore the rest of the Web site for style and function, as well as read the company's positioning information. Afterwards we can return to our Internet Sleuth list of results and follow another database for more objective information about the company and its marketplace. We can also refer to the list of companies from

199

Figure A.5
*Singapore Web
Sites home page.*

Figure A.6
*Singapore Telecom-
munications Ltd.
home page.*

our Yahoo search and hunt through the various databases for other links. Eventually, we'll not only find all the major players in the Asian telecommunications market, we'll know how they're presenting themselves online. Of the ones which have Web sites, perhaps we'll even be able to figure out who our prospective client is. If we're really lucky, *Advertising Age* or *Ad Week* may even tell us who designed the Web page they're dissatisfied with.

These databases and search engines are just the beginning of the options available to you.

Deja News Usenet Group Search

1. Using your browser, go to Deja News (http://www.dejanews.com).

Figure A.7
*Deja News home
page.*

2. Choose Power Search from the icons at the top of the page.

3. In Power Search, choose the list and sort by newsgroup options, and type in the word or words you want to search.

4. Click the Find button.

5. A list of topics sorted by newsgroup appears. In our example, we can see that some newsgroups seem to be more appropriate for a professional interested in the topic of digital photography than others.

6. Read some postings from your potential lists. Are the participants operating at a level that seems appropriate to your needs? If so, this may be the group or groups for you.

Figure A.8
Deja News Power Search form.

201

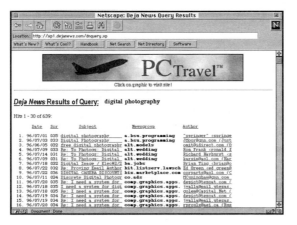

Figure A.9
Deja News results in list form.

Good Mass Marketing Career/ Job Sites

Career magazine's offering of career resource links.

> http://www.careermag.com/
> careermag/links.html

The Virtual Job Fair: a resume listing and job posting site.

> http://www.vjf.com

Contains ads from major U.S. newspapers in 17 major cities. A tremendous savings in time and energy.

> http://www.careerpath.com/

An ad agency for recruitment advertisers, this site is only useful for design-related positions with a strong technical component but is very good for that.

> http://www.monster.com

Sites with a Specific Agenda in the Arts and Design Fields

These are more rare than the plethora of general sites. Most of them are buried in larger sites with broader agendas. Some places to try first:

The Graphix Exchange is a directory specifically geared to freelance artists in all major areas, from photography to illustration to graphic design. Names link to email addresses and Web pages. This is an excellent place to publicize your own Web page, or to see what other professionals are doing online.

> http://bin.gnn.com/gnn/wic/
> wics/graph.14.html

A new Web area, 3DSite was created for the online 3-D computer graphics community. Its TalentHunter area has both a listing (http://www.3dsite.com/3dsite/service) and a job board.

> http://www.3dsite.com/3dsite/

Communication Arts magazine offers a full-featured site with job listings for design-related fields.

> http://www.commarts.com/

Design Online's Compass area leads to several topics, one of them being jobs and portfolios.

> http://www.dol.com/Root/
> compass/dcompass.html

Designlink is primarily a west coast site offering a no-charge listing for design professionals, and a for-fee portfolio space, which they will either compile from your material or will link to your Web site.

> http://www.designlink.com/
> designlink/

Foundation and funding sources listed for the visual arts.

```
http://www.artsusa.org/
hotline/vhlresrc.htm
```

ArtsNet: a nascent listing of arts-related jobs. Still very thin, but promising.

```
http://artsnet.heinz.cmu.edu/
career/careerService.html
```

How to Subscribe to a Mailing List

Most of the following lists have the same procedure for subscribing. Every list has two addresses, one with the name of the list itself, the other usually with the word LISTSERV or LISTPROC in it. The latter address is where you send your subscription request. Leave the subject line and the rest of your email header blank.

In the body of the email send:

sub [COMMAND NAME OF LIST] [YOUR NAME]

For example:

sub TYPO-L Rachel Martin

would be a subscription request to Typo-L Discussion of Type and Typographic Design.

Include no other text and delete your signature file if you have one.

Busy lists will ask you to confirm your subscription, and then they will send you an acknowledgement and a document with instructions on how to post or reply. Make sure to keep this document handy. I have a folder with my Internet software labeled ListServs where I save all my individual list instructions—they're NOT all the same. It's considered good etiquette to refer to these instructions when you need to leave the list—as you will if you're going on vacation or can't handle the email volume. No one can "take you off the list" without the correct email request from you to the LISTSERV address.

Suggested Mailing Lists for Artists and Designers

This list has been edited by the author for those mailing lists most likely to be useful for professional networking. For a comprehensive "list of lists" searchable by subject, try Liszt: Director of Email Discussion Groups (http:/www.liszt.com).

Art and Design Related Mailing Lists

Architecture
Architecture Forum

> Mail the command
> DIS-STD-ARCH to
> listproc@sc.ist.ucf.edu.

Association for Computer-Aided Design in Architecture

> Mail the command acadia-l to
> listserv@unm.edu.

Basic and Applied Design (Art
and Architecture)

> Mail the command DESIGN-L to
> `LISTSERV@PSUVM.PSU.EDU.`

Landscape Architecture Electronic Forum

> Mail the command LARCH-L to
> `LISTSERV@LISTSERV.SYR.EDU.`

Art

Art & Design Discussion List

> Mail the command art-design to
> `listproc@bilkent.edu.tr.`

204

Art Educators

Arts in Education

> Mail the command aie to
> `listproc@artsedge.kennedy`
> `center.org.`

Computer Graphics Arts and Design
Educators

> Mail the command
> cgad-educators to
> `listproc@sphinx.Gsu.EDU.`

Computer Graphics Education Newsletter

> Mail the command CGE to
> `LISTSERV@VM.MARIST.EDU.`

Fine Arts

Fine Arts Computing Group

> Mail the command ART193 to
> `LISTSERV@GWUVM.GWU.EDU.`

Film and Video

MEDIAWEB Film/Video Web Sites
Discussion

> Mail the command MEDIAWEB to
> `LISTSERV@VM.TEMPLE.EDU.`

Graphics

Discussion of Type and Typographic Design

> Mail the command TYPO-L to
> `LISTSERV@IRLEARN.UCD.IE.`

Graphic Design Discussion

> Mail the command GRAPHICS to
> `LISTSERV@ULKYVM.`
> `LOUISVILLE.EDU.`

Graphic Showcase Ezine Mailing List

> Mail the command graphics to
> `Majordomo@efn.org.`

Industrial and Other
3-D Design

Art-Tech

> Mail the command art-tech to
> `listproc@nmsu.edu.`

Discussion List On Environmental &
Outsider Arts

> Mail the command art-environs to
> `Majordomo@pobox.com.`

Industrial Design Forum

> Mail the command IDFORUM to
> `LISTSERV@YORKU.CA.`

Marketing

Marketing on the Internet

> Mail the command MKINET-L to
> LISTSERV@SUVM.SNCC.LSU.EDU.

Multimedia

Discussion of Interactive Music/Multimedia Standard Environments

> Mail the command MAX to
> LISTSERV@VM1.MCGILL.CA.

Interactive Multimedia Design and Development, Topics and Issues in New Media

> Mail the command mmdd-l to
> listproc@hawaii.edu.

Interactive Multimedia List

> Mail the command imm-l to
> listproc@scu.edu.au.

Macintosh Multimedia Discussion List

> Mail the command MACMULTI to
> LISTSERV@fccjvm.fccj.cc.fl.us.

Macromedia Director for Macintosh and Windows

> Mail the command DIRECT-L to
> LISTSERV@UAFSYSB.UARK.EDU.

Macromedia Software Discussion

> Mail the command macromedia to
> majordomo@acpub.duke.edu.

Media Authoring and Publishing Mailing List

> Mail the command mediapub to
> Majordomo@netbot.
> mindspring.com.

Multimedia Discussions

> Mail the command
> freebsd-multimedia to
> Majordomo@FreeBSD.ORGM.

Photography and Photojournalism

Adobe Photoshop for Mac or Windows or SGI platforms

> Mail the command photoshop to
> listproc2@bgu.edu.

Discussion of Photography in its various aspects: film and digital

> Mail the command photo-l to
> listproc@csu-b.csuohio.edu.

Electronic Photojournalism forum

> Mail the command mu-epj to
> listproc@lists.missouri.edu.

PHOTOART list

> Mail the command PHOTOART to
> LISTSERV@lugb.latrobe.edu.au.

Photojournalism discussion

> Mail the command PHOTOTUJ to
> LISTSERV@VM.TEMPLE.EDU.

205

PHOTOPRO - The Professional Photographers Mail List

> Mail the command PHOTOPRO to `LISTSERV@INTERNET.COM`.

PHOTOTECH - The Photographers Technical Mail List

> Mail the command PHOTOTECH to `LISTSERV@INTERNET.COM`.

APPENDIX B

List of Art and Design Associations

Advertising Photographers of
America (APA)
7201 Melrose Ave.
Los Angeles, CA 90046
800-272-6264
Email: apanet@aol.com
http://www.apanational.com

American Association of
Advertising Agencies
666 Third Avenue
New York, NY 10017
212-682-2500
http://www.commercepark/com/AAAA/

American Center for Design
233 East Ontario Street, Suite 500
Chicago, IL 60611
http://www.ac4d.org/

American Institute of Architects
735 New York Avenue, NW
Washington, DC 20006
202-626-7300
http://www.aia.org/

American Institute of Graphic Arts
165 Fifth Avenue
New York, NY 10010
212-807-1990
http://www.aiga.org/

American Society of Interior Designers
202 546-3480
http://www.wp.com/asid/

American Society of Media Photographers
Washington Park, Suite 502
14 Washington Rd.
Princeton Junction, NJ 08550
Phone: 609-799-8300
Fax: 609-799-2233
http://www2.asmp.org/asmp.html

Association for Computing Machinery
Special Interest Group on Computer
Graphics (Siggraph)
1515 Broadway, 17th Floor,
New York, NY 10036-5701
http://www.siggraph.org/

Association for the Graphic Arts
330 Seventh Avenue
New York NY 10001
212-279-2100

Canadian Association of Photographers &
Illustrators in Communications
Contact: Duncan Read (Executive Director)
100 Broadview Avenue, #322
Toronto, Ontario M4M 2E8, CANADA
Phone: 416-462-3700
Fax: 416-462-3678
Email: capic@astral.magic.ca
http://www.capic.org

Digital Graphic Association
408 Eighth Avenue, Suite 10A
New York, NY 10001
212-629-3232

Digital Technology International
500 West 1200 South
Orem, OR 84058
810-226-8438

Graphic Artists Guild
11 West 20th Street, 8th Floor
New York, NY 10011
212-463-7759
http://www.gag.org/pegs.html

Graphic Communications Association
100 Dangerfield Road
Alexandria, VA 22314
703-519-8160

Industrial Designers Society of America
1142 Walker Road
Great Falls, VA 22066
Phone: 703-759-0100
Fax: 703-759-7679
Email: idsa@erols.com
http://www.idsa.org/

Interactive Multimedia Arts &
Technology Association
P.O. Box 1139, Stn Q
Toronto, Ontario M4T 2N5, CANADA
Phone: 416-233-2227
Fax: 416-256-4391
http://www.ima.org

International Furnishings and
Design Association
P.O. Box 580045
Dallas, TX 75258
Voice: 214-747-2406
Fax: 214-747-2407
Email:IFDA@pic.net

International Interactive
Communications Society
IICS Executive Office
14657 SW Teal Boulevard, Suite 119
Beaverton, OR 97007-6194
503-579-4427
http://www.teleport.com/~iicsor/

International Interior Design Association
341 Merchandise Mart
Chicago, IL 60654
312-467-1950

National Computer Graphic Association
2722 Merrilee Drive, Suite 200
Fairfax, VA 22031
703-698-9600

National Multimedia Association of America
4920 Niagara Road, 3rd Floor
College Park, Maryland 20740
800-819-1335
http://www.nmaa.org/

National Press Photographers Association
Charles Cooper (Executive Director)
3200 Croasdaile Drive, Suite #306
Durham, NC 27705 USA
Phone: 919-383-7246 (or 1-800-289-6772)
Fax: 919-383-7261
Email: Steve Sweitzer (1995-96 President):
sweitzer@wish-tv.com;
Mark Loundy (Telecommunications Chair):
loundy@lightside.com
http://sunsite.unc.edu/nppa/

Organization of Black Designers
300 M Street, SW
Suite N110
Washington, DC 20024-4019
202-659-3918
http://www.core77.com/OBD

Professional Photographers of America
Andrew Foster (Executive Director)
57 Forsyth Street, N.W., Suite 1600
Atlanta, GA 30303 USA
Int'l Phone: 404-522-8600
U.S. Phone: 800-786-6277
http://www.ppa-world.org

Professional Photographers of Canada
1811 McKenzie Road, Bldg. 5
Abbotsford, B.C.
V23 3Z2, CANADA

Small Computers in the Arts
Network (SCAN)
209 Upland Road
Merion Station, PA 19066-1821
Phone: 610-664-3417
Email: scan@netaxs.com
http://moonmilk.volcano.org/scan/

Society of Environmental Graphic Designers
1 Story Street
Cambridge, MA 02138
617-868-3381

Society of Graphic Designers of Canada
VMPO P.O. Box 3626
Vancouver, BC V6B 3X6, CANADA
http://www.swifty.com/gdc/

Type Director's Club
60 East 42 Street, Suite 721
New York, NY 10165
212-983-6042

Naming Conventions for Files in Different Operating Systems

Macintosh

A Macintosh file name can be 31 characters long. The Macintosh is partially case-insensitive. The files TestThis and testthis will be seen as the same file but will display as originally typed if they appear in two different directories.

A Macintosh file name can include any element in the ASCII character set, including symbols and the space character, except the colon (:), which is used by the operating system as a separator in writing a folder path (directory tree). Leading or trailing spaces in a name are readable by the system, so a file name " here I am " would not be the same file as "here I am.

DOS/Windows

A DOS or Windows 3.1 file can be eight characters long, plus a period (.) followed by a three-character file extension. A file named in another operating system which is ported

to DOS/Windows 3.1 will have its name chopped down to the 8-character limit, with the last character being a zero (0) instead of all the missing characters in the name. If the original name included a space, the file may not be accessible because DOS uses the space as a command line separator. If it includes a period, DOS will assume that the next three characters of the name are its extension and chop the rest. A DOS/Windows file without a proper extension will often not open, even in the application it was created in. DOS is case-insensitive, so the file Windows2.txt and the file WINDOWS2.TXT are seen as identical and will display the same in a file listing.

File names in DOS/Windows are letters, digits, the underscore character, and the following symbols:

~ tilde

! exclamation point

@ at sign

number sign

$ dollar sign

% percent sign

& ampersand

( ) open and close parentheses

{ } open and close braces

' the inch mark

' ' open and close curly quotes (single quotation marks)

Windows 95

A Windows 95 file name can be 255 characters long. Windows 95 is partially case-insensitive. The files TestThis and testthis will be seen as the same file but will display as originally typed if they appear in two different directories.

A Windows 95 file can be named with any of the characters that are legal in a DOS/Windows name, as well as the space character. In addition, the following characters can be used:

+ plus sign

= equal sign

[] open and close square brackets

; semicolon

, comma

Leading or trailing spaces in a name are ignored in Windows 95.

Unix

Although most designers think they don't need to know Unix naming conventions, they are mistaken. Most Web servers run under the Unix operating system, so HTML files which are named with certain symbols can have loading and reading problems.

Unix is very different from the Mac OS or any of the Windows flavors. In theory, there are no limits on file name length, nor are there any characters that can't be used to create a file. However, a wide variety of characters, if used in a file, will cause problems because some piece of software running under Unix uses them as special command characters.

Unix is case-sensitive. The files TestThis and testthis will not necessarily be seen as the same file, depending on the specific shell and software involved.

The following characters should be *avoided* in naming a Unix file:

( ) The space character

/ forward slash (the directory delimiter)

* asterisk

? question mark

& ampersand

" double quote

' inch mark (single quote)

< > greater than and less than signs

$ dollar sign

! exclamation point

; semi-colon

In addition, the following characters should not be used as the first character in a file name, because many Unix programs use these characters to define specific actions or to hide files:

. period

- hyphen

These characters are perfectly legal any-where else in a file name and are used frequently.

213

Recommended Books

Storing, Mounting, and Archiving Artwork

Hart, Russell. *Photographing Your Artwork: A Step-By-Step Guide to Taking High-Quality Slides at an Affordable Price.* North Light Books. Cincinnati, 1987.

Scher, Paula. *The Graphic Design Portfolio: How to Make a Good One.* Watson Guptill. New York, 1992.

Snyder, Jill. *Caring for Your Art.* Allworth Press. New York, 1991.

Web-related Books

December, John and Ginsburg, Mark. *HTML and CGI Unleashed.* Sams.net Publishing. Indianapolis, 1995.

LeMay, Laura. *Teach Yourself Web Publishing with HTML in 14 Days.* Sams.net Publishing. Indianapolis, 1995.

Interactivity and Multimedia

Caffarelli, Fabrizio and Straughan, Diedre. *Publish Yourself on CD-ROM.* Random House. New York.

Johnson, Nels, with Fred Gault and Mark Florence. *How to Digitize Video.* John Wiley & Sons. New York, 1994.

Kristof, Ray and Amy Satran. *Interactivity By Design.* Adobe Press. Indianapolis, 1995.

Murie, Michael. *Multimedia Starter Kit for Macintosh.* Hayden Books. Indianapolis, 1994.

Lopuck, Lisa. *Designing Multimedia.* Peachpit Press. Berkeley.

Roberts, Jason. *Director Demystified: Creating Interactive Multimedia with Macromedia Director.* Peachpit Press. Berkeley, 1995.

Imaging

Blatner, David and Roth, Steve. *Real World Scanning and Halftones.* Peachpit Press. Berkeley, 1995.

Quay 2 Multimedia. *Photoshop 3: Training on CD.* Peachpit Press.

Sullivan, Michael. *Sullivan Scanning Tips & Techniques on CD-ROM,* 1996.

Business and Copyright

Brinson, J. Dianne and Radcliffe, Mark. *Multimedia Law Handbook.* Ladera Press. Menlo Park, 1994.

Graphic Artists Guild. *Graphic Artists Guild Handbook: Pricing & Ethical Guidelines.* New York.

National Information Structure Task Group, "Final Report," Washington, DC, 1995, `telnet: iitf.doc.gov`.

Scott, Michael with Talbott, James. *Multimedia: Law & Practice.* Prentice-Hall. New York, 1993.

APPENDIX E

The Netscape 216-Color Palette

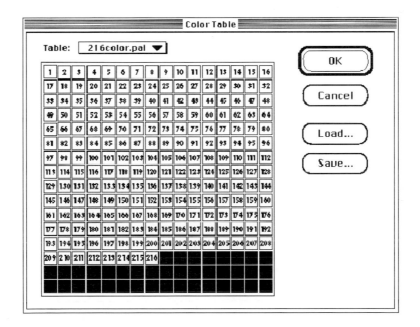

Palette	R	G	B	Hex Code	Palette	R	G	B	Hex Code
1.	255	255	255	FFFFFF	9.	255	204	153	FFCC99
2.	255	255	204	FFFFCC	10.	255	204	102	FFCC66
3.	255	255	153	FFFF99	11.	255	204	51	FFCC33
4.	255	255	102	FFFF66	12.	255	204	0	FFCC00
5.	255	255	51	FFFF33	13.	255	153	255	FF99FF
6.	255	255	0	FFFF00	14.	255	153	204	FF99CC
7.	255	204	255	FFCCFF	15.	255	153	153	FF9999
8.	255	204	204	FFCCCC	16.	255	153	102	FF9966

continues

Palette	R	G	B	Hex Code	Palette	R	G	B	Hex Code
17.	255	153	51	FF9933	47.	204	204	51	CCCC33
18.	255	153	0	FF9900	48.	204	204	0	CCCC00
19.	255	102	255	FF66FF	49.	204	153	255	CC99FF
20.	255	102	204	FF66CC	50.	204	153	204	CC99CC
21.	255	102	153	FF6699	51.	204	153	153	CC9999
22.	255	102	102	FF6666	52.	204	153	102	CC9966
23.	255	102	51	FF6633	53.	204	153	51	CC9933
24.	255	102	0	FF6600	54.	204	153	0	CC9900
25.	255	51	255	FF33FF	55.	204	102	255	CC66FF
26.	255	51	204	FF33CC	56.	204	102	204	CC66CC
27.	255	51	153	FF3399	57.	204	102	153	CC6699
28.	255	51	102	FF3366	58	204	102	102	CC6666
29.	255	51	51	FF3333	59.	204	102	51	CC6633
30.	255	51	0	FF3300	60.	204	102	0	CC6600
31.	255	0	255	FF00FF	61.	204	51	255	CC33FF
32	255	0	204	FF00CC	62.	204	51	204	CC33CC
33.	255	0	153	FF0099	63.	204	51	153	CC3399
34.	255	0	102	FF0066	64.	204	51	102	CC3366
35.	255	0	51	FF0033	65.	204	51	51	CC3333
36.	255	0	0	FF0000	66.	204	51	0	CC3300
37.	204	255	255	CCFFFF	67.	204	0	255	CC00FF
38.	204	255	204	CCFFCC	68.	204	0	204	CC00CC
39.	204	255	153	CCFF99	69.	204	0	153	CC0099
40.	204	255	102	CCFF66	70.	204	0	102	CC0066
41.	204	255	51	CCFF33	71.	204	0	51	CC0033
42.	204	255	0	CCFF00	72.	204	0	0	CC0000
43.	204	204	255	CCCCFF	73.	153	255	255	99FFFF
44.	204	204	204	CCCCCC	74.	153	255	204	99FFCC
45.	204	204	153	CCCC99	75.	153	255	153	99FF99
46.	204	204	102	CCCC66	76.	153	255	102	99FF66

The Netscape 216-Color Palette

Palette	R	G	B	Hex Code	Palette	R	G	B	Hex Code
77.	153	255	51	99FF33	107.	153	0	51	990033
78.	153	255	0	99FF00	108.	153	0	0	990000
79.	153	204	255	99CCFF	109.	102	255	255	66FFFF
80.	153	204	204	99CCCC	110.	102	255	204	66FFCC
81.	153	204	153	99CC99	111.	102	255	153	66FF99
82.	153	204	102	99CC66	112.	102	255	102	66FF66
83.	153	204	51	99CC33	113.	102	255	51	66FF33
84.	153	204	0	99CC00	114.	102	255	0	66FF00
85.	153	153	255	9999FF	115.	102	204	255	66CCFF
86.	153	153	204	9999CC	116.	102	204	204	66CCCC
87.	153	153	153	999999	117.	102	204	153	66CC99
88.	153	153	102	999966	118.	102	204	102	66CC66
89.	153	153	51	999933	119.	102	204	51	66CC33
90.	153	153	0	999900	120.	102	204	0	66CC00
91.	153	102	255	9966FF	121.	102	153	255	6699FF
92.	153	102	204	9966CC	122.	102	153	204	6699CC
93.	153	102	153	996699	123.	102	153	153	669999
94.	153	102	102	996666	124.	102	153	102	669966
95.	153	102	51	996633	125.	102	153	51	669933
96.	153	102	0	996600	126.	102	153	0	669900
97.	153	51	255	9933FF	127.	102	102	255	6666FF
98.	153	51	204	9933CC	128.	102	102	204	6666CC
99.	153	51	153	993399	129.	102	102	153	666699
100.	153	51	102	993366	130.	102	102	102	666666
101.	153	51	51	993333	131.	102	102	51	666633
102.	153	51	0	993300	132.	102	102	0	666600
103.	153	0	255	9900FF	133.	102	51	255	6633FF
104.	153	0	204	9900CC	134.	102	51	204	6633CC
105.	153	0	153	990099	135.	102	51	153	663399
106.	153	0	102	990066	136.	102	51	102	663366

continues

Palette	R	G	B	Hex Code	Palette	R	G	B	Hex Code
137.	102	51	51	663333	167.	51	102	51	336633
138.	102	51	0	663300	168.	51	102	0	336600
139.	102	0	255	6600FF	169.	51	51	255	3333FF
140.	102	0	204	6600CC	170.	51	51	204	3333CC
141.	102	0	153	660099	171.	51	51	153	333399
142.	102	0	102	660066	172.	51	51	102	333366
143.	102	0	51	660033	173.	51	51	51	333333
144.	102	0	0	660000	174.	51	51	0	333300
145.	51	255	255	33FFFF	175.	51	0	255	3300FF
146.	51	255	204	33FFCC	176.	51	0	204	3300CC
147.	51	255	153	33FF99	177.	51	0	153	330099
148.	51	255	102	33FF66	178.	51	0	102	330066
149.	51	255	51	33FF33	179.	51	0	51	330033
150.	51	255	0	33FF00	180.	51	0	0	330000
151.	51	204	255	33CCFF	181.	0	255	255	00FFFF
152.	51	204	204	33CCCC	182.	0	255	204	00FFCC
153.	51	204	153	33CC99	183.	0	255	153	00FF99
154.	51	204	102	33CC66	184.	0	255	102	00FF66
155.	51	204	51	33CC33	185.	0	255	51	00FF33
156.	51	204	0	33CC00	186.	0	255	0	00FF00
157.	51	153	255	3399FF	187.	0	204	255	00CCFF
158.	51	153	204	3399CC	188.	0	204	204	00CCCC
159.	51	153	153	339999	189.	0	204	153	00CC99
160.	51	153	102	339966	190.	0	204	102	00CC66
161.	51	153	51	339933	191.	0	204	51	00CC33
162.	51	153	0	339900	192.	0	204	0	00CC00
163.	51	102	255	3366FF	193.	0	153	255	0099FF
164.	51	102	204	3366CC	194.	0	153	204	0099CC
165.	51	102	153	336699	195.	0	153	153	009999
166.	51	102	102	336666	196.	0	153	102	009966

Palette	R	G	B	Hex Code
197.	0	153	51	009933
198.	0	153	0	009900
199.	0	102	255	0066FF
200.	0	102	204	0066CC
201.	0	102	153	006699
202.	0	102	102	006666
203.	0	102	51	006633
204.	0	102	0	006600
205.	0	51	255	0033FF
206.	0	51	204	0033CC
207.	0	51	153	003399
208.	0	51	102	003366
209.	0	51	51	003333
210.	0	51	0	003300
211.	0	0	255	0000FF
212.	0	0	204	0000CC
213.	0	0	153	000099
214.	0	0	102	000066
215.	0	0	51	000033
216.	0	0	0	000000

APPENDIX F

Web Editing Tools

Text-based Editors

BBEdit
$119
Bare Bones Software
508-651-3561
http://bbsw@netcom.com

BBEdit Light
Free
Bare Bones Software, for Mac
508-651-3561
http://bbsw@netcom.com

Gomer
Shareware
$15
Stoopid Software, for Windows
gomer@clver.net
http://clever.net/gomer

World Wide Web Weaver
$89
Miracle Software, for Mac
315-265-0930
http://www.MiracleInc.com

WYSIWYG Editors

Corel Web.Designer
$149
Corel, for Windows
800-772-6735
http://wp.novell.com

Front Page
$149
Microsoft, for Windows
800-426-9400
http://www.microsoft.com

golive Pro
$149
gonet communication, for Mac
415-463-1580
http://www.golive.com

golive (light)
Free
gonet communication, for Mac
415-463-1580
http://www.golive.com

Home Page
$99
Claris Corporation, for Mac and Windows
800-331-6187
http://www.claris.com

Hot Dog Professional
$99.95
Sausage Software, for Windows
714-250-7262
http://www.sausage.com

Hot Dog Standard
Shareware
$29
Sausage Software, for Windows
714-250-7262
http://www.sausage.com

HoTMetaL (light version)
Freeware
SoftQad Inc., for Mac, Windows, and Unix
800-387-2777
http://www.sq.com

InContext Spider
$99
InContext Systems, for Windows
800-263-0127
http://www.incontext.ca

Navigator Gold
$49
Netscape, for Windows
415-937-3777
http://home.netscape.com

PageMill
$149
Adobe Systems, for Mac and Windows
800-623-2320
http://www.adobe.com

Page Converters

BeyondPress
$595
Astrobyte, QuarkXPress to HTML, for Mac
303-534-6344
http://www.astrobyte.com

HoTaMaLe
Free
FrameMaker to HTML, for Mac, Windows,
and Unix
800-623-2320
http://www.adobe.com

HoTMetaL Pro
$195
SoftQuad Inc., for Mac, Windows, Unix
800-387-2777
http://www.sq.com

Internet Assistant for Word
Free
Word to HTML, Microsoft, for Mac and
Windows
800-426-9400
http://www.microsoft.com

Internet Assistant for PowerPoint
Free
PowerPoint to HTML, Microsoft, for Mac
and Windows
800-426-9400
http://www.microsoft.com

Internet Assistant for Excel
Free
Excel to HTML, Microsoft, for Mac and
Windows
800-426-9400
http://www.microsoft.com

Internet Publisher for Word Perfect
Free
Word Perfect 6.0 to HTML, Novell, for
Windows
800-321-4566
http://wp.novell.com

225

APPENDIX G

Software Contacts: Non-Internet

This appendix is by no means an exhaustive list. New programs are always being introduced. This is just a place to start exploring your software options.

Slide Show and Multimedia Software

Album
Shareware
ftp://ftp.amug.org/pub/amug/bbs-in-a-box/files/publish/m/megalomedia-photo-album-1.0.sit.hqx.
Imports graphics and arranges them in a photo album metaphor. Can attach text, frames sound, and run simple slide show.

BlackBeauty
Shareware
ftp://ftp.amug.org/multimedia/a-p/black-beauty-1.0.sit.hqx.
Multimedia slide show.

Gif Slideshow
Nick Gammon
P.O. Box 124
Ivanhoe VIC 3079
AUSTRALIA
Platform: Macintosh
Shareware: $20
Sumex
ftp://sumex-aim.stanford.edu/info-mac/gst/grf/gif-slideshow-15.hqx
Simple slide show.

Graphic Workshop for Windows
QuickShow Light for Windows
Alchemy Mindworks
alchemy@mail.north.net
800-263-1138
Platform: Windows
Shareware $10
Download at: http://
www.mindworkshop.com/alchemy/
alchemy.html.

HyperSlider
Platform: Macintosh
Wolfgang Thaller
Schillerplatz 9
A-8010 Graz
Austria/Europe
Shareware: $10
Download at: http://www.macworld.com/
cgi-bin/software.pl/Graphics/
software.460.html
Simple multimedia authoring tool. Handles
pictures, QuickTime movies and sounds.

JPEGView
Platform: Macintosh
Aaron Giles
P.O. Box 2967
San Rafael, CA 94912
Freeware
Download at: http://152.1.24177/
Teaching/manuscript/0600-0007,html

PICTshow
Slide show for picts, gifs, sounds and
QT movies.

ftp://ftp.amug.org/pub/amug/bbs-in-a-
box/files/art/art-tools/pictshow-
2.2.sit.hqx

ProView
E-magine
New York
$99.95 + S & H
voice: 212-665-0030, orders: 800-603-1474
http://www.e-magine.com/

SlideShow for Windows
CMB Software
cmbsoft@mcs.net
http://cmbsoft.pd.mcs.net
Shareware $20

Smoothie
Platform: Macintosh
Peirce Software, Inc.
1417 Selborn Place
San Jose, CA 95126
voice: 408-295-9760
fax: 408-295-9433
info@peircesw.com
http://www.peircesw.com/

SuperSlide
Hypercard
Platform: Power Macintosh
Javier D'az Reinoso
JSoft, 1994
P.O. Box 1712-574
Quito, Ecuador
xdiaz@pi.pro.ec

Authoring and Animating

Apple Media Tool
Apple Quicktime VR
Apple
800-950-5382
http://qtvr.quicktime.apple.com/

Asymetrix
Toolbook
800-448-6543
http://www.asymetrix.com/

Digital Box Office
Power Production Software
1233 Hermosa Avenue, Suite 302
Hermosa Beach, CA 90254
Phone: 310-937-4411
Fax: 310-937-4416
pps@netcom.com
http://www.powerproduction.com
Multimedia Software ($599)
Mac, Windows
http://www.powerproduction.com/dbo/
dbo.html

Director
Macromedia
800-288-4797
http://www.macromedia.com/

HyperStudio
Roger Wagner Publishing, Inc.
1050 Pioneer Way, Suite P
El Cajon, CA 92020
800-421-6526

Pierian Spring
Digital Chisel for Macintosh
$139
503-222-2044
http://www.pierian.com/

Presentation Software

Adobe Systems
Persuasion
http://www.adobe.com/

Micrografx
800-676-3110
http://www.micrografx.com/

Microsoft
PowerPoint
Mac, Windows
800-676-3110

Portfolio Utilities

Equilibrium
DeBabelizer
800-524-8651
Platform: Macintosh
info@equil.com
http://www.equilibrium.com
Graphics translation and optimization
program.

229

FBI
HighWater Designs Inc.
6 Bedford Farms
New Hampshire, NH 3100-6532
Fax: 603-669-7456
Commercial program ($395)
Download test version and free detector at:
`http://www.highwaterfbi.com/`

Graphic Converter
Shareware: $35
Thorsten Lemke
`thorsten lemke@sz2.maus.de`
`ftp://pub/mac/graphics`

PhotoBubble
OmniView
325 Oak Ridge Highway
Knoxville, TN 37931
voice: 423-690-5600
fax: 423-690-2913
`http://www.omniview.com/viewers/`
`viewers.html`

ProJPEG2.0
BoxTop Software
Photoshop plug-in for progressive JPEGs.
`ftp.agt.net/gst/grf/pshp/projpeg-`
`20.hqx`

GLOSSARY

Adobe Acrobat   A reader and creator of PDF (Portable Document Format) files, which enable you to view a document independent of its original platform.

alias   A small icon-duplicate file with a link to the original file. Available in Mac OS System 7.0 and beyond.

analog   A method of storing information using a technical process equivalent to the original information. An example would be sound impulses over a phone wire or music on a vinyl record.

AVI   Audio-Video Interleaved. Microsoft's standard for video on Windows.

bandwidth   The volume of data capable of being transferred at any specific time.

browser   A program used to view World Wide Web pages.

CD-R   Compact Disc-Recordable. A die-based technology for creating computer-readable compact disc masters.

CD-ROM   Compact Disc-Read Only Memory. The CD format readable on personal computers.

CinePak   A method of translating analog video data so that it can be played on a computer system. CinePak is compatible with both QuickTime and AVI files, although it is more efficient with QuickTime. It compresses information to create small files, then decompresses them as the movie plays.

color, 8-, 16-, 24-bit   A descriptive phrase referring to image bit depth. Bit depth is the number of bits needed to describe the color of a pixel. (8 bit=256 colors, 16-bit=32,768 colors, 24-bit=7 million colors.)

dithering   A method of using patterns made from an 8-bit palette to simulate greater color and quality than an image actually holds.

EPS   Encapsulated PostScript. A graphics file format based in the PostScript page description language.

Frame tag   An extension created by Netscape but supported by other browsers to create scrolling areas to display multiple documents at once.

FPO For Position Only. A printer's term for low-resolution artwork unsuitable for actual printing but used in a file to indicate position and scale of the higher-quality art that will replace it.

fps frames per second. The speed at which an animation, video, or film sequence runs.

FTP File Transfer Protocol. A method of transferring binary and text files to and from an Internet server.

GIF Graphics Interchange Format. A proprietary file format of CompuServe online service widely used to deliver graphics on the Web.

histogram A bar graph consisting of 255 individual vertical lines, each corresponding to a level of grey in an image. The height of the line refers to the amount of any given shade of grey in the image.

home page The root Web page for a browser, or the root Web page that acts as a door to your site.

HTTP HyperText Transfer Protocol. A method of transferring hypertext documents between Web servers and clients.

image map An image in an HTML document that has defined areas with links to other URLs. An image map is created by combining an image tag with an HTML link.

interface The computer environment that acts as the meeting ground between humans and the computer or computer program with which they are interacting.

interlacing The method in which a graphic on the Web loads on-screen, getting progressively more defined as more information is scanned.

interpolate To insert transitional material between an ending and a starting point. For example, a blend or color ramp is an interpolation between one color or value and another.

JPEG Joint Photographic Experts Group. A method of image compression optimized for continuous tone photographic imagery.

Lingo The native program control language for Macromedia Director.

link Specifically in hypertext, an element which, when clicked will bring you to another screen.

Lossless Opposite of Lossy. When image quality is maintained through the process of compression.

Lossy Opposite of Lossless. When image quality is degraded in the interests of file size through the process of compression.

moire Unexpected patterns in scanned images, usually the result of scanning material with existing dot patterns.

Mosaic   The first Internet graphical browser, created by Mark Andreeson (now a principal of Netscape) while a graduate student.

posterize   To decreate levels of value to up the contrast radically in an image, leading to sharply defined color or shade areas rather than continuous tone changes.

raster image   An image consisting of individual bits of information. A bitmapped graphic.

rasterize   The process of translating digital information into bitmap form.

registration   In printing terms, the exact alignment of layers of material, such as the Cyan, Yellow, Magenta, and Black separations of a full-color image. If these elements arc even slightly out of alignment, there could be gaps where no ink prints, or unacceptable color overlaps.

RIP   Raster Image Processor. The software that interprets (rasterizes) computer image information into a bitmap for an imagesetter.

rubylith   An overlay sheet consisting of a clear acetate carrier and a red film. Used in the pre-press process to create masked areas in artwork.

SMPTE Time Code   Society of Motion Picture and Television Engineers. A universal video standard for locating individual frames by numbering them.

spi   samples per inch. How frequently a scanner checks color and value while scanning. The more samples per inch, the more visual information will be available in the scanned image.

storyboard sketches   Roughly rendered still sketches of video or animation frames. So called from the traditional animation storyboard, which was a large panel that thumbnail sketches were mounted on for viewing.

substrate   In photographic printing processes, the receiving material for an image, usually but not always paper.

table tag   The HTML coding for laying out and aligning tabular material. Can also be used to create columns of text or images, with or without borders.

tag   The coding inside HTML open and close brackets (< >) that describes elements of a document.

Unix   A command-line computer operating system created for multiple users and capable of handling multiple parallel tasks. Invented in 1970 at Bell Labs.

URL   Uniform Resouce Locator. A pointer to an address on the Web.

vector   A line drawn between two points. In computer graphics, a line-based image consisting of specific points described as positions on a two- or three-dimensional grid, with lines drawn to connect them.

233

INDEX

Symbols

<IMG> tag, 166
3-D, 35
   design mailing lists, 204
   video capture, 35
216-color palette, 132, 217

A

advertising, 189-190
aliases (organization), 45
animation, 102-116
   see also interactive portfolios
animator portfolios, 15-16
animators (digital media), 37
anti-aliasing scanned images, 82-87
architect portfolios, 13-14
architecture mailing lists, 203
archiving printed work, 54
Ark Studios, 4
   Clark, David, 4
   Curtiss, David, 5
   Odegard, Robert, 5
art associations, 207-209
art mailing lists, 204
art sites, 202
artwork
   large format, 34
   mounting, 183
      recommended books, 215
   photographing, 51
   scanning, 71

   transferring to the Web, 125
assignment of rights (copyrights), 178
associations, 20, 207-209
attire (presentation), 192
audience
   chat rooms, 21
   digital media, 36
   email lists, 21
   group portfolios, 19
   networking, 20
   newsgroups, 20
   preconceptions, 33
   technophobia, 33
   Web, 117, 120
authoring software, 229
AutoCAD drawings, 34

B

backgrounds (Web), 130, 159
backups (organization), 52
bandwidth, 126
Big Blue Dot, 6
binders, 25-26
blank CD-ROMs, 115
books
   Graphic Design Portfolio: How To
      Make a Good One, 57
   imaging, 216
   multimedia, 215
   storage, 215
brochures, 27
broken hyperlinks (Web), 166
browsers, testing pages, 165

D

E

F

239

M

N

R

S

T

243

U

V